Hunting Upland Birds

CHARLES F. WATERMAN

Hunting Upland Birds

Winchester Press

Library of Congress Catalog Card Number: 72-79362
ISBN 087691-078-9

Published by Winchester Press
460 Park Avenue, New York 10022

PRINTED IN THE UNITED STATES OF AMERICA

TO OLD KELLY

*He wasn't the best bird dog in the world
but none ever tried harder.*

Contents

Introduction

THERE ARE SHOOTERS AND HUNTERS, not always the same people, and there are others to whom the bagging of game is an anticlimax to dog work. Then there are individuals in whom all these primary objectives are combined in varying proportions.

So those who follow upland game are certainly not all of the same mold, although they nearly always have an interest in conservation and outdoors, especially in the fall of the year.

Among the purest of the hunters are the ruffed-grouse seekers of the Northeast, some of whom have written perceptive books about that single bird in that single area, people who are willing to walk a long, hard day in cloying vines and clutching thorns for a brief glimpse of a bird that has somehow gathered all of autumn and shooting into an explosive bundle of brown feathers, and a single shot is reward enough for a long hunt. A continent away, the chukar lover scrambles along cliffs and slides for a jeering bird that has yet to build a tradition in this country, and when a chukar hunter meets a complete stranger in his playground of talus and cheatgrass and notes the other's scarred shotgun he feels enough familiarity to say, "Another darned fool, eh?"

Across the Atlantic, in a different situation but equally concerned about how the game is faring, would be a shooter who stands at a numbered butt and fires at birds driven to him by beaters. In some cases it has never occurred to such a marksman that studying the game and finding it with or without a dog would be a major part of the fun. In any event, he is there for the shooting rather than the hunting, and he never snags his tweeds. He has an opposite number in America who does his shooting at a preserve, leaving the shooting vehicle only when it's time to fire, and possibly is not interested in finding where the bobwhites have been dusting or how the pheasants have planned their escape routes.

And year-round, the dog fancier trains and selects for the moment when his charge points or flushes as generations of breeding have shaped him. This man can happily miss the bird if a point is staunch.

All of these and many more are the upland gunners, and perhaps we have a little something for all of them if we draw on our own experience and the experience of those who have gone before us as well as that of the specialists in birds, guns, and dogs.

CHAPTER I

Bobwhite Quail

So MANY THOUSANDS of gunners have found the bobwhite quail in so many ways and in so many places that it must be called a democratic bird, although fortunes have been spent in hunting it. Probably more money has been spent on this one small bird than on all the rest of America's upland game.

It is not that hunting bobwhites is so difficult, but that many bobwhite hunters choose to do it in an elaborate way and can afford it, and while quail shooting has been a sport of the rich and the social elite for more than a hundred years, the very things that make it possible to hunt quail with shooting wagons and matched mules make the quail one of the most important birds of all for the man whose equipment includes only boots and a shotgun. The reason is that the bobwhite can be reared in plenty if we give him space and cover, and wild bobwhites can be raised as a crop for the public as well as on the private plantation.

Nearest to the bobwhite in these qualifications would be the pheasant, but even the ringneck lacks the adaptability of the little fellow with the big chest muscles. You see, we can have the quail if we want it badly enough, for the bobwhite is fairly well under-

2

Tough shooting, even for experts. Bobwhite quail thus found at edge of heavy cover will nearly always head for the thickest brush.

stood and has been the subject of exhaustive study for generations. The ruffed grouse lives on the borders of farms and towns and is dependent upon management, but it's a slow process, one way or the other. The chukar lives on land we haven't found critically useful for the moment, and it has surprised us when it prospered in one spot, and surprised us when it failed in another. The chukar is largely on its own, as is the grouse, but the bobwhite lives closer to us, and a crop of bobwhites is readily achieved in a couple of years if we work at it. Thus, if worst came to worst, the quail might be the last bird left to hunt.

Game birds can be judged only by comparison, and eulogies come very easily. It is natural to call the bobwhite a bombshell, a rocket, and a gentleman, all of which are apt descriptions, but there are all kinds of quail hunting, and some of it very difficult while some is fairly easy. Judgment of any game is easy to make on the basis of very limited experience, and if there is one thing I wish to emphasize in this book it is the fact that all the birds covered can be easy or difficult as circumstances dictate. In short, it is difficult to say that the bobwhite is a better bird than the ruffed grouse or that the pheasant is better game than the prairie chicken. Different, yes. Better or worse, no.

The bobwhite has great acceleration when it flushes, and the mutter of its wings is so rapid that it gives the impression of even greater speed. A large covey can rise in a roar that sometimes causes experienced gunners to come apart, and a rigidly pointing pair of dogs can build tension instead of instilling confidence. It is not unusual to see an inexperienced shooter stop short of kicking up the birds, frozen in the anticipation of noise and speed and worrying about his shooting. Even veterans sometimes approach the birds as if they were intending to catch them by hand instead of shooting at them. It is a psychological advantage the bobwhite exploits to the utmost, and it is this tension that makes quail hunting exciting through a lifetime of gunning.

The quail, of course, does not fly as fast as it seems to. It is a small bird and its wingbeats are rapid and make a disconcerting noise. The concerted covey rise emphasizes all of these things, making it very difficult to shoot only one bird at a time, and the novice is almost invariably too hasty. If there is one thing that sets apart the master quail gunner, it is timing—an ability to tell when haste is really necessary (as in thick brush) and when there is time for a prompt but more careful shot.

There are times when quail can somehow draw on a reserve of acceleration and speed—real and not imaginary. Two of us once walked to the edge of a grove where our dog was holding a small covey on bare ground beneath an orange tree. When those birds went they drove off from solid ground, unhampered even by grass, and they had evidently been preparing to flush for some little while. I thought the speed was incredible but said nothing at the time. An hour later, my companion, who was a lifetime quail hunter, remarked that he didn't believe he'd ever seen quail go so fast. It was a combination of flushing situation, properly conditioned birds, and the fact they had been preparing to go for some time. They were ready.

The bobwhite quail (Colinus virginianus) has its own flushing and running traits. I believe the Mearn's quail, found near the Mexican border in the United States and in Old Mexico, comes closest to behaving like a bobwhite ahead of a dog, but the mountain quail and valley quail act much the same if the brush is quite thick.

There is much talk of the good old days when bobwhites held closely, seldom ran, and lived in more open country. Biologists sometimes tend to attribute these reports to aging legs that do not want to pursue running birds, older eyes that have difficulty pointing guns when flushes are just a bit farther out than ideal, and memories that cling to the good days and forget those of poor hunting and difficult birds. There is no doubt that these things contribute to yearning for other times, but the quail have changed, partly through pressure on individual coveys, partly through what we might call short-term evolution, partly through a process of elimination, and largely through a change of habitat.

Through the years there have been widespread introductions, a great deal of domestic hatching, and considerable live-trapping and moving. One of the persistent theories is that the Mexican quail, which were transplanted over much of the U.S. quail country in the late thirties, had a marked effect on the performance of native birds. The Mexican strains were said to be runners that refused to hold for dogs and contributed this trait to all bobwhites. It's been a long time now, and possibly there were minor differences in the behavior of the Mexican birds, but the transplantings were largely unsuccessful and any physical characteristics passed on to the native population have apparently disappeared. The Southwestern birds were of lighter color, but there is a great deal of difference in the shade of brown found in quail—so a lighter-than-usual bobwhite is not necessarily a direct descendant of a Mexican ground racer. I do not know that the Mexican birds ran more in the first place; it's one of those stories that persist and may have considerable truth.

Quail become wilder when subjected to hunting pressure, a wildness that can be expressed in several ways. Don Davis of Tallahassee, Florida, who has hunted quail and guided quail hunters for much of his life, puts it this way: "When they've been shot at, they tend to hold tight or fly. They are not likely to run much."

Other experienced men have told me much the same thing, and my own hunting bears that out, except that quail feeding very close to heavy cover are apt to move into it on foot after they learn that dogs and guns are about. This move may be only a few feet, but

Pointer makes a find in a brushpile at border of open field.
Gunner is James E. (Buddy) Pigg, Columbia, Tennessee. Such a point
is handled best by two shooters approaching from different angles.

they'll make it rather than sit in the open after they've heard
hunters coming.

Really wild flushes with no shooting opportunity at all can happen with hard-pressured birds, and certain coveys will sometimes
maintain a pattern of flushing. I know of one Southern field, bordered by heavy oak and underbrush on one side and a river swamp
on the other, where hunting is heavy, most of the hunting parties
driving the field slowly with four-wheel-drive vehicles while their
dogs work ahead. The quail do not live within the swamp or the
oak forest, but they stay fairly close to it. The field itself has grass,
a variety of weeds, and partridge pea. In midseason two of us drove
to the field edge, stopped our Jeep, and opened a dog box. As the
door thumped open we saw a covey of a dozen birds fly from near
the edge a full 150 yards away and drill into the heavy brush. The
covey surely hadn't been whittled down much, but it had learned

what a dog box sounded like. In the same place I have seen birds go up far ahead on several other occasions, but never as far away as on that trip. On later visits the dogs were released a short distance from the field and the rig approached at slow speed. That worked better, but we were no hazard to the quail population.

So thus we come to the "swamp quail," believed to be a distinct strain by many experienced hunters. Such birds are supposed to be larger and darker in color than the others and are believed to live in the heavy cover, especially in swamps. They are sometimes referred to as "the old native quail," since later generations are supposed to be of lighter color. Talk of swamp quail is common in the South.

There are swamp quail, all right, although they may be no larger or darker than the others. They do use swamps and heavy thickets a great deal, but there is no proof that they ever nest there or that they roost in the dark depths, except in dire emergency. Swamp quail simply live on the borders and use the nearly impassable terrain for escape when pushed from more open ground. Where hunting pressures are heavy, such birds survive better than do those with less dense escape cover; thus, there is a larger percentage of "swamp quail" as the season or seasons go by. Note, too, they are lightly hunted compared to more available coveys, and although neither group is necessarily overharvested, it's certain that the heavy-cover birds will have bigger coveys as the season ends.

Hunting birds that live on the borders of nearly impenetrable brush becomes a special art, and some gunners have become so proficient at it that a naturalist friend of mine insists quail-shooting hours should end at four o'clock in the afternoon. The routine goes something like this:

Both dog and man know the quail are likely to be quite close to the edge of heavy timber and brush, so they pay special attention to the edges. If the hunter is lucky, the dog might find game 50 yards from the edge, but if it's a typical bunch of "Tarzan quail" it is more likely to be 30 feet out. In any event, the shooter follows the first rule of the meat hunter and tries to walk up the birds while he is either facing the brush or moving parallel to its border. He knows the birds are going into it, and if he tries to cut them off from their escape route he is likely to have them fly straight at him, an experience much like being attacked by a swarm of bumblebees and not conducive to marksmanship. At any rate, he knows he's going to have a "one-shot covey" and isn't counting on finding any singles after the initial flush. The dog points, the birds go up and in, and he has one or two shots, after which all is still and, he hopes, his dog is hunting dead.

But in the depths of the swamp our covey is somewhat scattered, since they could not put down intact with so many obstacles. Back there a lone quail is temporarily safe, but it is unhappy, as that is not a place for roosting and certainly not much of a spot for feeding. If it's in there during late afternoon, it will probably start calling, and at the same time is likely to work back toward the edge of the cover. At something like an hour or two after the initial flush, individual quail and pairs are likely to be coming back out of the brush, probably quite near where they went in, and the covey might be scattered over a considerable area. If evening is coming on they're likely to be calling urgently, and it is the perfect situation for the hunter who has swung back to capitalize on it. Now he is likely to get the singles shooting he didn't have on the initial flight.

Single birds are seldom watched as they land in a swamp or thick brush, but it's known that they frequently land in open areas for convenience, and then are likely to walk into thick cover. If they are closely followed it is not unusual for quail to crouch in a fairly open spot, the theory being that they are thus able to take off easily. The real weedpatcher successfully follows quail into brambles and brushpiles and has dogs that cooperate in his closeup confrontations. He starts hunting where most gunners turn away. His techniques are special; we'll take them up a little later.

BOBWHITE RANGES

So much is said and written about the Southeastern quail hunting that some of the best of all bobwhite country has been almost completely overlooked until quite recently. Farming practices have led to exceptional shooting in Oklahoma and Kansas in recent years; it has been there all the time to some degree. Rolling farmland is good for quail, for it generally consists of grainfields broken by

Late-winter bobwhites found by Buddy Nordmann and Manon Halcomb in central Florida. The citrus grove in the background provides green shoots in February that attract quail.

draws and creeks, and these latter areas grow up to weeds and brush, making extended edges—and quail like edges where they are close to both food and hiding. The Kansas, Oklahoma, and Texas shooters wouldn't consider themselves part of the Southeast, but they're on the edge of it. Cold weather is what thins the quail north of Missouri and Kansas. The really stabilized populations are found as far north as southern New Jersey, Pennsylvania, Ohio, Indiana, Illinois, Iowa, and Nebraska. There is some excellent quail hunting considerably to the north—clear to the Canadian line in some spots—but those birds fluctuate with the severity of the winters. This is no Arctic game.

Kansas was home of a large quail, since extinct, that lived about a million years ago. The bobwhite of today has lived some 15,000 years, according to fossils found in the Southeast. At one time there was dense hardwood forest over much of what is now the best-known quail territory, hardly conducive to large populations. The first settlers of the East found quail, and there was report of a great many in Pennsylvania in the time of William Penn. Since much of that was mature forest then, the abundance of quail is hard to understand unless they have changed their requirements since.

More recent quail history has been tied to farm practices. In the South, pulpwood forests have become thick and burning has been neglected. Wherever grain has been replaced by pasture, bobwhites have decreased. Where fields have been made larger for purposes of mechanical farming, hedgerows and fenceline weeds are gone and quail have suffered. To offset these reductions of habitat, there are isolated instances of farming designed specifically for quail. On one quail plantation I watched a shooting-dog field trial in which 100 coveys were found in a single day. (It would sound more honest if it had been 99 or 101, but it came out exactly 100.) Such a plenitude is unlikely to be found on public lands or on farms where crop profits come before quail.

The bobwhite is found in forty states east of Montana, and some of the finest hunting is in areas that are considered marginal because of weather; severe winters can change that picture entirely. This bird has a strong allegiance to the United States, Mexico, and the Caribbean and hasn't done well in most foreign introductions. Success in southern Canada has been discouragingly spotty.

DOGS AND HUNTING

Pointing dogs are so consistently a part of bobwhite hunting that it is hard for me to realize that I had killed quite a few bobwhites before I ever saw a dog point, and that there are still numerous walk-up shooters who have never used dogs, most of them operating in cover with which they are completely familiar. They invariably hunt known coveys with known ranges, and the quail is such a creature of habit that a careful student can often walk straight to a bunch of birds if he has had some experience.

I know of some coveys that have been present with ghostly certainty each fall for forty years, for if the habitat is right there will be birds in a certain spot through the generations. When we consider that there is likely to be 70 percent natural mortality, shooting or no shooting, it seems probable that there will be quail in the best spots, even if the "home" covey should be wiped out by disease or predators. I assume that birds simply move in from a less desirable or "fringe" area in a poor year. In a certain hedgerow there will be a covey of some size every year, and a quarter-mile away there will be a spot that has birds only during a good season. If there is a bumper year, the hedgerow may have two coveys or one extremely large one. So a man without a dog is likely to be in business if he will walk a spot known to be a resting place, and he may find birds better during midday, whereas a dog man would prefer earlier or later, when quail are feeding, moving, and leaving scent.

Whether he is using a dog or not, a hunter looks for dusting areas or signs of a roost. Quail usually roost in a circle with their tails together, and the circular accumulation of droppings is a give-away. Tracks in dust are helpful, but there are so many birds leaving prints of about the same size that not everyone can tell a quail's tracks from something else.

If a flushed covey can be marked down, quite a few singles can be put up, even by a man without a dog. If he uses a flushing dog and can control it thoroughly, he may be able to kill a bag of birds over it once he has split a covey. The more the birds scatter the better, if terrain is suitable. I know of one man who collects his share with a Labrador retriever in heavy brush, but he's a hard worker.

The Southern quail dog is the stuff of which field trials are made, usually a lean pointer, often scarred by brush or palmetto, and capable of a reaching stride that covers a county. The rest of the gunning world hears of these dogs, learns of them in field trials, and assumes that hunters south of the Mason & Dixon line use them almost exclusively, following them on horses or in vehicles. It was never so, and it becomes less and less true as the hunting changes steadily to weedpatches and brush or follows the birds into the piney woods. The best shooting dogs vary their range to suit the conditions, and some of the most productive are seldom more than 75 yards from the gun. The pointer is the favorite in the Deep South, because it can withstand more heat, but the setter has its innings as a brushbuster if weather is cool. The German shorthair has come on strongly, especially as some breeders have produced something that runs somewhere between the plodding ground-trailers and those white streaks across the peanut patch.

Bobwhites are probably the best of all birds for dog work, and I know of no pointing breed that will not handle them if properly trained. The Brittany spaniel, although outclassed in speed on more open ground, has proved a good quail hunter in the brush. Many a top quail dog is a family pet, regardless of breed, and a meat hunter can do its job rather casually.

The slow-working dog is best for the weedpatcher or spot hunter, a man who knows the general location of certain coveys and starts his dog pretty close to the action on each bunch. After putting up one covey he may try briefly for the singles, then pick up his dog and drive to another location. This is a little different from the tactics of the hunter with wide areas to cover, possibly in new territory.

Dog stories can get tiresome but I have a friend who owns a matronly pointer with an ailment of the hindquarters that prevents her traveling much beyond a gentle trot. My friend has a pretty good idea of the general location of each covey and puts his dog down within a hundred yards of where he expects the action. She sniffs about casually and finally stops with mild interest, looking forward in a relaxed attitude. (If you have to stand in one place, you may as well make yourself comfortable.) My friend Milt Culp puts up the birds, which are usually in some modest brush, and we look briefly for singles, then go on to another spot. Patty is no show-off field-trial floozy, and the only sign of excitement comes when we put her in the car and head for home, at which point she wails mournfully despite Milt's comforting promises that we'll go again soon. That's not a typical rebel bird dog, perhaps, but it's a good one.

There's decreasing area for true vehicle hunting except on the plantation where quail are a major crop. The most common quail rig is a four-wheel-drive bobtail vehicle with a high seat to enable one passenger to see dogs at a distance. Even though the terrain might not call for four wheels of pushing, it's highly desirable because when geared down such an outfit will move very slowly, climb over logs and anthills with a minimum of fuss, and get out

Efficient quail-hunting rig is this customized Jeep at Tallawahee Plantation. There are two dog compartments and usually two dogs in use at a time.

of the occasional bad spot. A rig that must be gunned over rough spots is a nuisance. The high seat is usually mounted over or against the dog box, and it's usual to carry about four dogs, running them in braces so that nobody gets overly tired. Such an arrangement is good, even if most of the hunting is done on foot, for there are occasions when the dogs may as well hunt while the car moves from one spot to another.

You can divide these hunting cars into two groups—the ones that are run only when actually hunting, and those that must be used on long highway trips to reach the scene. The former are frequently battered relics that sag near the barn when not in use and will be towed if the trip is to be very far. The latter are often well-appointed vehicles capable of highway speeds, with comfortable upholstery, maybe air conditioning, and invariably a cab; the others are generally topless. They often have a shady but ventilated compartment for the game, covered gun cabinets, and two compartments to the dog box so that you can let out those needed for current hunting without difficulty from anybody else. Dogs can be watered from a spigot on many trucks. There may be a first-aid kit for the dogs and even one for humans.

Vehicle hunters usually endeavor to combine wide-ranging dogs with those working closer in. Manon Halcomb, a lifetime quail veteran, used to run three dogs when I went with him, carefully selecting operators of different ranges. His widest dog, in those days at least, was equipped with a radio, and there was a medium-ranger and one that stuck within 50 yards of the truck. I don't say Manon has always been able to keep a team exactly like that one, but it was ideal. His close-working dog was a singles expert, and the wide one had nothing but coveys on his mind. The radio business is a little spooky the first time you use it, and when the broken dots and dashes settled to a steady tone I couldn't believe we were actually headed for the dog, which I hadn't seen for ten minutes. But we left the Bronco where the going got a little rough and walked in the direction the radio said, the other two dogs pinching in to work closely for foot hunting. When they pointed I was quite prepared to put the radio away and forget the third pointer temporarily, but as we walked in we found they were actually backing our radio dog, concealed from us by a patch of palmettos. The birds were there all right. But maybe you don't like your gunning mixed with electronics.

As a matter of fact, careless use of the hunting vehicle on public (and some private) lands has been a major factor in the reduction of hunting areas. There is no objection to its use in the proper place, but having discovered such luxurious methods some sportsmen insist on doing their hunting sitting down and the devil take the fences, hillsides, and cover. They have turned some fields into what looks like a superhighway interchange, and this has led to prohibitions for obvious reasons.

Quail can adapt to vehicle hunting. Near the small town where we live there is a small patch of grass and weeds not far from a main-traveled highway with an oak hummock on one side, a patch of brush on one side, and a thick tangle of vine and briar on a third side. The fourth side is a frozen-out orange grove, and it is a perfect setup for quail. In spring, the male birds call constantly in the area and almost everyone knows they are there. Many of the vehicle hunters stop there on their way out of town or on the way home, put down a couple of dogs, and drive around the field. By late season, their tracks have made a thoroughfare of the field edges.

Buddy Nordmann, one of those quail students who can point out logical covey residences while being driven down an interstate highway at seventy miles an hour, told me that if I had a little spare time some evening to go out to that little field for half an hour just before dusk and get some shooting.

"The car hunters leave just a little too early," he said. "By the time those birds come out for evening feeding most of the all-day hunters have had a drink and are getting ready for dinner. You should find several coveys."

Feeling a little silly, I drove the family car to the field's edge, turned out my dog, who obviousy felt this was just for exercise, and began walking along one of the roads the hunters had pounded to dust. About 50 yards along the field's edge the dog pointed, and I found myself caught between a covey and the thick cover. I fired too soon as they flew into my face and I missed with my first barrel —then spilled a quail into the edge of the bushes with my second. A little farther along we found another covey that got up wild. Then I killed a bird from a third bunch—all within 200 yards of walking and all of the remaining birds leaving the field, apparently for good. Coveys are seldom that plentiful, but it was a good lesson in quail behavior.

When conditions are right and food plentiful, a bunch of bob-whites can fill their crops in a few minutes and move back into the thickets. They'll do it when there has been heavy pressure. The daily fall routine calls for feeding in both morning and evening, but weather can change that. On very cold mornings quail can be slow in getting into operation, and the same thing happens after a heavy rain. Although some moisture in the air is very helpful for dogs, a truly rainy day can find the quail sitting so closely that they are virtually impossible to find and putting out very little scent.

I went hunting at Tallawahee Plantation near Dawson, Georgia, guided by Grady Chambless on a rainy day. Driving out with the hunting car, we put up one covey that had been in the open near piney woods, evidently having moved out to feed, and although Grady knew we were in an area where dozens of coveys were located, we found hardly any. There was one single far out in a field alone. We moved a few birds in open woods but were not close enough to shoot. Around noon the weather cleared and there were a few to be found early in the afternoon. Then as things dried off, hunting became better and there was plenty of action in late afternoon, although the shooting was primarily in brushy sections. It is obvious that wet weather will keep quail pinned down, but the hard-and-fast rule will be broken by an occasional moving bunch like those we flushed on the way out and the single in the field.

I went on a rainy day with Jim Strader and Don Davis near Tallahassee, Florida, and it appeared nothing was moving, but our no-bird record was broken when one covey showed up in the middle of an open field. Three other bunches were at the very edge of the brush and ran or flew into it immediately. Such reports are not earthshaking but are important, because we *knew* our dogs were passing birds constantly as we were in areas of high concentration. In less productive territory we might have decided we had not been near any birds.

Once it has received its basic training, the worthwhile quail dog begins its self-education, becoming expert through experience. It may learn to head off running birds, it learns what good cover looks like and smells like, and if it hunts repeatedly in the same area it will learn through experience just where the various coveys hang out. In Louisiana, Bob Anderson's pointers covered the country well, but when they neared a known hangout of quail they would bear directly toward it and hunt it with special care, even though it looked much like the surrounding terrain. The geography was familiar. On preserves where ground feeders are used for quail, an experienced dog will learn to check every feeder in the area it hunts. This is brainy work and highly desirable, but a bird dog can become too smart, occasionally reaching the point where it feels it can wait for the others to find birds and then back with style.

The brush hunter for quail has much in common with the ruffed-grouse follower. He has an advantage in the number of opportunities he is likely to have, for there are more bobwhites than ruffs. In heavy stuff, bobwhite quail do less smashing through foliage and manage to evade more of it, so I believe you have a better chance of picking a quail's escape route. I believe the valley quail do more actual brush-breaking than do the bobwhites. There are times when a scattered bobwhite covey rises with very little noise in the brush, and they are surprisingly hard to see when flying close to a sun-dappled ground with leaves and branches overhead. Occasionally, quail will dive into brush while still within range and will simply disappear beneath your gun barrel.

One of the hitches in many plans for collecting scattered quail is their reluctance to flush once they have gotten into very thick weeds or brush. The fact is they're often in a spot where they can't fly without climbing over something first. Birds under a brushpile may be able to run but have a nearly solid cover overhead, and they can lead a hunter or two and a couple of dogs a ridiculous chase. If there are two hunters, they can get on opposite sides of a brushpile and one can try to push the birds to the other unless there are dogs willing to worm into the tangle. There's a simple gimmick here. When both shooters crowd the bush or brushpile they tend simply to push the birds to the center, and they will have no intention of coming out. It's better for one man to crowd the tangle noisily while the other stays back a little from the opposite side, giving the game a chance to fly.

There are circumstances in which quail simply refuse to fly. While hunting on John Cizerle's farm near Girard, Kansas, we put up a covey that landed only a short distance away in a field where very tall weeds and grass had been crushed down by heavy rains. The vegetation was lying almost flat on the ground, making a nearly level carpet but with enough space between the stems and the ground for the quail to walk, which they did. One of our dogs pointed and then cocked its head as if it was listening to something, which it was. The sound was like a bunch of mice running through a pile of hay, and it was the quail scampering around under the weeds. The dog forgot all its pointing instincts and began to stalk the birds carefully. Once or twice it put a paw down quickly like a feebleminded cat trying to catch a mouse under a carpet. We gestured to each other for silence, and whenever we'd hear the rustling we'd run over and try to kick up a bird. After a few minutes the covey was pretty well scattered and nothing had flown.

I began to look over my shoulder in the fear that someone might see us and send for help, but about the time all of the rustling sounds had subsided and I was ready to give up I heard a whir somewhere behind me and turned to find a single quail zooming back to where the covey had first gone up. I made a smooth swing and killed that bird in perfect form, the only bright moment of the entire foulup.

Quail are resourceful about hiding places. A wounded bird will crawl into almost any hole, but perfectly healthy bobwhites sometimes hide in unexpected spots. I once missed a straightaway bird that dived over a bank just as I fired, and when I went over there to see where it had gone I found a big trashpile with rusting buckets, tin cans, and auto bodies. The man hunting with me said it was quite common for birds to hide in that trash, and looking for them was useless.

Pete McLain, the New Jersey gunner and writer, has told of coveys going into woodchuck holes in severe weather and possibly when hard pressed by hunters. I have never seen healthy birds go into such a den but I once walked up to a pointer who had frozen near a gopher tortoise hole and plainly saw a single come up out of the hole in flight. It had been a frightened bird, for we had marked it down somewhere in the area.

It is hard to predict whether a covey will run. When they do, they are likely to fade away quietly, but they often carry on a running conversation and make no effort to hide. On good running ground you may be unable to put them up, even when they are in plain sight in the bushes, and this seems to be more likely on days when they aren't feeding. I have seen it most often in rainy weather, but this may be partly coincidence. You have to think of two kinds of running—birds moving ahead of hunters but not yet located, and birds that move after a dog has pointed. And herein is a much misunderstood dog activity.

When a hunter sees no birds and his dog keeps moving on a hot trail, it is natural to assume that the birds have been moving along some time before and the dog has not yet found them. A dog that trails for a long distance often gets marks for an exceptionally cold nose, whereas it may have been only a few yards from birds that were legging along ahead of it. Quail can run a considerable distance and often do, but I would say that 100 yards is a fairly long distance for a covey to run without flushing or hiding.

Quail prefer cover in which they can move rapidly, and if there is no running room on the ground, birds are likely to be scarce. Even some cover that is fairly low may be too thick for birds to walk through, and the densest thickets may have plenty of open area on the ground. Some grasses such as wiregrass may be too thick for quail to walk through but may mat down and bend over enough to make a series of miniature corridors and hiding places.

There is a rule that all fence corners should be hunted thoroughly. Not only is there likely to be a rather wide patch of weeds there, but birds that have run along the fence and come to the corner will be faced with a decision of direction and may hold or fly. For the most part, the more severe the weather the heavier the cover desired. In very cold weather quail often gather around abandoned farm buildings or even those that are in full operation.

Interpretation of quail calls is not complicated and can be helpful to hunters. There's little hunting at the time of year when the "bobwhite" mating call is heard, but the gathering call is recognized and imitated by many hunters. Some dogs know it, too. It's heard frequently when a covey has been split up and the members are trying to get together again, especially in late afternoon or evening. Imitators can get an answer or two, even though they don't actually pull in birds, and will be able to hunt in the right direction.

I have heard a great deal about the use of hawk calls in making quail hold or even to put them back on the ground when they're in the air. I've never seen it used on flying quail and haven't enough experience to know how effective it is when birds are on the ground, although I've known hunters who used hawk calls when afraid birds wouldn't hold. Hawks sometimes give away moving birds, as they frequently test a covey by swooping at it to make sure there are no cripples or sick individuals.

Most of the bobwhite country has rattlesnakes, but it is only in the South that they are likely to be active during hunting season. Until we get near central Florida or southern Texas there would be active snakes only on exceptionally warm hunting days, but much of the winter is warm enough for busy snakes in lower Florida. The killer is the Eastern diamondback, which can be a giant and quite capable of killing a horse with a perfect strike. Many bird dogs are lost to snakes every year. Caution varies with the dog. Some are curious about snakes and simply won't last long if hunted on hot days in snaky country. There are others that seem to avoid snakes religiously and some that pay no attention to them. A bird dog that grows old in service in the sand and palmetto country must have encountered many rattlers in its career, and its problems are multiplied by the fact that rattlesnakes and quail might look for similar hiding places on hot days.

Veterinarians tell me that a dog's reflexes are its best defense against rattlers, and that it is seldom that a snake kills a dog by hitting it around the nose, as the dog's head can be pulled back very quickly. Often it can't completely avoid the fangs but it gets away fast enough to avoid a full dose of venom. Antivenom serum can be administered by a few hunters who know the business.

I won't go into human treatments, but snakeproof boots are a good investment in the South. They're heavy and they're hard on your feet if they aren't perfectly fitted. Snakeproof leggings of aluminum, fiber glass, plastic, or screenwire and canvas will fend off the fangs, all right, although they have the disadvantage of catching weeds where the lower part of the leggings meets the boot or shoe, and the shoe or lower boot is not covered. It is possible, although not likely, that a snake can strike through the foot covering. There are snakeproof shoes that can be worn with leggings or with screen-lined pants. I have worn leggings of several kinds, but I've concluded the snakeproof leather boots are more comfortable and not much more expensive in the long run if you insist on snakeproof foot covering. Hunting is more fun if you aren't constantly in fear of snakes. You'll shoot better.

Are snakeproof boots complete protection? Well, not quite. It is possible for a snake to strike above them under optimum conditions, but the chances are strongly against such a strike. If you wear snakeproof boots and watch where you sit down or kneel you're pretty safe. If you hunt on hot days, you have to take a chance with your dogs. There are certain areas widely known to have many snakes and local inquiry can help you avoid them. The rattler is most likely to be where you're hunting, although water moccasins are about as deadly, and are sometimes encountered when a dog waters at a creek or seep.

GUNS AND SHOOTING

I have watched Manon Halcomb shoot quite a number of quail, sometimes when I should have been tending to my own marksmanship, and I was greatly impressed by his percentage of kills, enough so that I brought up the subject with Buddy Nordmann, an allround wingshot.

Grady Chambless kills a bobwhite on a foggy Georgia morning, using a skeet-bored 12-gauge.

"The thing about Manon," Buddy said, "is his timing. Unless the brush interferes, every bird falls about the same distance from him. I don't know if he could tell you just how far it is but he sure has a built-in stopwatch."

All of the very best quail shots have the knack of timing, whether they have fast reflexes or slow, whether they are high-strung or phlegmatic, and since those observations about Halcomb I have watched a number of them operate. No matter what their shooting style, they all have the timing.

A beginning quail shooter may do badly, even though he is a superior shotgunner, simply because he cannot adjust his timing. Quail flush fairly fast, but not nearly as fast as they seem to, and haste has saved many quail lives. The dead giveaway is when you have emptied your gun and the birds are still within easy range, whether you killed any or not. There is so much urgency about a covey flush that many men fire two shots before the birds go 10 yards. If they go up 5 yards from you (about average), you should have plenty of time to fire two shots by the time they have gone 15 yards—and 20 yards is about the ideal range for an open-bored gun on bobwhites. If they're in the open, you should be able to make kills out to more than 30 yards with regularity. If that 20-yard range seems to require lightning moves, remember that you generally hear the bird before it's really under way and that it may be climbing out of the grass before it really gets moving. Believe me, it is not difficult to shoot that fast if you have your gun at the ready —most quail hunters carry it at high port when walking into a point.

Of course part of this hurried business is true flock shooting, but even gunners with the presence of mind to pick out individual birds can get into too much of a hurry. It's natural to want to bag them all. Most beginners do better on single birds than on coveys. The obvious rule on coveys is to shoot one bird promptly but carefully and then do what you can about a second. Only veterans should attempt to kill three birds. Time is saved if the shooter goes for one of the first birds up, but it is natural to shoot at the nearest one—too near. The bunch is generally strung out more than appears at first. I think nearly all quail shooters either swing their muzzles through the birds' line of flight rather than using a sustained lead or simply spot-shoot when the angle is slight. Right angles or near right angles are not common in quail shooting, although they can occur when working the brush. In waist-high weeds, quail will probably go up several feet before leveling off, and the climbing birds are easily missed.

There is much talk of hip-shooting and of shooting birds just as they rise with a big pattern. I do know that a tightly bunched covey can be handled with this fast-gun method and one shot might get several birds. I'm not going to rant about sportsmanship, but it isn't as easy as it sounds. I knew one character who wielded a sawed-off 12-gauge automatic and made his dogs flush the birds so he could fire just as they jumped. I think he was good at getting them as they came up, being young and fast. If his "covey shot" didn't pay off, he still had plenty of time for two more orthodox attempts. If you're programmed for that sort of operation, more power to you, but you're likely to ruin some good dogs.

Even though the brush is thick, the beginning shooter should force himself to take his time until he has a routine shooting schedule. One of the most spectacularly successful shooters I have ever seen was a Georgia gunner who used 20-gauge pumps and kept two of them in the rig just in case something went wrong. I was trying to take pictures of him shooting quail in the brush (a very difficult thing to do), and he attempted to shoot a bird very close to the gun so that there would be lots of feathers. He missed and was completely crestfallen, but it was a simple matter of his having departed from his built-in timing schedule. Incidentally, picture-taking has thrown off many veteran shooters by making them nervous. This man wasn't nervous; he just did it a little differently and it didn't work out. Missing one quail is a small event to me, but it was a major catastrophe to him.

In talking about quail guns and shot we invariably run into the matter of sportsmanship, but as long as a man shoots them in the air and not on the ground and sticks to his legal limit I'm not going to make any accusations. For example, if he wants to use a cylinder-bored 10-gauge he might have a big advantage in "flock shooting" but the chances are the thing would be heavy enough to handcuff

Things happen fast when bobwhite quail rise in cover like this. Gun is an open-bored 20-gauge and shot will be made within less than 20 yards.

him the next time a single went whirring off through the pines, so it would even out. I use light 20-gauge doubles myself when I hunt quail, but I sincerely believe I can kill more birds with them because they are short and move fast. If someone else wants to use a sawed-off 12-gauge automatic it doesn't make him a bum sport despite some of the highflown remarks about gentlemen shooting. Sportsmanship is a quality of men and not firearms.

Some of the heavy-cover specialists use some frightening equipment, of course. I know a fellow who likes to shoot in thickets few dogs and no other hunters care to penetrate. His weapon is a cylinder-bored riot gun, 12-gauge, and he uses an ounce and a quarter of No. 9 shot. By the time those little pellets have traveled through a few yards of brambles there aren't enough of them left to mutilate a quail much.

Gauge is unimportant if you have 7/8 ounce of shot or more. As said elsewhere, the 28-gauge is adequate for quail, and the .410 should be used only by cautious experts at close range. Otherwise, it's a crippler. The 16-gauge is fine and quite popular in the South. I've used a 20-gauge with an ounce of No. 8 more than anything else, but when using an improved cylinder/modified double, I have used 1¼ ounces of No. 7½ shot in my tight barrel where I thought there might be long shots. I used a 20-gauge over-under skeet gun for a while, but decided I wanted something that shot just a little tighter. If you go to smallbore skeet borings, I believe you'll do better with No. 9. An ounce of No. 8 begins to get skimpy out around 25 yards.

There's no need for really heavy loads, and my ideal of a quail gun is around 6 pounds with nothing longer than a 26-inch barrel in a double. If you go to a real sawed-off gun I don't believe extra weight slows you up much because it's carried largely between the hands and swings fast. A *long* heavy gun is an abomination on bobwhites.

If the device doesn't interfere with your pointing, an adjustable choke on a pump or auto cut back to about 22 inches is a good combination. A ventilated rib will help keep the attachment out of your view if it bothers you. Such a gun isn't much shorter than a double with a 25-inch barrel. One big advantage of the double is the convenience in loading and unloading it when using a hunting vehicle or horse, and much quail shooting involves considerable

*Jim Strader of Tallahassee, Florida, finds some bobwhites in
the open, although his customized autoloader was originally designed
for closer work.*

transportation. I know there are a lot of loaded repeaters riding
in four-wheel-drive trucks during bird season.

Year in and year out, I suppose a 12-gauge loaded with 1⅛
ounces of No. 8 shot kills more quail than any other combination.
In skeet or cylinder boring, it's a tossup between No. 8 and No. 9.
In improved cylinder, I'll go for No. 8. In modified, No. 8 or 7½.
If somebody wants to shoot quail in wide-open country with a full
choke (some do it), he can use No. 7½ or even No. 6. Scatter or
brush loads don't print as even a pattern as the others but are a
big help at close range if your gun is modified choke or tighter.

I have known quail shooters who had somewhat more bend in
their bird gun stocks than they used in duck guns, the theory being
that these are quick shots and give less time for getting down on
the comb. Others say that quail tend to be rising when you shoot,
and the stock should be straight so the gun will shoot high. I don't
think either premise is important, but since recoil shouldn't be a
problem with light quail loads the gun that points most naturally
should be the choice.

BOBWHITE AT HOME

In late summer and early fall the family broods of quail begin to break up and large bunches form temporarily. These flocks, which may be forty birds or so, are not called coveys by biologists and their existence is shortlived. From these flocks the bobwhites begin to form true coveys, and the average covey is made up of around fifteen birds, although observers who don't count them generally guess a larger number.

The fall and winter covey is made up of birds from several families and possibly of a variety of ages, and this makes it unlikely that breaking up coveys is a help in reproduction. I've heard shooters say that shooting keeps family groups from inbreeding, but these aren't family groups, simply bands of birds sticking together for mutual assistance. The separation of the big bunches into coveys is known as the "fall shuffle," but it may continue all winter to some degree. Individual birds are likely to leave one covey to join another, and it can happen because a covey is broken by hunting or predation, or simply because some of the members decide to move on. Although each covey lives in a fairly small area, governed by the type of terrain and the amount of predation, an individual bird may go from covey to covey and end up many miles from his birthplace. Since a fall covey is made up of birds from several families, it is difficult to understand how a single small area can have a bunch every year, and it is an eloquent demonstration of the importance of exactly the right combination of food and cover.

As cold weather comes on, there may be a movement of coveys to more sheltered areas. Although they can withstand short periods of extreme cold, a long period of frozen snow can bring starvation, and blizzard conditions can actually freeze birds to death. Snow can be driven through their feathers and actually stop up their nostrils.

Traditional roosting formation is in a circle with tails together, and in cold weather a large covey crowds into a compact "pie" of quail with nothing much but heads showing under ideal conditions. If it is very cold the roosting formation may be employed at any time of day for the sake of warmth, and I have seen coveys engaged in what seemed to be a continual scramble for the warmest places when weather was severe. The crowding would become so energetic that those on the outside of the pod would brace their legs in continual pushing. Then as an outsider would crowd inside the group, those that had been pushed out would start the shoving. When such a bunch left there would frequently be a dead bird or two on the ground. As a kid I assumed they had been smothered, but they may have starved to death or frozen.

The spring breakup of coveys is in preparation for the nesting season and is announced by the male birds, who find good spots and then begin their "bobwhiting" calls in search of females. There's been considerable to-do about the earliest calls of the spring season, but when you get into southern Florida a stretch of very warm weather can touch it off at almost any time. It's accepted that weather and length of daylight periods combine to set off the breeding season, but I've heard reports of bobwhite calls in December from experienced hunters—a time when the gunning season was just getting under way.

Until they are mated, the males are especially noisy, and they continue their calls while the nesting process is under way. Late in summer the noisiest cocks are those that have not found a hen, and someone with the ability to produce a fairly lifelike hen whistle can call a male almost to his feet if he stays concealed. I know a naturalist who has called wild cocks into small clearings and has had one of them perch on his boot toe to look about for the elusive hen he'd been hearing. Male and female cooperate in building the nest, which is simply a shallow depression on the ground. They don't usually want their nests over thick debris, they don't want them under extremely high weeds and brush, and they want enough room to walk about in the surrounding vegetation. They do not often nest in the depths of swamps and briar tangles despite the reports of swamp quail.

The nesting cycle requires about fifty days. If the first nest is broken up, they'll usually try again, but as the season wears on the likelihood of success decreases, and late hatches are skimpy and often ill-fated. Birds surviving from very late hatches are often poorly feathered and poorly equipped for winter weather.

Mated pairs stay together before nesting and during egg-laying. While the hatching is under way the male will stay some distance from the nest but will be met daily by the hen when she leaves the eggs temporarily. In case of the female's death, the male may take over.

Northern quail definitely run larger than the southerners. In a list of average weights given in Walter Rosene's book, *The Bob-white Quail, Its Life and Management,* the largest birds came from Wisconsin and weighed 8.2 ounces, while the smallest came from Florida and Texas and weighed 5.7 ounces. Those are the northern-most and southernmost extremes, with the weights getting steadily heavier as the tally moves north.

Insects play a large part in the quail's diet during summer, espec-ially with the younger birds, but the quail is primarily a seed eater and so adaptable that the kinds of food found in quail crops run into the hundreds, and to select the contents of crops in one specific area as representative is misleading. Among the better-known foods are the partridge pea, beggarweeds, lespedezas, trailing wild beans, corn, wheat, and sorghums, but the quail is an opportunist of demo-cratic tastes.

One of the great changes in quail hunting is the closing of private lands and the reduction of public shooting areas. For generations there have been quail plantations in the South, large resorts of the wealthy where thousands of acres are managed for the benefit of bobwhites, and birds are hunted from shooting wagons and with mounted dog handlers. In most recent years, there have been a few plantations opened to public hunting for a fee. These are the cream of the game "preserves," and may provide both "preserve" quail and "wild" quail. In any event, the posters are going up and the man with a single dog who used to get out for a couple of hours after work is somewhat out .of luck. Perhaps there are not as many bird dogs around the small farms and city homes as there used to be.

If you look at this in the light of the American's traditional right to hunt for free, something has disappeared from the scene, but if you examine it in a practical way you can see that it will be re-stricted hunting or no hunting. It evolves into the importance of hunting for a given sportsman. Although only a rich man can con-tinually patronize the more expensive shooting preserves, the man of modest means who thinks enough of his sport can afford to make an annual trip the way he might take a big-game hunt or an off-shore fishing excursion. The costs are similar.

The bobwhite quail has proved the most satisfactory bird of all for the shooting preserve, and pen-raising is becoming more scien-tific. Some of the "preserve" birds are hard to distinguish from wild ones, although there is still low quality if they are improperly raised. One guide told me that some of the pen-raised quail will fly only about the length of a flight pen on their first flush, but would make much longer flights on the second rise. It was comforting to hear a pair of Tennessee veterans discussing birds on a preserve. Although they tabbed some of the game as pen-raised, there were others they couldn't decide about, and that's a very good sign.

It is no violation of confidence to say that there have been few fortunes made in the hunting preserves. They have come and gone, and most of those that stick are backed by money made in some other endeavor. A good hunting preserve is an expensive proposition and often a labor of love. Some of the preserve operators consider their efforts an attempt at saving something that would otherwise disappear, and they may well be right.

So when we say that the bobwhite can be raised as a crop we come to the matter of quail propagation and the quail hatchery, and we may now understand something of what it's all about. It's now been proven that a continual release program on public hunting lands is a waste of money. Hatchery quail released to supplant losses from a very hard winter or other quail disaster can be worthwhile. Adding to resident populations that have already filled their habitat to a natural level is a waste of birds. Millions have been spent on useless quail hatchery operations that were hard to stop in some states, long after biologists had learned they were of no help.

The hunting preserve is a somewhat different picture, and here we have a high concentration of hunting pressure. Call it put-and-take if you like, but there are many degrees of that. If there is any game that can be worthwhile in a preserve environment, it's the bobwhite.

CHAPTER II

Desert Quail

THE TRUE DESERT is hostile, violent, unreliable, and often frightening to visitors, with quivering heat in summer. It bursts into sudden bloom at the touch of rain and contracts to apparently lifeless browns and grays when normal drought returns. It is strange that such a place is crowded with wildlife, much of it delicate creatures that must adapt to times of plenty and want.

I list four kinds of birds as desert quail. The Gambel's quail is a dry-land equivalent of the California or valley bird. The scaled quail is a widely distributed ground racer, and the edges of its range get into country hardly ever termed "desert." The Mearns quail goes as a desert quail, even though it doesn't live at all in what would commonly be called true desert. Its home is grassy highlands, but they are within the desert's boundaries. I must list the masked bobwhite as a desert quail, although it is too scarce to hunt and may or may not return to huntable populations within the United States.

There are several things to be impressed upon new hunters of the desert. For one thing, there are many bird dogs that hunt a lifetime in true desert without ill effects. There may be individual dogs that cannot adapt to the many piercing, gouging, and cutting things the desert quail live in, but there are others that learn to take care of themselves within a few hours. Almost invariably a dog has some troubles at the beginning.

The same goes for the hunters themselves. They need good foot-wear, and they must learn not to sit down on cholla balls or lean against saguaro cactus, but it is seldom in hunting season that they are in serious danger from the poisonous reptiles or from the much-maligned peccary, which is just a shy little pig despite its tusks and the name of javelina, which is associated with overdrawn fables of mass attacks.

When the desert is hot it can be very, very hot, but it seldom is in quail-hunting season, and although much of it is trackless there is little need for the bird hunter to get so far from a road that he needs a guide. Usually there are enough landmarks to keep him straight, and he is more likely to complain about the encroaching sprawl of civilization than about the desolation of his hunting country. I can't think of any special equipment he needs, except the same pliers he carries to take porcupine quills from his dog in other areas. Here they might be used for cactus quills instead. The brush pants he wears in Wisconsin or Alabama will work in the

Desert country that accommodates both scaled and Gambel's quail in the Southwest.

desert. A real four-wheel-drive hunting rig might be nice, but he can hunt a lifetime from the family station wagon. Desert quail guns are a matter of personal preference; a skeet gun will do a fine job, and a full-choked reacher will work if that's the way you like to shoot.

My introduction to the arid uplands was pretty typical, I guess. I heard Gambel's quail talking at the edge of a superhighway rest stop, took my Brittany spaniel from the car and set him over the fence, then followed him without a gun. After he had worked the birds for a little while (they were apparently running, although I never saw them), I lost track for a few minutes and finally found him in a pathetic heap, so pinned by cholla cactus he could hardly move. He had, of course, tried to remove the tormenting balls with his mouth, and that too was full of needles. I carried him back, spent an unhappy quarter hour removing the spines, and decided regretfully that he would never be able to hunt in the desert. Two days later he was sliding through the cactus like a coyote and rarely collecting thorns at all. It was hard to believe he could learn that quickly, but I have no reason to believe he did so any faster than any other dog. I do not say that the desert isn't a hard place for a dog to operate, but the fears that he will be ruined seem to be unfounded. There may be exceptions.

GAMBEL'S QUAIL

The Gambel's quail (*Lophortyx gambelii*) has the same question-mark topknot carried by the California or valley quail. Like its relatives, it runs hard, sometimes flushes wild, and often holds tightly as a woodcock. It flies pretty fast but seems to lack the acceleration of a bobwhite. It will go a long way at times, especially when it can pitch down a desert mountain, and often forms large coveys. They split up well, seldom holding together for a series of flushes, and their scattering is both helpful, when you can find a bunch of singles, and frustrating, when they sometimes land, run in all directions, and keep going.

I got my start on Gambel's quail with Steve Gallizioli of the Arizona Game and Fish Department, a research chief, biologist, and hunter. I'll confess this is a much better start than most hunters would get and it was a long way from the fumbling approach I've made on other birds. Steve simply took us to the quail, explained the habitat, and told us why they were there. Under such circumstances a particular kind of hunting can appear pretty simple, possibly even easy, and it's tempting to be glib about it.

The Gambel's country Steve chose was very hilly, a part of the giant Sonoran Desert not far from Phoenix, and carried a vast variety of desert vegetation. The outstanding plants were the great saguaro cactus with uplifted arms. The arroyos were brushy, and we saw some Coues deer (desert whitetails) and very frequent sign of javelinas. The footing was very bad in places. It wasn't the kind of country where you'd fall off a cliff, but it was easy to sit down hard on any one of a variety of cacti, a good place to turn an ankle or smash an elbow, and a place decidedly rough on fine gunstocks.

We were running two pointing dogs, but they didn't hold a large covey at any time. They would put up a bunch, well out of range, and then we'd mark the birds. Usually they would simply cross over into the adjacent draw, and Steve could tell you about where they'd be without even looking. All he seemed to need was their general direction. Once they landed, the dogs did pretty well until it got hot and dry late in the day. Then the scenting conditions were evidently very bad, for I watched them work within a few feet of birds, upwind, without any indication of smelling them. A couple of times I saw birds flushed just after a dog had passed.

Of course I'd heard the stories that a dog won't help on desert quail, but on the first covey we had a pretty good dog demonstration. The birds went up wild and drifted into another draw, and when we followed them up one of the dogs pointed near the bottom. I went over there and several quail went out, one at a time, not exactly where the dog was headed, evidently having moved after it stiffened up. Those birds didn't seem very noisy as they left, each of them heading for the gully's rim, and I knocked down a couple in short order. When I went up the bank of the arroyo to encourage a dog that was pursuing a cripple, another dog pointed what I thought must be the wounded quail, but it was a healthy bird, and I got it as it skimmed the ground. I make a point of these three neat shots as they were not a good indication of the rest of my day's shooting. Although most of the covey disappeared, we flew several more singles, one of which held tightly within 5 feet of Steve's boots, where he discussed the situation with Bill Browning, the Montana wildlife photographer. While the pair talked, one of the dogs stood at Steve's knee in a strangely quiet pose and they decided it was pointing. Steve was so flustered that when he finally kicked up the bird he missed it, an event that caused me considerable satisfaction, since Steve misses very rarely, the only thing that keeps him from being a perfect host.

Later in the day we saw a large covey running ahead of us, hurrying along a high ridge with the dogs trying to point but continuing to move after a moment's hesitation. The accepted practice is to run at such birds, hoping to make them fly, but that can be an athletic endeavor and may not work anyway. When we lost track of that bunch our assumption was that they had walked off the ridge in the direction we last saw them, so we slid down off the top and hunted hard where they should have gone, to no avail. Incidentally, it is not unusual to see desert quail running, because even where brush, grass, and cactus seem to be extremely thick, there are invariably open avenues between plants. That's simply a matter of desert ecology—each clump of vegetation needing a considerable area to draw water from.

It must have been an hour later that we clambered back to our ridge to head back where we'd come from and found that our covey was hidden on the slope opposite from the one we'd descended. They were no more than 50 yards from where we'd lost track of them. A single bird lost its nerve first, zoomed down into an enormous valley, was followed by half a dozen birds, and then the entire covey. That set off a chain reaction, and quail continued to plunge from the slope, possibly more than a hundred driving downward to become dots against the blue haze of the canyon and then become invisible except for silver specks where the sun caught their wings. They spread out broadly (in fact they had been widely scattered when they left) and began calling almost immediately, so we started down, slipping and sliding on small rolling stones, and careful not to fall into prickly pear or barrel cactus. We found quite a number of individual birds, although the vast majority escaped. By then it was late in the day, very dry, and the quail hadn't put out much scent. The dogs didn't look good at all.

Gambel's quail live in the Southwest in the desert lands of

Nevada, Utah, Colorado, California, Arizona, New Mexico, western Texas, and northwestern Mexico. They roost in dense thickets and nest on the ground, laying ten to sixteen eggs. They're usually found near water, leading to some reports that they cannot survive far from it. Some observers, however, say they will live a long way from water and fly to it occasionally. At any rate, a very dry year in the desert generally means a poor crop of Gambel's, and the guzzler, a cistern type of watering device, is one of the tools of management. There is no outstanding predator, although owls, hawks, coyotes, foxes, and wildcats can kill adult birds, and skunks, rats, rocksquirrels, Gila monsters, and snakes (the Sonoran Desert has about 170 kinds) may destroy nests. But if the weather is good, resulting in satisfactory plant growth, the quail almost invariably prosper. Hunting itself has had little effect on the population. It is human development in a booming Southwest that has become the biggest threat.

Undoubtedly the Gambel's quail might like some of the things eaten by its relative, the valley quail, but in the desert it shows a strong preference for mesquite and deervetch, primarily the seeds. The Gambel's will stay with us if the desert stays.

SCALED QUAIL

In some areas the scaled quail (Callipepla squamata) lives with the Gambel's quail. Some observers say that it can stay in more barren desert land than the Gambel's, but it also appears in what I'd call fairly arid country that certainly isn't desert. It's a resident of the Southwest and is collected as far north as Kansas, but it doesn't live as far west as California.

It is also called blue quail and cottontop, and this one is the track star as far as I am concerned. Scalies fly fast, generally tending to go higher into the air than the Gambel's quail. Steve Gallizioli pointed that out to me early in my desert-hunting career, and my experience certainly bore it out. I've seen scaled quail going some 150 feet high on occasions.

Sometimes they hold but they're more likely to flush wild, and you'll read that dogs are useless except to recover dead and

This scaled quail's name is appropriate. In some areas their range overlaps that of the Gambel's quail, although it also extends farther north.

wounded. I think they're harder for the dog than Gambel's or valley quail, but I'll take the dog if I can control it. Even when they're whistling along the sand with their legs hardly visible in blur I'd like to have a dog, and after I've lost sight of the danged things I like to have someone with a nose to get them going again. And if the dog gets birdy it may even be wise to call it off and make a big circle, coming on the fugitives from another direction. It doesn't work very often, but nothing works very often on cottontops.

You can have a break now and then. When my dog went lame in Arizona I had a try at them on my own, saw the usual blue-gray shadows sliding through the brush ahead, and made my creaking version of a sprint toward them. That time I got them up, although they were well out of range, and I watched them go fairly high and swing around behind me to where there was extra cover along an arroyo filled with the loose sand of violent desert cloudbursts. I hurried back there and they went up at long range, still scattered from their landing. One of them skimmed the ground and I spilled him with my duck gun, which I'd taken in the fear there would be no near chances.

I have repeatedly found scaled quail in desolate country where there is little inviting vegetation, but there is a tendency for them to stay where the brush is just a little higher, the grass just a little denser, and the cactus just a little closer together, even though none of it looks thick enough. I found later that the scalies that flew to the brush around the dry wash were likely to do the same thing on another day.

As to the method of running at scaled quail—or any running bird for that matter—the best method is to gain gradually if you can. You see them moving along ahead of you, probably keeping the same distance, and by speeding up just a little you may gain appreciably, possibly getting within range before you ever make your break. Then when you go, go fast, and whether you yell or not is a matter of personal preference. What you yell probably doesn't make much difference either, but many of the things I yell at desert quail make me feel much better. Shooting into the air might help

Steve Gallizioli hunts in Gambel's quail country where dogs and humans must be careful of several kinds of cactus.

to get them airborne, but unless you're toting a repeater it can leave you short of ammunition when they do jump, if they do. If you have no dog and they scatter instead of flying, you have tough work ahead of you, for there's no telling how far the individuals will run. Once they do scatter, make a quick survey of the places you would hide if you were a scaled quail and kick the stew out of those places. They can go right up your shirt front sometimes.

Many scaled quail are shot on the ground while running, a practice frowned upon by most upland gunners. It sure isn't wing-shooting, but I doubt if it's much easier than shooting cottontails, which hardly ever fly. I don't shoot scalies on the ground but I won't help lynch someone who does.

Like most other quail, the cottontop nests in a hollow under a bush with nine to sixteen eggs. It departs most widely from quail custom in its eating habits, consuming much more animal matter, including grasshoppers, ants, beetles, true bugs, leafhoppers, and spiders. One of the interesting things about the diet is that lists of crop content are almost completely different when reported from different parts of the range, an indication that the bird is highly adaptable. The same sort of condition exist with bobwhites.

DOGS FOR GAMBEL'S AND SCALED QUAIL

I am considering the Gambel's and scaled quail separately from the Mearn s because I consider them very different, and dog requirements are rather unusual. I consider dogs a great help in all but a few upland situations, and the running quail is something special in desert country. I am inclined to prefer a close-working dog, simply because the first flush is likely to be wild anyway, and although you might not get a shot, you can at least mark down your birds more easily if the dog is in fairly close.

You want a dog that will indicate strongly when it is making game, for you may not get many staunch points and the indicating dog can get you stumbling in the right direction. It must be readily controlled, for you'll often want to put it on birds you have seen and that it has missed. You want it to hunt dead carefully, for dry desert air sometimes doesn't help it much and there are a lot of awkward places for a bird to fall.

Short hair or long hair? We can fuss for a long while about this. A shorthaired dog will get visibly scratched up and won't have much protection from the thorns, but a longhaired dog will turn into a pincushion before long, simply because everything sticks to its coat. Weather is usually warm, and the shorthaired dog has an advantage there. You need a calm dog, even if its hunting is a little lazy. Wild ones get a lot of minor injuries in the desert. There is snake danger in warm weather, little during most hunting seasons.

GUNS FOR GAMBEL'S AND SCALED QUAIL

As for guns, I notice that Steve Gallizioli wears an over-under 20-gauge with a carrying sling. His is modified and full-choked, and he does well with it but remarked that he felt his tight barrel was a little too much so. He was shooting a light load when we were with him. On the Gambel's quail I used a 12-gauge over-under, improved and modified, at first, simply because I thought I was shooting better with it at the moment. Later, I decided a 20-gauge was just as good, in the same boring, but I think 1⅛ ounces of No. 8 or 7½ shot is the best medicine for quail that tend to get up a bit wild.

The carrying sling is an excellent idea in that type of country, but few American shooters will consider them. As in any rough country, you need a light gun. When I was walking up the scaled quail I used a modified and full gun with high brass and No. 7½ shot. In most cases the cottontops can be waited out if you have to, and in many cases they're a long haul away to begin with. Right now, I am touting a double, bored improved cylinder and full, for all desert birds. There would be no question of my choice in a repeater. It would be a modified boring with No. 7½ shot and quite a bit of it. For a better shot the full choke might be better, but I doubt it.

MEARNS QUAIL

In much of the desert bird hunting you can look upward and see a quick graduation from a true desert ecology to the mountain

Mearns or harlequin quail, found in high, grassy country like this near the Mexican border in Arizona, behave much like bobwhites.

slopes, possibly grassy areas that grade into conifer timber and peaks, sometimes snowy in hunting season. Up there you might even find blue grouse in some of the northern parts of what we call the desert, but in the Southwest, near the Mexican border and on into Mexico, is a quail that follows the bobwhite pattern ahead of a dog and lives in a unique habitat.

It's the Mearns or harlequin quail, confined to a small U.S. range, and hunted by only a few gunners who use bobwhite methods and dogs that would be equally at home with bobwhites. You don't hear much about that sport because there isn't much of it. In Mexico it's the Montezuma quail.

The terrain is higher than the true desert, and in Arizona it's made up of hills carrying tall grass and scrub oaks. Nearer the equator in Mexico I understand the altitude is likely to be much higher. The Mearns quail *(Cyrtonyx montezumae)* is especially un-usual in its food choice, for although it has adapted to grain where that's available, as have most other quail, it does a great deal of digging for tubers or bulbs, the chufa tuber being listed promi-nently as crop content. Where the harlequin has been digging, it leaves a gouged-up area that resembles squirrel excavations. The bird's feet are especially designed for it.

The Mearns quail has about the same silhouette as the bobwhite; it holds tightly and perhaps runs even less. On our first hunt for it, I walked away from our little van camper to exercise the dog, stepped into a covey of quail, and watched them whir away over the grasstops, looking and acting like bobwhites. This would be simple, I thought, but we hunted half the following day without results. We stuck to grassy draws spotted with scrub oak, and the first harlequin I saw that day did what everyone had told me he wouldn't. The spotted little rascal went softshoeing out of an old fallen treetop and disappeared into a rough patch of rock and grass while the dog snuffled helplessly on its trail. While I scuffed about to make it fly I heard its takeoff somewhere in a clump of oak.

Tall grass such as this makes ideal cover for Mearns quail.
This is hilly country with scattered live oak.

That afternoon we worked waist-high grass along some ridges, and when my dog disappeared I finally found him frozen in grass so tall and thick he was only a shapeless light area. When I went to him the quail went up from under his nose and I managed to wait until it had leveled off well above the grass tops and bagged my first harlequin. I did it again a few moments later, obviously having worked into a scattered covey along the ridge. Then I had another point and half a dozen birds went up, boring downhill for the oak clump in the draw below me. I missed twice in my haste at getting them before they disappeared, then watched them go into the cover while I stood with an empty gun. Obviously my timing hadn't been too good, and I looked around to make sure no other members of the party were watching. It was the same old story of knowing I had to hurry a little and then overdoing it.

I think that is typical of hunting Mearns quail. It acts like a bobwhite. The dogs should work it like bobwhites, and the gun that works for bobwhites should be perfect for the harlequin. Perhaps it is because I have killed only a few, but the beautiful little bird in its high country of tall grass and scattered oak draws has a special glamour, perhaps a glamour of rarity. The harlequin cannot stand much hunting, for it has a small range and there are few of them. Its call is different—a rather tremulous and highpitched owl-like sound.

Harlequins nest in the grass with something near a dozen eggs.

MASKED BOBWHITE

The masked bobwhite is another desert quail and for some time was absent in the Southwestern borderland. It looks like the common bobwhite, except that it has a black mask over most of its face and head. For a time it was believed extinct, but in a dramatic search of northern Mexico U.S. biologists found a few, brought some back, and are trying to reestablish it north of the border. They say that it was a stray bobwhite feather in the nest of a cactus wren that put them on the trail. But it will probably be a long while before we hunt U.S. masked quail, if ever.

CHAPTER III

Mountain and Valley Quail

VALLEY QUAIL hang around towns, stroll about under bird feeders in back yards, and stage military parades on the shoulders of main-traveled highways. Apparently they aren't very wild and not particularly afraid of people. My efforts at hunting them would indicate they needn't be afraid of me.

My very first experience with them was a forecast of things to come, and I should have quit then but I mistakenly believed the whole thing was a fluke. Using a good pointing dog in Hun and chukar country, I put up a covey of valley quail in sagebrush that was about waist high. They got up like a swarm of big bees and pitched right back into the sage, possibly thirty of them, and I wasted no time taking after them for I'd heard they might scoot out of the country if I was slow. I hadn't fired on the first flush, although I later reasoned they were within range. Apparently only part of the bunch had gotten up the first time. The little hilltop was swarming with them.

My dog pointed in front of me and five or six birds got up behind me, fluttering over the sagetops and in no hurry at all. Just as I got on one of them, they dropped to the ground and I shot too high.

*Mountain and valley quail country in eastern Washington.
I found these birds the most difficult targets when they were hunted
in thick brush along river bottoms.*

I actually saw them running haphazardly around in a little open place, evidently looking for the best spots to hide, so I rushed at the opening to make them fly, but nothing happened, and I looked wildly about to find my dog pointing staunchly 20 yards away. He had his head tipped downward as if the bird was right under his nose, which it was. When I walked up, the quail fluttered around a little at the bottom of a sage bush and disappeared again. But it looked like a perfect setup now, for the bunch had to be well scattered and I was sure there would be plenty of shooting.

Then I almost stepped on a bird and it buzzed away to dive back into the cover. I missed that one twice, and the dog pointed again. I kicked and shook the sage where he was aimed, but nothing came out and I assumed the bird or birds had run. After that we hunted for ten minutes without seeing a bird, although the dog pointed firmly twice and I kicked the bushes until I nearly fell on my neck. Then we put up a bird accidentally and I killed it before it could dive back into the sage. End of episode. I never saw another quail. By that time they had either found such good hiding we couldn't move them or they had walked away from the scene. Every time I get into a bunch of those birds I swear that I'm having an off day of shooting and that I've been unlucky, but I'm beginning to conclude that valley quail are just not my kind of birds. Oh, I like them all right. I just can't score very well.

The California quail *(Lophortyx californicus)* is also called the valley quail, but there are a number of races of very similar birds, all of them found in the West, and only a biologist with a library can really straighten out the Latin. Generally, it's California quail near the coast and valley quail inland. The Gambel's quail is quite similar in appearance and a close relative, but I consider it separately because it is primarily a desert bird.

Where they are found together, the valley quail (I like to call it by that name when it isn't in California) and the mountain quail *(Oreortyx pictus)* behave about the same, except that the mountain quail doesn't form huge flocks as the valley quail does and has a somewhat different flight pattern.

There is always difference of opinion about the airspeed of birds, especially those that make only short flights, and I have heard that the valley quail is a slow flyer and conversely that it is the fastest of all the quails. Here we're into the business of gearshifting. I'll agree that it can flutter above the tops of the bushes like an undecided wren, but when it streaks across an open space at top speed I'm inclined to think it goes as fast or faster than any bobwhite. But then, I have seen supercharged bobwhites that made incredible speed. Let's not get into the speed arguments.

VALLEY QUAIL

The most miserable showing I have ever made on valley quail was in the Snake river valley on the Washington side not far from Lewiston, Idaho. That is a typical riverbottom tangle of trees and brush, but there are some open avenues between the clumps and I should have done better than I did. I was hunting alone with two dogs, and they started things off by pinning a big bunch of quail in an old brushpile, left from some clearing operations. Unfortunately for me, it was right against some really thick stuff. The main body of the covey left in a roar in such a way I couldn't get a shot and then individuals kept spewing out in all directions. I missed twice and then stumbled to a new position with a better view.

In my new position I guarded a fairly broad open space and finally a bird took that course and I got it. The rest of the hunt was made up of similar adventures, and it was the worst scare I have ever made on any birds as far as I can recall. Under such circumstances, your best chance is to mark some birds down in a spot where the brush is low enough so they'll fly over it instead of through it. Stick near the edge of heavy cover and chances are that you'll sight a landing where you'll have a reasonable shot.

Valley quail will sit in trees after being flushed from the ground and sometimes are in plain sight, a situation that has never contributed to my mental attitude. Like any other bird flying from a tree, they can get added speed in diving downward but are addicted to little 20- or 30-foot flights to other branches. Before putting this down as easy shooting, you should try it. If you're like me, you aren't programmed for that kind of move.

Valley quail are especially deceptive because of their apparent tameness about country roads in hunting areas. They are most in evidence in early morning and late evening and like the road shoulders for grit. They seem almost as tame on these roads as they are closer to town where there is no shooting, but they are surprisingly hard to bag by road hunting or trail hunting. I have stopped a hunting rig on a trail with a bunch of quail standing all over the area, some of them staying put within 20 feet of the truck. They will make a half-dozen kinds of call and scatter, evidently without plan, but often two or three will stand in the trail and gawk. Put down a dog and load a gun and it is amazing how many things can go wrong.

Undoubtedly, the numbers of California and valley quail have been greatly reduced by civilization. They were pursued by market hunters up until the late 1800's, and there are records of as many as 100,000 being bought in a single year in San Francisco. During

Mixed bag of pheasant, valley quail, and chukar in eastern Washington. All can sometimes be found together on the shoulders of draws next to grainfields.

dry weather it was possible for commercial hunters to kill birds by the thousands at isolated springs.

These quail nest on the ground with more than ten eggs. They roost in bushes, usually off the ground, and will find rather thick places at night, somewhat different from bobwhite roosts. The bobwhite seems more concerned with being able to get out fast if necessary. The valley or California quail seems more interested in finding a place where he won't have to make a getaway.

Valley quail and mountain quail have a very similar range, although the valley quail is found in a somewhat larger area. Both are found all along the Pacific coast from the Canadian border clear into Baja California, although the valley or California quail are found somewhat farther south on the Baja peninsula. Valley quail are as far east as Utah. Both birds are shot in Washington, Oregon, Idaho, Nevada, and California.

Valley quail are primarily seed eaters with filaree seed and leaves high on their list. The menu also includes turkey mullein, barley, clover, lupine, bur clover, and deervetch. Mountain quail will eat some of the same things, and their crops often contain brome grass. Nests of both birds are targets of opportunity for various predators, and coveys are frequently "tested" by raptors—the various eagles and hawks. That is, the predatory birds swoop at a visible flock to make certain all members are healthy and capable of escape. If all birds are active it is probable the big bird will leave them alone. Both mountain and valley quail may make short migrations to avoid unpleasant weather.

MOUNTAIN QUAIL

I once had a covey of mountain quail dead to rights. It was a very steep mountain draw in chukar country, and two dogs pointed with a confidence that left no doubt. It was a narrow patch of scrub oak and rosebush in a groove of mountainside and there was no other cover near. The slope was mostly bunch grass and slide rock, so I found a perfect spot for shooting and then moved a little toward the notch. Mountain quail squealed and chirped and came out by ones and twos, giving plenty of time for reloading between flushes. It was a perfect setup, and it was too bad the season didn't open until the following day. I could have murdered them.

The mountain quail is the largest of our quails and wears a plume that sticks straight out of its forehead, whereas the various valley quails and the Gambel's quail have questionmark plumes that curve forward. The mountain quail is commonly found at higher elevations, but its range overlaps that of the valley quail so much that they're frequently hunted together. Mountain quail do not bunch into the huge flocks quite common with valley quail. Like the valley quail, the mountain model is quite willing to run instead of fly. When it does fly it is more likely to rise somewhat higher into the air before leveling off. Perhaps it's because the mountain quail is larger, but it doesn't seem to go quite as fast. It goes fast enough.

Hunters after these birds for the first time are surprised to find not many of their kills are the fully plumed and uniformed adults. Young birds of the year are likely to have abbreviated plumes and drab colors, and when you first shoot one you're likely to think you've bagged another species entirely.

It may be that both mountain and valley quail are capable of wide ranging, but they will often stay in a very small area, even when hunted. I've chased both kinds back and forth when the cover was right. Of course it's the same as with other birds. The more you harass a covey, the smaller it becomes as individuals walk away or find really secure hiding places.

It's fun to watch a mountain quail making its getaway when you happen to catch sight of it on the ground if it's really on the lam. I remember one big rooster that scooted across in front of me, his plume almost straight up. He went over a little bluff and I got there soon enough to see him pace without hesitation to a fallen log, almost obscured by brush. He ran the full length of the log, jumped with a few wing strokes to another smaller one, moved through the lower part of a bush as a silent shadow, came to a 10-foot open place, flew across it, hurried along another log, and somehow disappeared. You know this sort of thing goes on constantly, but it's seldom you get to watch 50 yards of it. I remember that I was trying to make him fly all the time, and anyone who thinks he could have bagged that bird during the 10-foot flight just wasn't there.

Wing shooting is traditional in upland game hunting, and that's the way it's done, so it's stylish to have a list of insulting names for a ground-sluicer. I don't shoot birds on the ground, but I'm the first to say it would sometimes be harder to hit a running mountain or valley quail than it would be to hit the same bird in the air. It's a little like shooting bobwhite quail with a .22 rifle (generally illegal). Although that's considered poor sportsmanship, I can't say it's easier to hit a running quail with a .22 than it is to hit a flying one with a shotgun. And then we come to mountain grouse. I was almost ostracized when I shot some blue grouse with a pistol and a shotgunner told me I was a game hog. It didn't make any difference that it was harder to hit a blue grouse in the top of a pine with the handgun; the blue grouse was upland game and intended to be shot with a scattergun on the wing. Anyway, although I don't shoot them on the ground, I don't necessarily look down on someone who bags an occasional quail that way. He just isn't imbued with wing-shooting tradition.

Mountain quail are usually found in brushy draws if there are such places, but they seem to run or fly out into the open occasionally when hard pressed. I get the impression that they have decided the hunt is going along the draw and it will be safer to get out of it. In Idaho I once worked a small and brushy draw thoroughly with the dog birdy all the way. Then the dog wandered out into the sagebrush and pointed. The only birds I killed were out in the wide open where the sage was only a couple of feet high. I am convinced they went out there because our hunting pattern was definitely following the draw.

On the same hunt, I got a covey moving along a creek bottom where the willows were thick but followed the creek very closely and only 20 feet across. The birds kept leapfrogging along the willow clumps, making no effort at long flights and sticking to the bottom. Eventually, we probably passed nearly all of them, for the dog was inefficient with the birds above him in the willows. I don't think I bagged but one bird from that covey. I actually saw a small willow move a little and shook the bird out of it.

Mountain quail nest on the ground in the brush with five to fifteen eggs. They're not supposed to have a stable feeding range, but I have repeatedly bounced what appeared to be the same birds from a very small area, and they certainly stay very close to a preferred spot for several weeks at least.

DOGS

Dogs are a great help with valley quail, and there are many places where you'd be lost without them. A pointing dog will discover the coveys and often pin singles very closely. Here, as usual, it is good to have dogs that will work wide when the country is fairly open and close in when cover is tight. I've found that coveys frequently won't hold at all, but once the band is split up the single hunting can be good and a dog is essential. When I've found either valley or mountain quail in thick brush, a flushing dog might be superior to a pointer, unless the pointer is of the pheasant type and willing to keep moving as long as the game isn't definitely pinned down. I have heard shooters claim that flushing dogs are much better for mountain quail, the main problem being to get the birds into the air. The same goes for valley quail sometimes. It is small consolation to have a staunchly pointing dog if you can't make the bird fly.

As one Western quail hunter once told me: "What you need is a dog that will crowd as close to the bird as it can get. When hunting valley quail I've had to part the sage as if I were looking for Easter eggs instead of quail. Sometimes you'll actually look down in there and see the bird hanging on for dear life as you shake the branches. Then when it flies it may just go to the next bush."

The pattern in real bramble patches can be about the same with both valley and mountain quail. You'll see the birds running in there, but they'll manage to scoot out the other side where you can't get at them. By the time you've skirted the thickest area, they may have disappeared on you. The dog may be able to locate them again, but if they retrace their steps a couple of times and stick to the same bramble patch the scent becomes so confused that the dog isn't much help. That's the problem. Work it out for yourself. I have a poor track record.

GUNS

For most of the valley-quail shooting I've done, the typical bob-white-quail or ruffed-grouse gun is best. Shot sizes of No. 7½ or 8 are about right, and an ounce of shot will probably be enough. This gun is generally short, light, and fast-handling. If you're operating in creek or river bottoms, much of the shooting will be quick. Occasionally, there will be long chances on open slopes, but the open gun will be best most of the time. I have chased valley quail with a gun bored improved cylinder and full, but most of the shooting was with the open barrel, and there have been times when I wished I had brought a skeet gun. I recall one debacle in which I tried three different shotguns on three successive days—a blatant repudiation of my own policy of trusting the firearm and correcting the human error—but I just couldn't believe that I could be that bad.

In brush shooting it's the same old story of looking at the target and ignoring the intervening screen of foliage—the same system as used with ruffed grouse. I am very poor at that kind of shooting and am sure that most shotgunners would bag more quail than I would under the circumstances.

Mountain quail are more likely to be caught in the open, and many mountain-quail hunters shoot full-choked guns by preference. One successful pumpgunner told me he didn't know what choke he had but that it was probably full or modified. Modified would be my choice for the more open-country mountain-quail operations, and the conditions are similar to those of chukar hunting.

It's a lot of work and a lot of fun. With my record I have no business instructing.

CHAPTER IV

Pheasant

T̲HE FIRST WILD PHEASANT I ever saw was a long-tailed rooster drilling his way through spitting snow down a Colorado slope. He crossed fast at about 50 yards, then set his wings and swooped out of sight in some cottonwoods a quarter of a mile away, and I didn't even shoot. It was something of a shock to anyone who had expected the labored rise of an overweight bird at close range. I stood there for a minute and thought of the stories of twenty ringnecks with twenty shells, and the advice that I should count to three before moving a gun toward a rising pheasant lest I damage too much meat.

Like most game birds, pheasants can be almost too hard and too easy, so they shouldn't be judged on the basis of a single trip. There isn't much excuse for missing one that goes up under a dog's nose while flailing tall grass, but nailing wild-flushers in a cornfield can be man's work. And although many birds are collected by hunters who barely recognize what they're after, there are pheasant hunts that require heavy thought and planning.

Of all upland birds, the pheasant is the people's choice. There are thousands of shotguns used for no other purpose than an annual ringneck expedition, and their owners would consider any other game a poor substitute.

A cock pheasant rises from a western irrigation ditch where weeds offer good cold-weather cover. It is often necessary to block off such a ditch or the hunter will never catch up with the birds.

Pheasants can be hunted without dogs, and in some areas pheasant season is a social event with large parties of gunners holding mass drives in a variety of carefully planned formations. Where the ringneck prospers, most of the populace tends to ignore other upland game, and I am sure the colorful Asian has substantially lessened hunting pressures on other birds. That can be a complicated relationship, for the pheasant has partly taken over from native game when land uses made survival difficult for prairie chicken and sharptailed grouse.

WITHOUT A DOG

If you must hunt without a dog there's a lot more to it than shoving your muddy boots through the thickest brush and listening for a cackling rooster. One of my first pheasant trips was with a character who was raised with them but had never owned a bird dog. He was amazed that his tactics weren't known to all, but it took some time for me to understand them, even when we hunted together.

Most of the birds were in a river bottom clogged with heavy brush and great patches of willow but with large open spots with grass and weeds too short even for pheasant concealment. We'd heard pheasant talk coming from the place, but I wouldn't have tried it if I'd been alone. It looked too tough for me.

My buddy said we'd better separate before going into the thick stuff, explaining that two hikers operating apart would put up about twice as many birds as if they stuck together, whereupon he clumped off into the tangle. He'd come back out in an hour or so, he said. It looked simple enough, so I walked in myself, heading in a different direction.

Once I was sure I heard something scooting through the willows ahead of me, and after five or six more minutes I distinctly heard a bird take off up there somewhere. About that time I heard my friend shoot over in another bend of the little river, and my enthusiasm rose. It was possible, after all, to find pheasants in that brush. I struggled along for another ten minutes. Bang! Over in my friend's area. Maybe I wasn't getting in where it was thick enough, so I turned into rougher going. Maybe I had been too poky, so I hurried it up a little in spite of the gobs of half-frozen mud that dragged on my boots. Bang! Maybe my cohort had accidentally picked better cover. Maybe the rat had done it on purpose. Bang!

Once I heard a floundering rise from the top of a fallen tree and had a glimpse of a shadow with a long tail, but it was on the other side of a screen of willows and my futile shot brought down nothing but a shower of twigs. After an hour of stumbling about, I returned to the open field where we'd separated. My buddy was there with his limit of birds, genuinely concerned that I'd had no success. It was about that time I began to suspect there was something going on that I didn't understand and I began to ask some pointed questions.

Like many other modest souls he was reluctant to advise me for fear I'd think he was presumptuous. He was also doubtful that he knew anything I didn't know about pheasants. His procedures had been so basic, he thought, that anyone would know about them anyway.

"Maybe you didn't wait long enough for them to fly," he finally suggested.

"Wait, hell!" I said. "What're you talking about?"

Then he saw he might as well start from the beginning.

He'd kept in mind that pheasants are primarily movers when danger is near, and what he had executed was a one-man drive. He would enter a patch of thick cover and move about it rather slowly but remembering that his object was to herd birds toward an open area. He knew the birds were there, and he wasn't concerned much about whether he saw them running or not. When he came to an exceptionally thick strip of cover he would wander about it in such a way that runners were not likely to reverse the route and get behind him. He didn't sneak and he didn't make extra noise. Too much noise might cause wild flushing, he said, with the birds getting up out of range. If he sneaked too carefully he might pass a lot of birds that simply held tight.

As he neared an open area he would quarter back and forth as if herding a flock of birds ahead of him. In some cases, the "flock" wasn't imaginary, even though he never saw it. Then, when he got within easy range of the opening, he'd stop dead still and stand motionless. He was "waiting for them to fly."

The pheasant psychology was fairly simple. The birds, if there were any, had been listening to his progress through the cover and had moved slowly ahead of him until they came to the border of the open area, which they had no intention of crossing on foot. At that point they tended to squat and hide in the hope he'd simply walk on past them. But when he stopped they assumed he had sighted them, and after a few moments their nerves would crack and they'd take off with the usual cackles, often flying right across the open area. This was very tough on pheasants, for my friend didn't have his 12-gauge along just to ward off the brush.

The sudden stop and long pause will cause many varieties of game to flush. This seems the direct opposite of the situation in which a fast-going bird dog will stop suddenly on point and freeze a covey of birds that might otherwise run away, but the quick-stopping dog sometimes flushes birds that would run if he sneaked. Probably because they are conscious of their own sounds, a moving pheasant will often stop when you stop and begin to run again when you resume travel.

I do not say it always works, but my friend's procedure on those river-bottom birds was a lot more successful than my wanderings. The pheasant is the best subject if you want to learn something of how a bird dog feels.

Ordinarily, a wide river bottom isn't the best location for two dogless hunters. Their ideal setup is a narrow draw or creek bottom, a brushy irrigation ditch, a hedgerow, or a weedy fence line bordering a grain field. They must keep in mind that cocks prefer walking to flying and that their preferred movement is toward heavier cover rather than away from it. In following a strand of cover one man takes either side. If possible, he walks in the cover, but if it's too thick, as is often the case with cattails or rosebushes, he simply stays close to the edge while remaining in the open.

If there are three hunters, one of them can do most of the brush-busting, preferably lagging just a little behind the wing men, who generally walk pretty well in the open. The idea is to put up birds along the route, but it's smart to move in a direction that will move them to where the cover will peter out—walk away from the heaviest of it. A strand of any cover that runs out from a river or creek bottom and leads toward a stubblefield or cornfield is a natural route to be followed by pheasants for morning or evening feeding. You're more likely to make them fly if you hunt out from the bigger mass of brush. If you go the other way, you tend to drive them in deeper and deeper.

Red Monical, who has done a lot of Western pheasant hunting, showed me a smooth way of handling a small, brushy draw when only two shooters are present. We'd walk with one of us on each side of the cover until we neared the end of the draw, where we assumed most of the running birds would be congregating. Then one of us would hurry ahead by a roundabout route and approach the end of the draw quietly. For the last 100 yards it would be a matter of driving birds to each other. Some of them would run out of cover and fly into the open. Others would double back and fly over the man who had stuck with the original line of march. When you get between them and desirable cover, even mature roosters will sometimes give close-range passing shots.

A dogless hunter needs some special study of his area and must remember that the smaller the patch of cover the better his chances. Some excellent pheasant-holding areas fairly scream to anyone who stops to examine them but are ignored by hundreds of hunters. Since a few birds are nearly always seen in easily hunted country the tougher spots may be passed up for an entire season. They can be bonanzas, for as the season progresses more and more birds leave the easy places and crowd into the tough spots. "Crowd" isn't too strong a term in many instances.

Red and I found ourselves in pheasant headquarters late one fall on the Judith River in central Montana. The Judith flows through pasture and wheat land and where we hunted, not far from Lewistown, has extremely high bluffs on both sides. The bottom is filled with brush patches and some grazing area. The grain fields are mainly at the tops of the bluffs, where the land is pretty level although it bulges into occasional brushy knobs. The country is heavily hunted in the early season, with some shooters sticking to the easily walked irrigation ditches and the obvious fencelines and weedy hills. A few of them get down into the river bottom, where the advantage is with the pheasants. I figure that if pheasants ever disappear from the Judith, hunters won't be to blame.

But right at the top of the eroding bluffs and only a few yards from the edges of the grainfields there is an almost endless series of brushy notches, sloping so steeply down toward the river that you have to dig in your heels to stand up. Red and I had made an early-morning check of the grainfields and had seen a couple of birds scuttle into one of the notches, so we decided to hunt them out.

We carefully scooted down off the edge of the rim and laboriously clawed our way through the brambles and weeds, but we hadn't gone far when the pheasants began to flush and go sailing on set wings toward the river a quarter-mile away, gaining speed as they went. It was a memorable shoot, and the birds had evidently been undisturbed there all fall. Outraged cackles floated back up from the river bottom, where most of the cocks ended their flights in thick willows and cattails. A few sailed clear across the river and alighted in pockets on the opposite side, near duplicates of the ones they had just left.

That year at least, the rim notches were perfect for pheasants. They were within a short stroll of waste grain in the stubblefields. They had water ready at hand because there are seeps all along the Judith bluffs. They had roosting cover, and they had an obvious escape route, all of it downhill. And apparently no one had bothered them. It wasn't easy shooting, but there were plenty of chances. A kill was likely to end up in a stiff scramble downhill.

Years later I found a similar situation while using a dog, but about all it accomplished was to help find downed birds. It wasn't much good to have a dog point on that slope when you couldn't see it. A flushing dog would have helped more.

Midwestern cornfield hunting is frequently a matter of drivers and blockers, the blockers moving very little and waiting for a line of beaters to fly the birds over them. That's not the easiest shooting in the world and it puts a premium on range judgment. It also puts a premium or safety. Upland gunners aren't too strongly addicted to orange vests or caps, but something bright should be worn for pheasant hunting, as there's no other game bird more likely to get between you and your friends. I'll admit that birds aren't colorblind and that they can see you better when you wear something gaudy, but the safety factor makes it worthwhile.

DOGS

No one is ever going to describe a perfect pheasant dog, for performance that would earn ribbons in some circles would fall miserably flat in others. I feel that this is the best place of all for the flushing dog, but there are times when a pointer is superior. You can list illustrations until the season ends, but you can't be conclusive about pheasant dogs.

Many cornfield hunters who prefer driving and blocking methods and generally do their hunting in large parties would consider a dog a nuisance except for retrieving purposes. Their choices are retrieving breeds, dogs often kept at heel until the shooting is over.

Flushing dogs are best of all in very thick cover, and there are times when horsepower is almost as important as a nose in rousting out tight-holding cocks. One of the worst situations is heavy cattails, which are too much for most pointing dogs and for many flushing spaniels. I've seen some bull-shouldered Labs that delighted in crashing through such obstacles. It wasn't a very aesthetic performance, but the pheasants came out. I've felt helpless when a pointing dog zeroed in on a clump of cattails but ardent stomping and stumbling failed to bring anything to the surface.

Red Monical (left) and Bill Browning contemplate their bag of pheasant roosters in central Montana. The muddy Brittany is Kelly, who pointed eighteen species of upland birds during his lifetime.

At risk of offending almost everyone concerned, I'd say the pointing dog is invaluable where birds are scattered widely and where the thick clumps of cover are reasonably small. I have seen a good pointer go into what was supposed to be hunted-out cover and locate a limit of birds within a few minutes. The pointer tends to lose its magic when both birds and brush are thick.

There are times when birds will not hold at all for a point, and in such circumstances the dog's best procedure is to keep its cool and move behind them slowly enough so that it doesn't run away from the hunters. If the shooter is educated, he'll follow the dog, read its actions, and be on the job when the bird flushes. The ideal situation, of course, is for the dog to be cautious enough so that it does not bounce birds on its own. If one does take off, the sharp move is for the dog to stay put in the hope that other birds may decide to stay on the ground, providing the hunter isn't immediately available. That's plenty of mental strain for any canine, and some of the best will blow their stacks when the first squawking rooster leaves. Pheasants have ruined a lot of dogs, and after a few have run, flown, and cackled, an otherwise staunch pointer often refuses to hold when a bird finally does things the way it's supposed to.

It's often a long while between the time a dog first scents a pheasant and time for the shooting. Last fall two of us were hunting some stubble land stripped with hayfields and irrigation ditches and bordered on one side by a cottonwood river bottom. On one side there were steep hills with narrow draws carrying strips of willow. There was sagebrush on the hill faces. There is no part of the landscape that hasn't been known to hide a late-season ringneck, and dogs and men should enter such scenery with open minds.

One of our two dogs was making a long cast through a strip of stubble when it caught a scent from a weedy ditch 60 yards away, turned sharply, and ran that way, slowing gradually to a near point at the edge of the partly snow-matted weeds. The other dog came up and they both worked into the ditch, indicating extreme birdiness. Then they worked the ditch for 100 yards, alternating sides. Part of the time they moved rapidly and part of the time they milled around uncertainly. We'd found the rooster's tracks where they first reached the ditch, so we'd been trotting along dutifully, expecting anything or nothing. There was one place where it appeared we'd really lost our bird; possibly he'd flown for a few yards, but the dogs then turned hotter than ever and almost shouldered each other along on what had to be a fresh track.

Finally we came to a spot where the cover was considerably wider than elsewhere, and farther along it narrowed considerably. It was a logical place for the bird to hide and hold. It was also a logical place for him to turn and backtrack and a logical place for him to flush. The dogs pointed, moved, and pointed again. Then they seemed to be working back in the direction we'd come from, and I scuttled into the ditch ahead of them to thwart backtracking. My friend found a good high place to shoot from. Then both dogs stood in uncertain points, turning their heads a little from side to side, and one of them (a real old-timer at this business) rolled his eyes up at me. I interpreted that correctly as meaning I should stomp hell out of things, which I did, and a big cock pheasant came up, the wind from his wings flicking my sleeve a little and his harsh cackle having the usual effect on my nerves. Part of the weeds were shoulder-high at that point, and although it appeared I could have beheaded that bird with a pool cue I failed to down him when I

A bunch of pheasants goes up from a draw in North Dakota. From this cover they were only a short flight or stroll from grainfields.

shot too quick while he was going almost straight up. I saw the charge of shot riffle his breast feathers, but I managed to wait a little for my second try and collected him.

The dog performance on that occasion had been far from classic, but it had worked. Pheasants are opportunists, especially the old roosters, and it might pan out entirely differently next time. That had been a pretty conventional cock, and I don't know how he had lasted so far into hunting season except that he may never have been worked by good pheasant dogs. Put him up without a dog? Forget it, unless you stepped on his feet by accident.

Jim Smith and I got into some birdy country along an old railway spur where someone had mowed a single swath of heavy weeds and grass. It was early season, no snow, and we supposed the pheasants would be appropriately naive. We saw one bird take off far ahead of us, but that was standard procedure and no indication there weren't plenty more. Then our dog pointed suddenly as if he'd caught strong scent without warning and he stayed put. He was facing right at the swath of mowed weeds and I was unable to find anything where he was facing. Then both the dog and I heard a faint rustling from some distance and we figured out that a cock was scooting along under the fallen stuff and making a getaway.

For lack of anything better to do, I told the dog "Okay!" in the hope he'd put up the bird, which he finally did after jumping around the downed stuff like a cat after a mouse. Moving under mowed hay is no novelty for pheasants, but you generally expect such operations from cripples instead of healthy roosters with long spurs. One of the most extended cripple hunts I ever viewed occurred when a smart dog learned that a winged rooster was under some very heavy stuff that had been beaten down by rain. For a while the dog ran around on top of the cover, looking, listening, and sniffing for the bird, but when that didn't work he got under it and stayed under it until he caught his quarry. None of this wins field trials, but it sure gets pheasants.

Making late-season pheasants fly can be one of the major obstacles. Perhaps they are smart enough to know the ones that fly get shot, and perhaps the easy flushers have already been bagged and only the runners seem to be left. Anyway, we like to think the runners and unconventional performers are the smart ones. At least they're harder to come by. Some English gamekeepers prefer pen-raised birds to wild ones because they fly better.

Ben Williams and I once started up a creek bottom with three Brittanys, one of which was a pup and required considerable vocal direction. It was a wide strip of cover, probably 50 yards across, with plenty of opportunity for passed birds, and we weren't very quiet about our progress, figuring a little commotion might get action otherwise missed. It was obvious the dogs could smell running birds all of the time. We got some conventional shots when birds flushed wild and doubled back or held for the dogs, but after we'd trudged for a considerable distance I saw a moving shadow on a grassy hillside 200 yards ahead, looked closely, and decided it was a pheasant rooster legging it away from the cover and across the closely grazed grass. Then I saw another and another. They were running as if they meant business, with their necks out in front and their wings cupped just a little to keep balance at high speed. They weren't running to better hiding; they were simply running up the hills and then taking off by air for parts unknown. Now pheasant psychologists could have a field day with that, and the logical explanation is that they knew they'd be shot at if they flew at close range. Do they figure that out? I have heard stories of roosters that refused to fly under any kind of stress, even when caught by dogs. I've always thought there was something wrong with them but can't prove it.

Leaving the best cover on foot is nothing novel for pheasants, and most hunters have experienced epidemics of it. On many occasions I've had a dog suddenly abandon a streak of good cover only to move over and point at a scraggly patch of something or other hardly calculated to hide a bobwhite, let alone a ringneck rooster. I have seen the birds abandon better hiding for such spots, but in most cases you learn the story through the dog's actions, and sometimes there's enough vegetation between the hiding places to cover the retreat. Choosing skimpy cover over good cover must be a pet gimmick of experienced pheasants.

But they do stupid things. Another hunter and I caught a gaudy rooster feeding in the middle of a wide-open field at midday. We sighted him from a distance of 200 yards, and he could have walked to a nearby creek or taken off at his leisure and flown away without difficulty, but he showed indecision when he sighted us. We stood and watched while he hid in a clump of grass that barely concealed his tail and we walked up to easy range before he flew. Our dog pointed him, but I don't know if that helped hold him or not.

Most of these instances are chosen from occasions when birds weren't particularly plentiful. I believe the scarcer the birds the more helpful a dog can be in the hunting. Where birds are running about by the dozen, as I have seen them in Nebraska and South Dakota, I have found dogs so confused that they were not only hampered in hunting but actually failed to find hard cripples in the confusion of crisscrossing trails and possibly visible birds. Early in my pheasant career I knocked a hard-hit cock into a patch of rosebushes and my dog was after him in an instant. A half-dozen pheasants flushed from him as he sought the cripple and he lost his cool *and* the cripple.

The disappearance of pheasant cripples is one of the unhappy wonders of hunting for me, and when shooting without a dog I am so obsessed with clean kills that I pass up chances I'd take instantly if a dog were standing by. Natural camouflage of all game birds has always amazed me, but when a cock pheasant almost as long as my shotgun and with all the colors of the Central American flags crashes down into 6 inches of grass and disappears forever I no longer have any comment at all. I think with shame of the dogless hunt of many years ago in which another fool and I collected one-third of our downed birds, blasting away in happy innocence at long range and short, whether cover was heavy or nonexistent. As I

Bill Browning exhibits a late-season pheasant taken at a time when the "easy" birds have already been bagged and the survivors have become real strategists.

look back on that day I realize that most of those shots should never have been taken at all.

In the first place, a pheasant, especially a seasoned rooster, is incredibly tough where shooting is concerned. Shot from the rear, as the majority of them are, a pheasant has enough viscera, heavy bone, and muscle to contain several good-sized shot long enough to make good an escape. If you're not equipped for cripple-catching, you're stretching things any time you shoot from the rear at more than 40 yards. Make that 35 yards unless you shoot a tight gun and big shot.

Unless a dog is on the job immediately, a winged pheasant has become a highly unlikely part of the bag. If you want to do it the sporting way, keep shooting until he quits moving and forget any romantic notions about running down a winged bird on foot. I vividly remember the first winged rooster I saw hit the ground and come up running with a long-legged and athletic young guy pursuing him in hunting boots. It was no contest, and if the bird hadn't tried to hide in a brushpile it would have been another lost cripple.

Almost all pheasant gunners have stories of the bird's tenacity toward life. A speeding cock is hard hit well up in the air and begins to slant for the ground. As he sails toward what appears to be an inevitable crash landing his legs begin the unmistakable motions of a running bird and keep it up until he strikes. Even when he still has 100 yards to coast, the legs are generally pumping. Perhaps this is in anticipation of the getaway; perhaps it is a test of the injured bird's escape equipment from which he will decide his procedure when he strikes the ground.

Even the dying convulsions of a pheasant seem directed toward escape and concealment. I recall having a hard-hit bird from another gunner fall almost at my feet, and the wings flapped a little as it died. The spurred legs pushed some too, and to my surprise it disappeared under some dead leaves in its last five seconds of life.

Because of the difficulty of recovering cripples and the bird's toughness, pheasant hunting has some special requirements in sportsmanship. If you don't use a dog, you must use a great deal of judgment if you are to collect more than half of your kill. The story of the hunter who arrives on hard-hunted terrain with a good retriever and finds he has a limit of birds before he uncases his gun has been told enough to be boring, but it has been true many times. There are that many unrecovered kills and cripples where hunters are careless.

PHEASANT HABITS

If they're not badly disturbed, pheasants have feeding periods in morning and evening, and some of the best spots are located by driving back roads slowly and watching closely. It's not unusual to sight dozens of birds in cultivated fields, often in close flocks, and although charging across the open farmland with a shotgun at the ready probably won't get you within range of such feeding bunches, they're likely to disperse to spots where you can get at them by a more conventional approach.

The ideal setup includes a grainfield that can be reached by the birds with a short walk from suitable resting or roosting cover, generally tall weeds or fairly thick brush, and with a water source nearby. Although birds will often fly for considerable distance to a feeding ground, the ideal setup involves only a short stroll from food to water to rest.

On quiet mornings and evenings, you'll often hear the cocks cackling, for a big mouth is one of the pheasant's weak points, and many birds have been located by listening for them. Wild-flushing birds sometimes call attention to themselves with this racket and make it possible to mark them down for later attention. The clattering squawks have disconcerted many a gunner and possibly many another predator, but not every rooster knows just when to turn them on and when to keep quiet.

Hard-hunted birds regroup and adopt new habits after a very few days of pressure, even when it's still early season. Probing tactics can sometimes unearth surprising concentrations of ring-necks in unlikely places, especially in the case of roosters, which seem to be much more wary than the hens. That's not a blanket statement about game birds and I'm referring only to pheasants. I have heard this explained as simply a case of the rooster being shot at and becoming wild, but I think wariness and wildness are just the nature of the rascal, and I think a mature cock will figure out brand-new escape routes and destinations while a hen is still fluttering around the same old weedpatch and wondering who all the people are. More about hens and roosters elsewhere.

When shot begins to rattle through the willows a savvy ringneck is likely to head for the hills if there are any. Hunting in the grain-fields and hayfields of one valley, three of us found that the birds had thinned out greatly after only a week of open season. There seemed to be nothing but hens in the coverts that had blossomed with glossy cocks on opening day, and it was hard to believe more than a small percent had been plucked.

The valley was bordered by honest-to-gosh mountains with snow on top, and we tentatively worked up a slope until we were half a mile from any grain. We put up a rooster, so we went farther and

Almost a hopeless situation with a pheasant rooster being pointed. The bird will almost certainly run or fly deeper into the tangle, and if he goes up the shooting must be quick. (Photo: Bill Browning)

finally had fine hunting along steep little draws full of willows, far up the mountainside. It was a simple case of the birds going where the hunters weren't. In limiting out with cocks, I do not recall our flushing any hens at all. Apparently they stayed in the valley, even though one hen was allowed in each daily bag.

Pheasants travel considerable distance under pressure, but if completely undisturbed they often move no more than domestic chickens. While hunting quail in Washington, we saw the same pheasants in almost the same spot each day while heading for quail cover. One cock seemed to stick to a few yards of a stubblefield that was bordered by a wall of brush and vines, seeming a perfect escape route. Sure of his safety, he'd stand and glare at our truck as it went by, and he was so sedentary we decided he must be a cripple, but I took a dog over there and found him hiding a couple of feet inside the cover. He flushed almost straight up in order to clear the brush and was an easy shot, even for me. Examination showed there had been nothing wrong with his health and his crop was stuffed with grain. He'd evidently gotten overconfident with his escape setup, but from my experience with male pheasants I'll bet that he'd have changed his tactics immediately if he'd gotten away, and the next hunter would have found him long gone as he approached the field's edge.

GUNS AND SHOOTING

Hundreds of once-a-year marksmen who swear they can't hit grouse or quail have little trouble collecting their limits of pheasants, but those who say pheasant shooting is like a barnyard poultry harvest have had limited experience. It's true that a ringneck held close by a pointing dog in waist-high cover comes out like a damp Rhode Island Red chicken, but anyone who finds it too easy when high-crossing pheasants have a tailwind must be a very fine shot.

The driving and blocking systems used in some Midwestern cornfields will give you a wide assortment of ranges and angles, and before the day is over most of us will find an angle we don't hit too well. Where driven game is pushed at gunners over high hedges or rows of trees, I understand the pheasant becomes tough enough for almost anyone and clean kills on "tall pheasants" are well remembered.

Whether it comes up out of a muddy cornfield or is a product of meticulous game farming and sails over manicured grounds, I am inclined to believe the "tall" pheasant isn't as tall as we like to think it is. The fact is that the Chink doesn't believe much in altitude, and unless there's something to push it it'll travel only 30 or 40 feet up by choice, even when it's going a long way.

I don't believe I've ever seen a pheasant higher than 100 feet from the ground, and I've seen very few higher than 70 feet. There's a good rule that overhead birds are closer than they appear and that crossing birds are likely to be farther than they look. Anyway, in puttering through some shooting books that contained photos of high-flying pheasants I did some measuring, using photographed objects of known size as a basis, and came to the conclusion that however high those pheasants looked, none of them was more than 90 feet above the shooters. However, some birds have been known to get 100 yards up and go far more than 2 miles.

Besides those missed because of routine shooter errors, like lifting the head from the stock and stopping the swing, there are some pheasant misses that demand special attention.

First, of course, is what I call the "big-bird miss," which happens with Canada geese, oversized sage chickens, and wild turkey. It's simply a case of the bird being so large and apparently so slow that the shooter points carelessly, neglects to swing, and assumes that no lead is necessary. Perhaps the best remedy is to concentrate on the bird's head, convince yourself that it can fly as fast as a teal, and try to decapitate it. The cock pheasant has a special protection in his very long tail. It is very difficult to shoot 4 feet ahead of a thing that appears to be almost 5 feet long and barely moving, and the bemused hunter subconsciously considers the flowing tail as part of the bird's vitals. Where birds are hard-hunted there's a ridiculous number of fat and healthy roosters without tails. People simply shoot them off.

Whatever else the pheasant may have going for it, it doesn't take off very fast, especially if there's much cover to surmount before being airborne. Its wings belabor the vegetation, it cackles inanely, and when it comes up it seems to hang helplessly for an endless while. A trigger-happy hunter is likely to shoot too soon, and he is likely to neglect any sort of lead at all. If he connects, the range may be short enough so that all he collects is feathers, but he's quite likely to miss. I have, on occasion, missed both shots from my double before the bird was at a suitable distance. In self-defense there are times when they get up pretty far out and there may be some need for hurry.

When it gets up 20 or 25 yards from the gun I can't say the ring-neck is precisely a simple target. Usually it is rising steeply, and since it's already some distance out, you often want to shoot before it levels off. High-shooting upland guns often take care of the up-ward allowance. Given a choice, I suppose you'd want the pheasant gun to be a high-shooter, but if it shoots very much too high it's something that must be remembered at other times.

It is seldom that a pheasant rises facing the direction it intends to go if there's much vegetation to come up through. As a rule it continues briefly in the attitude with which it leaves the cover, and then swings to the direction of its escape. If the cover is quite high there can be a pause at the top of its rise before it lines out for its destination. For an instant it can hang motionless and it's an easy shot, but it doesn't always do it that way. Your best bet is after it's leveled off in most cases—at least partly leveled off.

Save your dainty loads and small-gauge guns for something that will come down with one or two small pellets. A pheasant takes a lot of killing, and a duck musket is often a better choice than a quail gun. I think ultralight loads are poor conservation with any game—with the pheasant they are barbaric. Unless conditions are carefully controlled, I think it takes 1⅛ ounces of shot as a sensible minimum for pheasants. I generally use 1¼ ounces, and I have needed 1½-ounce short magnums in a 12-gauge. You can use the whole list of chokes dependent upon the shooting conditions. Ad-justable choke devices are excellent, for the cover can change completely with a few steps. My pet combination of improved cylinder and full choke in a double gun is pretty good.

In cover where everything is likely to be short-range, especially with pointing dogs on birds that haven't been hunted hard, you can get by with a skeet or improved-cylinder gun using No. 7½ shot. That's a typical upland situation, and a light 20-gauge will work, but if you can't restrain yourself when something unusual occurs out there at 35 or 40 yards you'd better have No. 6 shot and something like 1¼ ounces of it. I'd say the all-round pheasant gun should be a modified choke, that the 20-gauge is about as light as

Dr. Jim Smith, Livingston, Montana, dentist, finishes some wet walking. His gun is a custom Bernardelli.

you want to go, and that it should be a 3-incher for most hunting; and although I am a double-gun addict myself I have seen many cases in which a quick third shot is badly needed.

As I look back, I can't recall very many doubles on pheasants, and I'm proud of it. Certainly there's enough time if you put up several birds together, but the importance of keeping an eye on a target until it hits the ground and bounces surpasses any need for a double in my book. And when you feather a bird and he keeps going, however raggedly, shoot again and then reload before you go to pick him up.

Even when you're not deliberately driving them to each other there are many instances in pheasant hunting when a bird will come to you from another hunter. There is also an unwise pheasant stunt of flushing and peeling back over a shooter. There are some occasions when birds come at you from great distances, and now and then you can get down or even hide behind something in the hope a bird will come close enough for a shot. Many of these are flushed a long way off by hunters who never see them at all, and although they're alarmed, they're thinking mainly of the guns they are escaping instead of any they might be approaching.

After being moved by dogs or hunters, pheasants occasionally get knocked off from duck blinds. The first time I ever sighted a flying pheasant from a duck stand he was coming straight at me across a considerable expanse of water, and until the last instant I couldn't have told you if it was a Canada goose or a crested titmouse. By the time I had identified it, decided the pheasant season was open, and got my pumpgun sorted out, it had flown 5 feet past my ear and kept on going back of the blind somewhere. A year later a similar thing happened, but that time I quickly figured out that it was a pheasant and dropped it. The inability to identify familiar birds in unfamiliar surroundings comes up repeatedly, even with experienced hunters.

Pheasant guns seldom need the speed required in grouse cover, although the walking can be long and tiresome, often in snow and mud, and the light upland weapon can be welcome if it carries enough punch. The most common shot size for pheasants is No. 6 but No. 5 and even No. 4 are excellent for wild late-season birds if big shot can be used in guns that shoot tightly enough to make it effective. Plenty of pheasants are bagged with long and heavy trap guns, although most target guns carry too long a stock for a hunter who is likely to be wearing almost everything he owns on a cold November day. A short stock helps the gun to come up.

PHEASANT MANAGEMENT

Pheasants live differently and can be managed differently from other upland game birds. Biologists are constantly on the pan with one group or another where pheasants are concerned, partly because pheasants are so highly valued as game and partly because they are so big and showy that people see them the year round.

Two things are especially important. For one, the cocks are so different from the hens that is possible to set cock seasons with little danger that many hens will be killed accidentally. Then, the breeding procedures do not involve a pairing off each spring, as happens with so many other birds, and the tribe is highly polygamous. This means that the population of males can be pretty well shot off with no permanent effect on the overall population. The necessary number of cocks for satisfactory reproduction is subject to some argument, but it's pretty well agreed that seven hens to one cock is a satisfactory proportion. Ten to one has been reported a workable arrangement under some conditions, and even more one-sided counts have worked.

Now if there is satisfactory cover it is very difficult to overshoot the roosters in most cases, and even where it seems there are "no roosters left" you'll probably see one for every seven hens flushed. Not only is there no harm in shooting most of the cocks, but extra roosters left after the hunting season are simply gobbling the food that might as well be used by productive hens and taking the places of young birds that could just as well be reared for the next hunting season.

From the game manager's viewpoint, the ideal situation is to have the cocks harvested down to a minimum, for the fewer cocks left in the cover the more chance of a big crop of young birds. The plan is to have as large a turnover as possible, and if the production potential for a given area is 100 birds for the hunter each year and only 50 are bagged, there are 50 wasted from a game-management viewpoint. The extra birds left in the weeds will either be lost to natural causes or will carry over and replace the new birds that should be coming on.

There are pheasant areas where only a slim resident population exists and game managers feel that introduction of a batch of cocks each fall will sweeten the bag. But remember that these are put-and-take birds, and it's to be hoped all of them will be harvested. If so, they will have no effect on the next year's crop.

Many pheasant limits include a hen, and this is one of the most common causes of friction between landowners and management personnel. There's common sense on both sides. Where there is an overpopulation of pheasants or where there are too many hens for the supply of roosters, the hen harvest can be desirable, but it's hard to agree on what's an overpopulation, and some farmland has been closed to all hunters because game managers insisted on legal hen shooting.

You can't have different hunting regulations for every farm, but pheasant populations often vary widely, even in limited areas, and the problem of whether or not to shoot hens can get complex. It's tied in with the mysterious requirements of pheasant habitat and hunter psychology.

For example, let's take a hunting area with a sparse but continuing pheasant population. The pheasants never really boom, but they're nearly always there, and hunters count on them although limit kills aren't common. Perhaps there is another form of shotgunning in the immediate area, and although the pheasants aren't really thick enough to be the basis of an all-out hunt they make a supplement to rabbit, quail, or duck hunting. Because there are larger pheasant populations nearby, the limit includes two roosters and one hen—but the catch is that they aren't necessarily bagged in that order.

Now the hen pheasant is not as hard to bag as the cock. She seems somewhat less adaptable to hunting, she tends to lie a bit tighter under dog pressure, and is less likely to evacuate the area when guns begin to boom. All of this means that your average hunter figures he isn't going to bag a limit in the thin area anyway, so he shoots the first pheasant that gets up, generally a hen. The hens are easier to come by and they are the most plentiful, so the crime is compounded. The take isn't a ratio of two to one at all and may be lopsided in the other direction; possibly several hens are taken for every rooster, since most of those who kill a hen may never get a shot at a second bird. I know of places where it works like this and the hen season makes bad management. We might end up with more males than females.

The pheasant is a farm bird, and although there are some that live in comparatively wild country, all the large populations are close to man's operations. They are primarily grain feeders, and their lives appear to closely parallel the domestic chickens that they sometimes join at feeding time. Pheasants tend to be plentiful in corn or wheat country, and the first impression is that all they need is grain, water, and some escape cover, but it hasn't worked out that way. Here's a bird that has been managed for centuries over much of the civilized world, but there are still big gaps in pheasant knowledge, especially where habitat requirements are concerned.

When the Chinese pheasant first got a good hold in this country, following an introduction in the Willamette Valley, Oregon, in 1881, professional and amateur biologists began trying them almost everywhere else there was room for a bird to stand. There were hit-and-miss introductions, but a pattern began to emerge. They didn't seem to do well south of northern Oklahoma at their southernmost point. In the East they insisted on staying even farther north, so the immediate conclusion was that warm weather simply didn't work for them. All sorts of pheasants were tried in the South, where the bobwhite could stand a little help, but it didn't work. Then, when pheasants prospered in isolated spots of the Southwest where temperatures often became extremely high, it began to appear that excessive humidity was the problem farther East. But that wasn't the whole story, for there were some unproductive spots where there was plenty of grain, considerable cover, cool weather, and moderate humidity.

It appears now that soil fertility and composition is the controlling factor in more places than we realized. It isn't enough for the soil to be productive of sufficient grain; it must produce other things too, probably suitable grass and weeds in suitable quantities, but that's about where the biologists bog down. Pheasants prosper best on fertile soil, but exactly what that soil must produce is something of a question. Lime seems desirable. We believe now that it isn't necessarily warm weather they can't take; we think soil that is not subject to thorough freezing isn't often suitable. Glacial soil has a good record in pheasant production. Arid sections with extensive irrigation are noted for pheasant crops, possibly because well-dried soils have a reputation for fertility.

Successes of pheasant introduction are many, but the outstanding failures have come from the Southeast, where a wide variety of strains have been tried. Some of the introduced birds have been of startling color and came from little-known parts of Asia where the climate appears to be the same as that of Alabama or northern Florida, but it just hasn't worked out. The game-management people show no sign of giving up, and Dixie hunters haven't lost hope either. Consequently, quail or turkey hunters occasionally meet exotic apparitions in the field, lower their guns, and wish the best for the strange, bright things that occasionally cackle up from ahead of their pointers.

Pheasants are big enough and showy enough that they crop up frequently in history. It's believed they got to Europe from the Caucasus in southwestern Asia, and the Greeks had a crop of pheasants. The Chinese spoke of them much earlier. The English got their "English pheasants" from Europe and have had them for several hundred years. The "native pheasants" spoken of by early Americans were actually ruffed grouse for the most part, and some American hunters still refer to them by that name. Although there were attempts at rearing the exotics in America long before that time, the birds really got their start in the Willamette Valley. Those were Chinese ringnecks, and there was an open season ten years later. Although they have since been mixed with other kinds of pheasants, the Chinese birds seem to be the basis of most American populations, and ours are called simply *Phasianus colchicus*.

Although there are some in the Southwest, most American pheasants live in the northern United States and in southern Canada as far as 400 miles north of the border. They have undoubtedly displaced grouse and quail in some areas, but they've been here long enough now that hunters feel they've as much right to the land as the original residents have. They're tough and resourceful game, highly adaptable as to diet. Until recently I thought a pheasant rooster was very nearly head man against any upland game smaller than a turkey, but a report on pheasants in the sandhills of Nebraska by Ward M. Sharp and H. Elliott McClure states that the salty little sharptail grouse can chase a cock pheasant away from winter feed. Surprised me. But evidently the pheasant can get along in close proximity to a variety of game. I have found them living alongside, if not actually among, quail, prairie chicken, ruffed grouse, sharptails, Hungarian partridge, sage hens, and chukars. There appeared to be no competition during hunting season but I don't know what happened as the winter got cold.

Since it is not particularly difficult to raise ringnecks in captivity, there are innumerable introductions by farmers who enjoy handling colorful birds for fun. Pheasant raising is a pet project of youngsters preparing for farming careers. After informal observation of the results of such projects, I am wryly convinced that the birds tend to seek their own levels and most of the introduced birds simply disappear unless they are released as gun fodder just as a season opens. Some of the experiences would be funny if they hadn't involved so much honest effort.

A young student farmer released a batch of young pheasants on an area that appeared to be ideal pheasant cover and sold some memberships in a hunting club. A friend and I bought memberships and were on the scene when the season opened, several weeks after the birds had been released. We worked the place carefully with three dogs and shot some pheasants, all right. Fact is, we collected most of those we saw, but after a couple of hours it appeared we'd pretty well worked the area over, and I was about to suggest we leave some for someone else when my more perceptive buddy took an appraising look at our birds and announced that none of them were young enough to have been part of the release. After that we hunted very hard in hope of finding some of the club pheasants, but we found none at all, and I have no idea where they went. The assumption is that they had either perished to natural predators or had been chased off by the resident birds, who weren't looking for company. A similar project by another sharp young farmer turned out the same way.

A rancher who had Hungarian partridge on his property invited me to hunt the place just as pheasant season opened. Since I'd never seen any ringnecks during a number of Hun expeditions, I was a little surprised and cross-questioned him a little. The explanation was that the fish-and-game people always released a number of pheasants each year several miles from his place and that they traveled across his land in "leaving the country." The usual route was up a wooded creek bottom and past some grain bins. There were pheasants there, all right, but just for a few days.

The business of learning where put-and-take cock pheasants are to be planted each fall becomes something of a game with hunters, and farmers or ranchers who are to get a supply of pen-raised birds often take delight in keeping it secret from all except a few close friends. Then, come the season opening, the landowners call up a few of their cronies and have some undisturbed shooting before the general public has located the bonanza. Most game departments have found that the releases should be postponed until just before season opening or a large percentage of the birds will simply disappear.

Some years ago, a friend of mine wangled a big bunch of pheasants for his ranch, after what he considered a series of strokes of political genius. The birds would be put out several days before opening, and since there were already some pheasants on his land, my friend was quite confident they'd stick around long enough for some sport. It didn't work out, though.

"Hell," reported my buddy, "not only did the new birds leave, they took all of the others with them."

Opening day was a complete blank, and it was a long while before there were any pheasants on the land at all.

Pheasants have some rather unusual grouping tendencies. Although they don't pair off in spring as do many other birds, there is a general mixing of the sexes. Then, as fall comes on and after the young are flying, there is a rough grouping as to sex, and it is possible to find bunches made up almost entirely of hens or entirely of cocks, a separation that becomes more definite as the winter deepens. Such groupings can give amateur observers a false idea of the population.

Although hen pheasants do not commonly hatch more than one brood a season, it is possible that they will try again if early nests are broken up. Pheasant nests are crude affairs, generally only shallow depressions, if that, and early nests are likely to contain more eggs than late ones. April nests often have twelve or thirteen eggs, but the tail end of the hatching season, which often comes in September, finds nests with considerably fewer eggs, and this condition has been reported over a wide variety of range. The incubation period is about twenty-three days.

The fall population is made up mainly of birds of the year, and in good years about 70 percent of the hen population has been hatched the previous spring or summer. Even if there is no hunting, natural losses figure out to something like 70 percent, a figure that keeps cropping up in game-bird ecology.

Despite the usual association of large pheasant populations with grain fields, the adult can get by on very little food if necessary. It can also survive severe weather if there is any sort of windbreak, although blizzard conditions have resulted in extensive losses.

Pheasants can burrow in snow or thick vegetation and go without food for a month.

Predation seldom has a great influence in the population. Skunks, coyotes, or foxes will destroy some nests, and hawks or eagles are responsible for some losses, mainly of young birds. Feral house cats have proved the major killers in some areas. Dogs can kill young birds and destroy nests. Hens show a strong preference for hay, especially alfalfa, as a nesting area, and the mowing machine is one of the most consistent killers. As hatching time nears, the hens become increasingly reluctant to leave their nests. Because of their need for grit in their crops, pheasants gather on roadsides and are victims of highway travel. This weakness is capitalized on by poachers or legal hunters simply too lazy to walk.

What is a good pheasant population? It must depend upon the cover and food, of course. Although any experienced hunter can take a quick look at 100 acres of land and tell you very nearly where the birds will be bunched at a given time of day in a given season, the number to be put up from a given clump of willows isn't much of an indication. It usually figures out that one bird per acre for a large area is a very potent population indeed.

The pheasant is a brassy, garish Oriental type, hardly a gentle-man's bird as it is hunted in this country. It is certainly not the hardest bird to hit and seldom the hardest bird to find. Its ability to carry shot is hardly a recommendation, for there is a larger per-centage of crippling loss with pheasants than with any other species. Admittedly the ringneck is one of the most intelligent birds of all, but it is so large and colorful that despite its mystic methods of concealment it can be pretty well hunted out if the cover is thin.

But all of this is offset by the fact that the pheasant can be farmed like any other crop, and given the food and cover it will be with you when many other birds have disappeared. There is no rise quite like the clattering, squawking catapult of the Chink, and although expert scattergunners may sneer, the surveys show it generally takes more than three shells per pheasant in the coat. It is also the subject of considerable planning on the part of the hunters, some of whom do it without a dog, and anyone who thinks pheasant hunting is simply a matter of walking through the weeds and shooting birds should go out with a true expert and compare

bags after a few hours. Pheasants are preferred table birds, probably because they have a lot of white meat and are short on the
"wild" taste. A mature cock will weigh about three pounds and a
hen about two.

The ringneck has found a home here, but that's nothing new, for
he has been spreading over the world for thousands of years.

CHAPTER V

Hungarian Partridge

THE DOZEN GRAY BIRDS leave the ground with minor twitterings. For several hours they have been on the edge of a narrow draw, one of a series of deep grooves in the mountainside.

There is a trickle of spring water in the draw and a few patches of snow in the shade of the scattered willow clumps. The partridge have avoided the thicker weeds and willows, spending most of the day high enough on the shoulder of the depression so that they can see for a considerable distance, and their feeding has been desultory, mainly on weed seeds. Most of the chilled grasshoppers are gone now, but earlier in the fall they were a mainstay of diet.

The covey has been resting out of the wind, but they take off into it, then turn steeply only 10 feet from the ground and drive down the slope. A thousand feet below them are orderly patches of yellow wheat stubble and some cropped green-brown alfalfa fields with neat haystacks. The ranch roads are dark streaks between the wheatfields, and there are tiny silver dots marking a small river, largely hidden by its cottonwoods and alders.

The downhill flight takes only two minutes—over the sage flats dotted by black Angus cattle, past a sprawling structure of sheep

These Hungarians just happened to swing back past the shooter when they flushed wild on a windy day. Where grass is short like this, the Hun can be almost impossible to approach.

pens, and over the irrigation ditches that have drawn water from the river farther upstream.

The covey does not appear to have a leader and goes in a compact wad, hardly distinguishable from blackbirds at a distance. It makes one sharp turn and drops into a field of stubble, its wings giving off one quick glint from the low November sun. For a minute or so, several heads show alertly above the stubble level; then they all disappear for the serious business of gleaning scattered wheat kernels. Now they are where Hungarian partridge are supposed to be—in a grainfield. But a bird that may sometimes choose an 8,000-foot snow-spotted slope of the Rockies in late fall, within plain sight of a warm fertile valley, is not easily catalogued.

When two studious Hun hunters (there are only a handful) compare notes, there are few arguments but much amazement, for the Hun is so adaptable it fits situations undreamed-of in its native Europe—and thus it replaces prairie grouse, outlasts pheasants, and frustrates men and dogs.

The Hungarian or gray partridge *(Perdix perdix)* came from Europe in a series of poorly recorded introductions, many of which failed, and it is hard to name the exact source of a given population. For example, the birds of the northwestern United States are believed to have resulted largely from Alberta plantings, made after U.S. introductions nearly petered out. Huns had been tried in the eastern United States by many early settlers, but it was in the first ten years of the twentieth century that they really adopted the slopes and flats of the West and northern Midwest, and it is there that they are most plentiful today.

Those who have identified them only with grainfields are surprised to see them hale and hearty on the sage hills, many miles from agriculture. I have found them living and flushing with chukars on a high, sun-toasted Idaho ridge, and I have seen them go ahead of a bewildered dog together with a cackling Chinese pheasant from Montana bottomland. They will feed beside pheasant or sharptail, and although the larger sharptails will chase them away from choice spots, persistent partridge that keep returning will finally be allowed to stay, perhaps a reflection of the bigger picture in which the tenacious little birds replace prairie grouse. I believe that no one understands them well—and when I have discussed them with a European gunner I found that our experiences hardly overlap at all.

In Europe, they are gunned expertly from numbered butts ahead of thoroughgoing beaters, and in Europe their culture is highly successful, but I doubt that they have been truly *hunted* at their perplexing best. If you intend to do that, you should condition your legs, get on terms of mutual tolerance with your dog, and try places like Washington, Oregon, Idaho, Montana, the Dakotas, Alberta, and Saskatchewan. There are very good populations east of there along the northern U.S. border—but you must make a great deal of local inquiry.

For that matter, all local inquiry anywhere must be thorough and explicit, for the Hun lives an unobstrusive life, hunting it has never been commercialized, and many ranchers who have grown up with Huns do not know them by any name unless they call them "little chickens." In the best Hun-hunting country I have ever worked, I have been told by a game warden that there were not enough of them to bother with, and in one of the best areas, the ranchers told me I was welcome to look but they couldn't recall any birds answering to my description. With this backdrop of mystery, you may be able to accept the vagaries of Hun behavior with less annoyance.

The Hun is about twice the size of a bobwhite quail, and the body shape is almost the same. The overall appearance is gray or tan, and it is seldom that the gunner sees the halfmoon of buff or brown on the adult bird's gray breast until the game is in hand.

Speed of flight is about the same as that of the bobwhite, although the beat of the rounded wings is somewhat slower and I believe the Hun has more change of pace. I think the bobwhite can take off faster. I have seen Huns fly along at what seemed to be the same speed as that of the chukars they accompanied, and I have seen them beat a sharptail grouse for the first 50 yards, although I doubt if their sustained speed is greater. They quickly leave a rising pheasant, but when the pheasant gets up speed there is probably little difference. I do not consider the Hun an erratic flier, and even when it attains top trajectory and teeters slightly on set wings it goes on a fairly straight line unless flipped by the winds it often lives in.

A startled covey that has been surprised at rest will go in a clump, and their reddish-brown tails are much in evidence. It is a noisy rise, not only because of the flailing wings but because of an invariable series of squealing chirps. There is a tendency for them to change course after climbing 10 or 15 feet, a close-formed covey seeming to wheel as one, but discipline is evidently shortlived, for many bunches disintegrate for scattered landings, especially in rough country. The first flight is seldom much more than 300 yards and may be less.

Most Western Hun seasons open in September, when there is a wide range of size among the young birds. I have seen hens on lupine-bordered nests late in July, although the normal hatching season is much earlier. Even in their northern range, there may be pairing as early as February, a process well-completed in March. Birds shot from a covey as late as early October may be of three distinct sizes, adult birds as well as at least two ages of birds of the year. There is no doubt that a female may nest a second time if her earlier efforts are broken up, but there is no proof that ideal conditions will bring off more than one hatch, and such a performance would be highly unusual.

Early coveys are usually family groups, but later there is a combining of small coveys, and occasionally there are very large flocks, especially late in the season. The average early covey in a good year numbers around fourteen birds. A hen may lay as many as twenty eggs in a sparse ground nest, usually in a clump of vegetation, but the nest may be surrounded by fairly open country and is generally near to water. In one Montana area we found several nests along a small creek in grazing land, almost exactly the same distance from the stream—about 20 yards. The nest is probably located near where a covey will live, but that is not a fast rule. In fact, the fast rules are discouragingly scarce.

After hunting late fall coveys for years, one shooter firmly believes that any covey made up of members of several broods is likely to split up by families when hard pressed. He is convinced that each family breaks for an area with which it is familiar, probably where it was reared. I have watched this process (if that's what it is), a large bunch gaining altitude and then dividing into

Hun country can be big, and Huns generally settle it sparsely. Dedicated Hun hunters must be willing to walk, and it's often a long way between fences. Dr. Jim Smith finds himself in an awkward position as Huns take off in a bad direction for a left-handed shooter.

two separate contingents, each of which sticks pretty close together.

Huns will frequently roost in shallow draws, sometimes assuming the circular pattern of quail coveys, and sometimes squatting in groups of two or three and separated by several feet. They may live on the very edges of grainfields—or they may live on mountain slopes and fly down to feed. Those that come from the heights at feeding time are likely to fly back upward when moved by hunters, and these are some of the longest flights I have seen.

Given a creek bottom or weedy ditch as a home, the birds will stay on the edge of thick vegetation, penetrating rosebushes or buffalo-berry bushes only under unusual conditions. When approached by dogs or hunters, they often actually move to more open ground, evidently for a better view of their surroundings, an opportunity to run faster, and a chance to fly without the handicap of heavy cover. But tired or flustered birds, especially singles, will pitch into the thickest brush available, evidently having no plans of flight.

The same locations support coveys year after year, fewer birds when there have been poor hatches, and there will be a "beaver-pond covey" or an "old-shack covey" or a "grainery" covey through the seasons. Even though the partridge cycle (if so definite a term can be used) is at low ebb, the old established covey sites will be occupied, and some hunters believe that the places are nearly ideal homes, occupied by a new bunch immediately when abdicated for any reason. At least in some instances, the birds are strongly territorial, but it can be a shifting territory, less rigid than that of some other birds. Perhaps this is one key to the Hun's hardiness. I have known a group to live close to abandoned farm buildings for a decade, apparently keeping other groups away, although the roosting sites were somewhat scattered.

I have found a covey in one small creek bottom for six consecutive years, and although it may be found at widely separated points along the draw, it has invariably flown to the same small, rocky canyon after the first rise. Above all, the Hun prefers a "thin" population, and Hun country has many acres to the covey, even in the best years. In bumper years, there is a tendency for displaced birds to appear in unlikely places, and in mountain country this may mean high altitude. The individual coveys insist upon plenty of elbow room and tend to travel until they get it, even if the conditions are not ideal. The best sites continue to be occupied through good years and bad, but some of the poorer cover will be completely devoid of birds if there's a bad hatch. I have made some long trips to hunt birds where they had been plentiful, and when there are none there I can usually see that it had been simply a haven of displaced birds. Although the Hun is often described as a follower of the grainfields, I am sure there are coveys that live and die with no access to grain.

Abandoned ranch buildings such as these often have a covey of Huns because of the winter shelter and volunteer grain. There is nearly always one bunch at this spot.

The attraction of unused farm buildings for Huns is well known. Not only will there be a variety of volunteer grains about the place, the birds may actually use old buildings for concealment in severe weather. Shelter belts of the north country, tight rows of trees on the north side of occupied or unoccupied farm buildings, are perfect cover for the Hun, giving it protection from the slanting snows but leaving it room to move and look about. And adult Huns may share the premises with skunks, barred owls, or hawks, apparently watchful enough to remain safe among their enemies. In Alberta, where modern machinery and large holdings have caused abandonment of hundreds of weathered farm structures, I have seen a platoon of fat birds scuttle around the corner of a crumbling house and disappear somewhere about the rusting machinery and lopsided barn, tenants of what was the cozy farm home of another era, its builders gone for forty years. And in the high country, I have found my dog frozen in a point against the side of crude sheep shelter with Huns streaking across the musty interior to leave by a broken door, roar off down the slope, and disappear in a bend of the arroyo.

The partridge often forage until quite late, and a rancher friend swears that he has seen an entire covey feeding in the grass late at night and illuminated by the rectangle of light from his window, certainly accepting man's works as a convenience.

There are Hun failings, sometimes exploited by careful hunters, and the very best of the gunners are those who hunt the same areas and the same coveys year after year. Although this year's covey may be made up of totally different birds, it is likely to follow some of the habits of last year's flock. There are some groups that slavishly follow a given sequence of flights, even through as many as five flushes, if they can be followed that long.

On one of my earlier Hun hunts I watched a bunch flush wild from a fallowed field and sail off over a sage and rabbit-brush flat, disappearing somewhere in a creek bottom. I followed with a restrained Brittany, and he caught the scent but before he could point there was another wild flush, which ended in heavy sage. That time we were able to get close enough that I killed one bird and was able to mark the covey for the third time. After their third landing, the birds ran for a long way with the dog trailing laboriously; then they took off too far away for a shot. On the fourth

Ben Williams gets on a Hun that had been pointed in this draw between cultivated fields. His dog, Gina, is confident there'll be a retrieving job.

landing the dog pinned part of them and I walked to easy range. It was exactly where they had been when we first found them. On later trips after that particular covey I was able to guess their next stop, even though I could not see them down. The circular course is common, but it is seldom a covey can be followed that far without disappearing over a hill.

There is some strange relationship between Huns and snow. Like some other upland birds, notably the ruffed grouse, alarmed Huns are quite willing to fly straight into a snowdrift, and they can use loose snow for shelter during severe storms. I saw a large covey of Montana birds fly from a gravelly hillside as I approached and sail over lower ground to pitch out of sight into a soft drift. In seconds, the drift was speckled with their suspicious heads, but they were not handicapped in their next takeoff, for they went almost straight up together, beating the powdery snow as an aid in their acceleration.

Then I came upon a single patch of snow on a hillside, all other snow in the area having melted. It was a chilly day, and Huns seem to have no aversion to 100-degree heat for short periods in summer. But on that single patch of snow sat an entire covey, somehow preferring snow to lush grass. I have heard that they play in snow, but I have not seen it. I do know that Huns are very alert in shallow snow and inclined to fly before a hunter can approach them, evidently feeling they are easily seen.

Much less vociferous than the chukar, the individual Hun can remain quiet for long periods, even when separated from its flock, but there is a "lost" call, a thin, reedy sound much like a loose fencewire sliding through staples in a high wind. Few hunters and few dogs recognize the squeaky signal, almost certain to be heard in late evening if a covey has been broken. Ben Williams, the Montana Hun expert, loves to stay on his favorite grounds until dusk for that reason. A rapid walker, he runs three bird dogs, and quickens his pace as nightfall nears. At least one of his dogs appears to recognize the "lost" call.

It is a shameful truth that a large percentage of the Western bag of Huns comes from road-hunting with the birds shot on the ground. Around four o'clock each afternoon in fall, many coveys seek gravel and dirt roads for grit and are likely to return daily to almost the same spot if undisturbed. Their neck-stretched curiosity of passing cars is likely to be fatal, and under such circumstances they often bunch closely, so many a casual shooter gets a "mess of chickens" with a single shot without leaving his car. This is no reflection upon road drivers who locate hunting areas and then go on foot for the shooting.

Anyone who drives much in Hun country for very long is bound to come upon a covey along a road or trail. They stand and gawk or simply patter off a little way and stand to watch. There are several procedures to be followed, any of which may be wrong. I used to leave dogs in the car, grab a gun, and step out, whereupon the birds usually do one of two things—either they disappear in grass or weeds, or they flush and fly for a short distance, perhaps no more than 30 yards, and drop back into the cover. I used to leave dogs in the car because I didn't trust them with birds in plain sight, especially if the dogs were fresh and eager. After one of those abbreviated flights from the trail, however, I have had very poor luck getting any shooting without a dog. The game simply fades into the undergrowth or flies again before I'm near enough to shoot. There are exceptions, of course, but unless you think your dog is too excited to be reasonable, you'd better put it on the ground when you step out. On some occasions, when I've waited until I've failed to put anything up on my own, it was too late for the dog to score. The birds would simply run out of the area, probably scattering as they went.

I've had similar experiences with several other kinds of upland game, although the Hun is an outstanding example of a bird's reaction to vehicles. If the birds have been gathering grit on the trail or road for most of their lives, they are probably used to cars, trucks, and farm machinery, and simply get out of the way for them. A man walking toward them is something else. Bobwhite quail are noted for similar performances.

DOGS

In a very good year, it might be possible to bag a respectable number of Huns by diligent hunting without a dog. The procedure would be to learn the locations of specific coveys by long observation and then to hunt only those spots where birds had been seen, preferably where there were definite attractions such as small creeks or weeds at the edges of stubblefields. There are very few Hun hunters who operate without dogs, and most of those do it only as a sideline to other kinds of shooting.

A good Hun dog should hunt wide, for it has much land to cover. It sounds like a job for an English pointer, and if I had to choose a Hun dog by breed, that's what it would be. I am aware that there are some circumstances where a close-working dog is best, but the overall picture calls for the big-goer. When you do get close to the birds, a high degree of dog control is necessary, because the

Ben Williams collects a Hun from Michael McGillicuddy, the star performer of his kennel of pointers and Brittany spaniels.

Hun as a runner is in a class with chukars and pheasants. Only a few canine sages have learned deliberately to head off a sprinting covey, and I have never owned one of those treasures, although I have seen the miracle performed a few times.

Flushing dogs are welcome along weedy farm fences, but when the terrain is wide pastureland, even the lean English pointer probably can't cast too wide. There is no bird hunting I know of where reading a dog's actions is more important, and a strange dog, however proficient, may become a mysterious creature, even to the old Hun hunter. As the dog finally stops after a prolonged period of birdiness, it is hard to tell whether it has actually pinned game or has simply gotten too close to running birds and has decided to wait on them. You may call it a point if you like, but it may be better than a point, for there are some staunch stylists who will remain in a classic pose while the birds casually walk over into the next arroyo, plucking an occasional weed seed on the way. In any event, it's good to walk in promptly when Huns are pinned, for they can become restless in a hurry and it's no time to wait for a gunner who is some distance off. Courtesy probably won't pay, and as long as everybody understands, no feelings should be hurt.

There was the time in Montana when the birds held tightly on a grassy slope almost under the dog's nose. There followed a concerted rise, which gave me easy shooting, the birds swinging over a strip of stubble and disappearing on the other side of the hill with me and the dog in what we thought was close pursuit. There indeed was excellent cover, the sparse grass the Hun prefers bordering a few willows and some juniper clumps in a deep draw, and the dog prowled industriously to no avail, although it appeared he was endeavoring to ground-trail in several places.

It was when I returned to the truck, parked only a hundred yards from the first find, that I had dog trouble, the persistent rascal refusing to load up and insisting upon retracing his steps to the scene of his triumph of half an hour before. When whistle, endearment, and strong language had failed to bring him from a classic point, I left the gun in the truck and stomped after him. As I

Somewhere on the slope in the background are several coveys of Hungarian partridge, probably just below the snow line. Bill Browning and the author finish their lunch before beginning the hike.

A perfect Hungarian rise at easy range. Much of the time
they'll be farther out. Bird at far right is coming down. Birds often use
back-country roads like this one for grit gathering.

reached for his collar to yank him away from the lingering scent
of the long-gone covey, they rose in a noisy cloud around my un-
armed person, having simply walked around the hill in a return
to the place where they had started. It was not a freak occurrence,
for I have seen it repeated several times. A pointing dog in Hun
country should be attended with a ready shotgun, and it should
never be doubted until proven wrong. And proof is not always
simple, for when you release it from its point after you've been
unable to flush anything, it is likely to ground-trail for a while and
then stare forlornly about. It is hard to say whether they have been
there or not, and if so when.

There is the top-of-the-hill tradition, too, one of the more reliable
Hungarian performances.

Flush the birds and watch them swoop gracefully across a valley,
tower upward in dying speed, and drop gently into the grass near

*Ben Williams hurries toward dog, knowing that Huns are
likely to run up the arroyo. This is typical Hun territory in grazing
country of the West.*

the ridgetop across the way, somehow disappearing in cropped
brown grass and small, scattered bushes. Rush headlong down the
slope and pantingly up the other side and they will fly out of range
and over the hill, for they have never stopped watching you.

Or follow the rule and leave them time to walk unseen over the
crest. Once over the hill and out of your sight, they may be at ease
and simply begin feeding. Now you stealthily climb the hill behind
them and, best of all, the wind may be in your face, a boon to your
curbed dog, who probably wonders what's going on. Then when
you top out, you proceed cautiously, and the chances are that there
will be birds on the other side, not far from the top.

But often there will be a quivering point, a sputter of wings, and a single bird will show you its red tail and streak off down the slope, and after you have killed it or missed it you will stand with your warm gun, gradually tensing up until all your marksmanship is gone, and wait for the covey to roar up. But it will not appear, and the dog will sniff uncertainly and roll its eyes at you, and you'll eventually trudge off after a new covey. I don't know where they go.

And there is the reversed field, less frequent but almost ghostly in its final effect.

Jack Ward and I put up a veritable swarm of Huns in a small patch of sage, and they whirred away toward a little arroyo and pitched over the edge and out of sight on locked wings. They did not reappear on the other side, so we estimated twenty-five birds down in a 30-foot-deep dead-end notch. One of us walked toward the open end of the depression and the other proceeded dead ahead, while the dog quartered nervously to the tune of verbal cautions.

We came within range of the little swell and limped along with the hesitant gait of a nervous shotgunner trying to keep his left foot forward as much as possible. We caressed the safeties and our palms sweated. We twitched violently when a meadowlark came up out of the spot at the bottom of the little draw where there was a little streak of weeds, higher than the other cover. We told the dog to go on down the little slope and wondered why he had evidently forgotten how to point, but no birds came out. We glared at the opposite side of the declivity, unable to believe the Huns had run out, for the ground there was bare except for scattered grass blades. We turned and walked back the way we had come, prepared to hunt in another direction, and the dog trotted out before us.

And then two Huns flushed, fanning the sage tops at full speed, their nerves apparently cracked by the ordeal of walking back past us while we were stalking them in the other direction. My friend caught one in the easy swing of a man who has not had time to tighten up, and by that time the dog had pointed back near where the main covey had first flushed. The sage patch was full of them, an entire flock that had flown into the little declivity and then scattered to walk brassily back in the direction they had come from, somehow eluding two alerted hunters and a quartering dog. They came up as singles or in twos and threes and we hunted for two hours in no more than five acres of cover. Even so, we never flew the entire covey.

In the open Hungarians are like other birds, restless in a high wind, but the wind is not all bad, for it indicates the best hunting spots will be on the lee sides of cover. But once a covey begins to land on the very tops of bare ridges on a windy day, they can be almost impossible to approach. I have heard there is no use in trying to get a shot on the first flush of Huns, but it simply is not true, for there are times when they hold tightly, even when they are adult birds and completely fresh. There is, of course, the racing dog that strikes body scent at top speed and plows to a stop, causing birds to freeze with the sheer shock of its presence.

GUNS AND SHOOTING

For most of us, the typical lightweight upland gun will be best, and if we must split hairs, perhaps the perfect choice would be a double with one barrel improved cylinder and the other full choke or improved-modified, a rather unusual combination with more merit than is usually recognized. If there is a typical Hun situation it is birds rising a trifle wide, perhaps at about 15 yards, and flying over open country. At first, the choice would seem to be a full-choked gun, but only a cool hand does his best with it. If he waits until his careful swing scores well, he will fire his first shot at around 35 yards and then must hurry on the second. Less accomplished marksmen will generally do better with a fairly prompt shot at around 25 yards and then a deliberate try at longer range with a tighter barrel. Modified boring is probably the best choice for repeaters.

Some of the most frantic Hun debacles occur when a rare covey allows the shooter to walk into its very midst in a narrow draw, and then flies up about him like gargantuan bumblebees with the usual reproachful chirps. In such a situation an entire bird may disappear into a pink haze before a properly pointed full-choke charge, but most full-choke shooters will not score without steely nerves and the ability to count to three before doing anything.

Very small guns are generally out of place. The Hun deserves no less than an ounce of shot, and I generally shoot 1¼ ounces of No. 7½ in a 3-inch 20-gauge over-under that is bored modified

A Hungarian partridge is a pretty bird, but the dog wants to get the photography over with and go on hunting.

and improved cylinder. A slightly smaller charge, 1⅛ ounces, will do almost as well, but I have never used 1-ounce loads, needing all the help I can get—and it is very rare that one of my birds is too hard hit for the oven. To get into the fine points, if you use a full choke, No. 6 might be a little better, retaining enough density out to more than 40 yards in a tight barrel. Most of the hunting takes considerable walking, often in tilted country, and heavy guns make it harder. Still, the very light gun is unnecessary for the shooting itself, and there is no problem of brush except in rare instances. I have hunted them with duck guns, but would rather not carry that much weight.

My pet for Hungarians weighs 6¼ pounds, and a friend uses a 5½-pound 16-gauge that he is careful not to leave within my reach. Two shots are enough for most covey rises, although there are times when a widely scattered covey is found while feeding, and these sometimes go up as pairs and singles. A repeater can be a help here, but some double users swear it's a disadvantage, claiming they can reload fast enough actually to get off four or more shots faster than a repeater can accomplish if plugged to three shots. This is a matter of individual training, and the argument can never be settled.

Now and then a covey will split up with individual birds holding incredibly tight, getting up almost at your feet and giving straight-away chances. For some unexplained reason, the singles tend to leave closer to the ground than the freshly flushed coveys and they also seem to maintain a straighter course. Perhaps the individual birds within a covey are affected by their associates' behavior. At any rate, there seems to be more swerving. You can compile all sorts of figures about Hun speed, but they have a remarkable change of pace. I have never understood the occasional flush in which there seems to be no hurry at all. Then, there are the explosions.

The Hun has unusual habits that vary with its environment—adaptability that allows it to prosper where the birds of pioneer history have failed. And perhaps this adaptability comes from the selective breeding of centuries in tightly settled communities of the Old World, an environment the prairie chicken or the heath hen could not face. Now the Hun takes over where its naive predecessors have faded before the tractor and the automobile.

CHAPTER VI

Chukar

CHUKAR PARTRIDGE ARE DIFFERENT, so different from our other game birds that they are developing their own cult of hunters, but so far they have been largely underharvested. Hunters are very slow to accept new species of game birds, and thirty or forty years of American chukars simply is not enough to convince pheasant or quail hunters that the Asiatic import is here to stay.

The chukar has turned its back on what some hopeful promoters were sure would delight it. The Midwestern grainfields seemed an obvious heaven for an Indian pedestrian who had been trying to make a living on sunbaked semidesert for a few thousand years, but after the widespread Eastern and Midwestern introductions had fizzled, the biologists finally realized that the chukar wanted what it was used to. It gratefully accepted the near-desert country of the West and prospered on rocky slides amid cheatgrass, rabbit brush, and sage, apparently preferring land that wasn't good for much of anything else and displacing no native birds. So far, it has been rather difficult to get the hunters to follow him. There are chukars that die of old age without ever meeting a shotgun.

Eastern Oregon generally has chukars in plenty, and if a short

Chukars are big birds. The gun is a Bernardelli, bored improved cylinder and full choke for the unpredictable ranges at which chukars are shot.

climb won't get you to them, a longer climb will. The better the season, the less the effort, of course, and we took a camper, a four-wheel-drive rig, a shotgun, and a Brittany spaniel to Vale, Oregon, during a good year. The map shows Vale in a pretty blank area of the road map, far enough from any large city that we were unprepared for the crowded trailer park. There were electric lines across electric lines, there were four-wheel-drive trucks, there was a waiting line at the washroom, and a background of dog noises. Since I'd been led to believe the Oregon chukars were lonely and neglected, I made inquiry as to where all the chukar hunters had come from.

"Aw, those aren't chukar hunters," said a man exercising two German shorthairs. "The pheasant season opens tomorrow."

As elsewhere, the ringneck is the magic bird in Oregon. A few of the gunners may be looking for chukars before the pheasant season begins, but once that happens the chukars are largely left alone.

My wife and I started out the next morning with Warren Mc-Gowan of Vale as an impromptu guide. I'm a little vague as to just how we moved in on Warren, but I'd heard he knew about chukars and I'd asked information for his number, warned him by telephone, and then went to Vale and knocked on his door. We bounced out of town, going West on U.S. 20, and after several miles Debie inquired: "Is that a chukar up there on that rock?"

"Sure is," Warren said. "Just pull off here and we'll see what we can do about it. There's a little road that runs around behind him."

The chukar had been standing in plain sight on a bluff that overlooked the road, obviously attending to sentry duties, and Warren explained the next move. There were probably several birds, he said, possibly a big covey, and they weren't likely to fly across the road. We'd get downhill back of them and walk toward the highway in the hope they'd fly downhill over us. That's what we did, the dog picking up bird scent almost immediately. He worked well ahead and pointed up the slope, but before we could get to him, birds began to flush and bend back toward the draw behind us. It was about the third one that came pretty high and nearly overhead. I got him in the edge of the pattern and Kelly picked up my first chukar within plain sound of the highway traffic going by on the other side of the little bluff, only 75 yards from the old International Scout. Not all of them have come that easily. In fact, we hunted the rest of the day and Warren got one bird. Efforts at following up the rest of our first covey failed completely, so I guess it was a bad day for scent.

We drove up into rounded mountains, somewhat below the snow, and stumbled along over volcanic rock and through tilted patches of tall sage. Once we saw running birds cross a sandy dry wash near the rocky Jeep trail, and we scrambled sweatily through some grotesque erosions in trying to get above the birds, but they and their scent had faded away in the dry breeze. Then we heard some calling on a wide sagebrush flat; even saw a couple fly off into a steep slope, but no shooting. This had become more like the chukar hunting I'd heard about.

Warren couldn't get away with us the next day, but he directed us to some BLM land that sloped steeply up to rocky overlooks high over the Malheur River. It was mostly sage and rabbit brush cut by rocky ravines, not really bad walking, and there was a Jeep trail that went up to within a few yards of the river bluffs. I got up there, put the dog down, and heard chukars immediately, apparently disturbed by the little truck's arrival and fussing petulantly.

The chukar's call, generally a rather delicate rendition that sounds like its name repeated without variations of pitch, is hard to locate. When I have been very close to calling birds, the sound has always been softer than I expected, but it somehow carries undistorted across hazy canyons. It is invariably hard to locate exactly, and when I hear the calls I simply try to select the general direction and approximate distance and then look for an ideal spot for chukars to ·be and head for it.

But up there over the Malheur River the calls seemed to come from all around me, which they did. Somehow I had driven into the midst of a great scattered flock, birds at the very highest point of many square miles, and chukars are firm in their policy of walking upward and flying downward. These were not sufficiently frightened to flush but disturbed enough to set about hiding and

A typical spot for chukars. Rocky outcroppings are especially productive at midday when birds are resting.

sneaking, moving nervously about for better concealment but continuing their conversational calling.

A brisk breeze whipped about the crags, and the dog scented birds instantly, pointed, and then changed directions, moved a little, and began confused ground trailing. I stepped around a jumbled pile of boulders, perhaps 20 feet high, and came face to face with a chukar sentry sitting erect on a great rock and about even with my face. It was a little startled, only about 20 feet away, and remarked, "Chukar, chukar-r-r."

Despite a long history of disgraceful misses on birds that I see before flushing, I half-mounted my 12-gauge and told it to leave, so it hopped down from the rock and walked away into the sage. The dog hurried up and pointed in the direction my bird had gone, standing on a bare patch of rocky ground. While he pointed, a chukar strolled across about 3 feet behind him, looking alternately at the dog's stern and at me.

About that time the birds began to flush, seeming to come from all directions but definitely heading down over the cliffs. I was completely unnerved and missed wildly. On at least two chances I swung carefully as the birds roared toward the dropoff and then fired hopelessly over them as they dived over. Then I indulged in a little psychoanalysis, told myself that these were nothing but birds, however exotic and disconcerting, and that they were killed like all other birds by shooting ahead of them at the proper range. I waited until one was about 35 yards away (I suspect most of my misses had been at less than 10) and swung a little ahead and under as he neared the abyss. There was a little explosion of feathers and it went pinwheeling down toward the Malheur River, a gleaming streak far down there in the gorge.

It was a little difficult to get my dog headed over that cliff, but as with most of those impossible precipices, there were some ways down. The fact is I found that bird before the dog could and got ready to climb back on top, but a little covey of chukars sailed high over me and landed a third of the way down to the river, setting their wings and dropping into a little sagebrush arroyo, even steeper than the rest of the slope. I worked down on them from above and the dog pointed. Then I saw some furtive shadows flick across a sunlit patch of gray sand, trying to turn uphill, and when I thundered and crashed through the brush toward them they lost their composure and flew again, swinging up to get a few feet of altitude and then banking off toward the river. That is when I braced my feet in the sliding sand and shale, swung my over-under firmly, and killed two chukars. I killed two chukars, by golly, and even when Kelly refused to bring them up the mountain to me, I smiled and told him "good dog" for bothering to find them. I went slithering and sliding down to get my birds and heard a derisive "chuka-r-r" above me, where strays from somewhere were scuttling back up toward the rimrock. I made a fake charge toward them, then backed off and climbed up on top again, taking a circuituous route in the hope I'd meet them up there somewhere. An hour later I sneaked along the rim, heard some calls up ahead, and froze when I saw another sentry atop a boulder, its sharp gray-and-black uniform bright in the low sun, but it and its friends pitched off the precipice and for all I know went clear down to the river.

And at this point I find I am doing what so many others do when they recite chukar experiences—I am making it sound very, very difficult. Because the birds do live in some rugged country, some of it so difficult that my only advice is to forget it, there's a tendency to make too much of chukar-hunting hardship. I'm the first to say that a chukar hunter wears out his boots rather fast and is likely to have skinned knees and a shotgun that looks as if it had been used for prying rocks out of rabbit holes, but about half of the chukars I have killed were taken with a minimum of climbing, and about a third of them with no more hardship than is suffered on a bobwhite-quail hunt. By this time I have probably revealed the chukar is one of my favorite birds, if not Number One on my list. In all fairness, however, I'll confess the bird is more predictable than most, and anyone who follows instructions of experienced hunters should be in business within a few hours if the birds are there.

Now chukars are sometimes road-hunted with success, usually on back-country trails where a bunch of birds can be located from a vehicle and then followed into a flushing situation, with or without a dog. The rule of "walk up and fly down" is adhered to very strictly, and "up" can sometimes be only a gentle incline. I have often followed birds up a hill that didn't even interfere with my breathing only to have them take off in approved style when they ran out of uphill and were reluctant to start down. The pattern is

A band of chukars glean in the stubble. At such times they are likely to be nervous and often flush wild.

the same as on a near-vertical mountainside or canyon wall, where you hang on with fingernails and belt buckle—they walk up and fly down.

During dry weather, the streambeds are the favorite places for locating birds. They're down there for water, and you can walk or drive along the bottoms and jump birds or sight them running up the canyon walls. Because this system works so well when there's little rain, there's a tendency to cling slavishly to it when there's rainwater in every rock pocket in the country. Rainwater turns the birds loose, and I have found that they tend to operate high on the slopes, often at the very top of a canyon wall. When water's easy to come by, there's a tendency for them to feed in early morning and late evening and rest along the upper slopes most of the remainder of the day.

In Oregon, we found that a small grassy or sage-filled notch in the top of a canyon wall is likely to hold birds. In such a spot they are protected from high winds and have only to flip over the canyon side to make a fast escape. The notch needn't be more than 20 or 30 feet wide, but it should have some vegetation for cover. They don't need much but they want some. Much of the chukar shooting I've done has been in eroded canyons rather than on the slopes of more conventional mountains. The canyons nearly always have a creek or river at the bottom and often border good feeding areas. In Washington, for example, it is possible to walk miles of stubble-field with a precipitous dropoff only a few yards away, and although chukars can live without it and prefer to spend most of their time nearer to rock and cheatgrass, they are glad to feed on grain when it's available. In other areas, the canyons are bordered by thick sage and grasses that provide quite satisfactory rations when there's no grain around. Remember, they don't have to have grain.

Birds caught by a pointing dog in a notch at top of a canyon would normally be expected to flush down over the rim, but they often elect to run upward if they're not at the very highest part. I recall one good example in Oregon when the dog pointed at a shallow draw that simply ran out into a dropoff of several hundred

In chukar country like this, the hunter watches his footing as well as the birds and can't afford a slip. This cliff is in Oregon.

feet. I walked in and several birds flushed, one of them giving me a good shot as it headed downhill and I got it. Some of the other birds had run around in the sage in plain sight, but then disappeared and showed no inclination to fly, and for a time I couldn't figure what had become of them. Then the dog became very birdy and started away from the canyon, working up until the little draw petered out into a gentle uphill slope. He had gotten well ahead of me and I suppose the birds were peeling off one at a time and hiding in the grass, but he finally pinned two of them temporarily at the very top of the hill and probably 300 yards from where they had begun to run. One bird swung so wide I couldn't get on it, but the other towered straight up for some 40 feet and turned toward the canyon behind me. I shot it at the very top of its climb, when it was almost stationary in the air and closer than it should have been. I'm afraid that one was pretty badly mangled.

In Washington, we hunted chukar near Clarkston, just across the Snake River from Idaho, and Don Steele, a local game protector and bird hunter, filled us in on some of the local habits. My wife, Debie, was determined to make photographs of flushing chukars after many failures and was clutching a motor-driven Nikon. Chukars in the air with a grim hunter in the foreground are a tough picture to make, since flushes are so unpredictable, occur in upended country, and often result in low takeoffs that head downhill and merge into the foliage.

There's a different feel to that Washington country. You drive along a valley and then turn up on a winding road until you're in the high wheat country, yellow stubble running off as far as you can see in the haze, broken occasionally by enormous gashes of erosion with streams at their bottoms. Here and there is a cloud of dust made by farm machinery, or a farmhouse set far out on the prairie with few or no trees and frequently abandoned in this day of large operations.

The chukar pattern was pretty obvious. They fed in the stubble or topside draws, but they lived on the steep slopes of the canyons, slopes so steep that sometimes the grass simply couldn't hold them and allowed slides. There were frequent outcroppings of dark stone that made perfect resting places for birds, but some of them preferred to stay very near the top, some of them actually resting on the edges of the wheatfields at midday.

There was one bunch of six chukars that spent nearly all of its time at the upper edge of a canyon. As you approached the spot, a typical little grassy notch, the birds would take off and go sliding silently over the rim. Apparently they'd begin to walk back up immediately, for two hours later they'd be there at the same old stand. It was on the route that we drove our Bronco to and from hunting, and although we plotted long and arduously as to how I could get a shot, nothing ever came of it.

I met a single hunter on one of the slopes, and he tried to discourage me from the stubblefield shooting. There had been too much hunting of those birds, he said, and they flushed so wild there was no chance of getting a shot. Our first trial bore that out, for when you walked or drove along the edge of the stubble the birds would take off 75 yards ahead, dog or no dog, sometimes accompanied by Hungarian partridge. They seemed able to find enough waste grain within 100 yards of the canyon, and I don't believe I saw any birds farther in than that.

My plot was to restrain a couple of dogs and move slowly along just below the edge of the canyon in the hope that I wouldn't be seen from on top. When the dogs showed special interest in the uphill terrain, I'd let them run and follow as closely as possible. If I intercepted climbing chukar that hadn't yet reached the field edge, that was all right too.

It wasn't perfect but it worked. Some of the birds had gotten far enough into the stubble by the time I passed them that the dogs didn't get birdy, but as dusk and closing time approached the dogs went shaky and drooly and I let them come up over the edge with me panting close behind. We'd come up at a point where there was a narrow patch of uncultivated land between the canyon and the stubble, evidently a seepy place that was difficult for machinery, and the dogs went stifflegged and tense across that patch of weeds and grass, pointing solidly some 50 yards in from the edge. I walked ahead of them and at first couldn't put up any birds, so I let the dogs break their point and help me. The chukars went up in clouds and in ragged skeins. I shot two birds and let all others go so that I could be sure of my kills in the confusion. Even after we picked up I could hear strays calling in the weeds, but shooting hours had ended.

Remembering that chukars walk up and fly down, a careful

gunner can do well by dropping down from the top of a canyon and maintaining about the same altitude as he walks parallel to the rim. That's a trial-and-error proposition, but there's a tendency for the birds to be resting at about the same level, and when you see some fly you can be fairly certain others will be at nearly that altitude. Now, if two men are walking the face, one can go at about the level he thinks the birds are and the other can stay downhill but walking parallel with him. That's a good way for everybody to get some shooting. If you can get your dog to work above you, you're sitting pretty as long as you have it at about the right level. Whether it points them or simply bumps them, you're likely to see birds. It often comes as awkward overhead shooting at a downward-plunging target, but it's a lot better than no shooting at all.

Where the ridges are not too high and not too far apart, it is possible to circle moving coveys of chukar and come at them from above. Younger and faster men than I have been able to run them up from below in really steep country, but for an old gaffer like me that means an occasional glimpse of vague shadows, a steady chorus of chukar calls, and a covey that somehow evaporates just as I think it is about to fly. Although I have had dogs work very well above me, I have very rarely been able to get uphill to a staunch point, a simple matter of the birds becoming restless before I can get there. I have a personal rule against chasing chukars uphill, although I'll do it if the incline is slight enough.

There are occasions when the birds will go around the end of a hogback and make a confusing pattern of something that has looked very simple. In some sage hills near Boise, Idaho, I had a chukar-happy dog that pricked his ears and refused to hunt mountain quail as long as the chukars would call, no matter how far away. Those hills were rounded on top and not particularly steep, but the sage was very high and I never did see any running birds. I'd hear them calling and then try to get above them and walk down among them, but on those round hills they'd often make an end run and end up on the other side of the mound. There I would be able to get the dog on them from above with a little luck, and they might hold pretty well.

Incidentally, chukars seem to mix well with Hungarian partridge. Not only have I found them in the same habitat, I suspect that I have bounced mixed coveys on several occasions. I confess I couldn't actually see the birds feeding together, but when I put up what I thought was a covey of chukars on an Idaho slope my first shot got a Hun and after missing something I wasn't sure of at that point, I then knocked down a chukar, apparently from the same spot. On the following day I heard chukar talk from there again and nothing but Huns flew. Mountain quail, valley quail, sage grouse, and a few stray pheasants are often found in chukar country.

Running coveys of chukars tend to scatter and disappear, even as do many other kinds of birds. They seem to hold together pretty closely as long as there is no good place to hide, but once they get into good cover they can spread out. On a slope, the ideal spot for chukar is a rocky outcropping, and I am guessing they choose these places because they can see the surrounding territory. The sentry system is very prevalent. Chukar roosts are often in jumbles of talus, and when weather is severe they actually hole up in mountain caves.

You'll hear that chukars always call when separated, but it isn't so. For that matter, sometimes a covey that's merely moving along feeding will keep up a constant calling, but there are other days when you can stare off into the indistinct depths of a chukar canyon until your eyes and ears hurt and never hear a thing. The calling is most prevalent in late evening when a covey has been separated. There are artificial chukar calls that work sometimes, and some chukar hunters can get a response with a purely vocal effort. Although flushed birds come up with some unusual alarm sounds, I've never been able to interpret the other calls. Some of them undoubtedly are efforts at reunion; others are simply conversation.

A wounded chukar is hard to find but probably less difficult than a Hun, partly because it is bigger. Even a good dog sometimes has difficulties when a cripple is dropped in an area where numerous birds have been feeding. Chukars are not noted for tight holding, but I have seen some examples that would shame a bobwhite or a nervy ringneck.

While we were hunting in Oregon my wife announced she had found a pictorial spot and wanted me to pose with an especially pretty chukar I'd just bagged. The picture took considerable maneuvering, and I suppose we stood there for more than five minutes while our dog was held back at the camera. My posing finished, I broke my gun to reload it and continue hunting when several chukars flailed up from within 10 feet of where I had been standing. It must be assumed they had been there all of the time. The cover was nothing but a little cheatgrass and some runty sagebushes. I still don't know how they stayed out of sight, but I reasoned that we had approached them from uphill without too much commotion and they had tried to sweat it out. Somebody got jumpy. When one went they all went, for the dog was unable to find any more. It was some time before I could get the shells into my gun.

The finest chukar hunting I've had has been in broken country but where the canyons and draws are fairly shallow. In a 50-foot draw a chukar is likely to act about the same as it would in a 500-footer. It runs up the side of the thing and then flies. In moving through such country by four-wheel-drive we've often come upon flocks in the trail, and after trying it several ways, my conclusion is that it's best to grab a gun, jump out, and run at them. On the occasions when I've carefully put a dog on the scent and followed cautiously, the birds invariably faded away or flushed wild. When I ran at a herd of chukars it took me quite a piece to put them up, and the single bird that fell wasn't the one I'd shot at, so I guess I was a little flustered. Run fast and yell.

GUNS AND SHOOTING

A double gun wih double triggers is nice for chukar, because I don't know of any bird that's less reliable as to the distance he takes off from. If you're quick at picking a barrel you can score better.

I have used No. 7½ shot more than any other, but if the gun's fairly tight, I'd go to No. 6. I don't think the chukar is particularly tough, but it's a bird about the size of a ruffed grouse, weighing more than a pound in the larger editions.

Your gun should be light and fast, simply because of the rough walking and the occasional climbing, and although I don't practice what I preach I'm sure a shoulder sling would be a lot of help when you're climbing. I never liked the look of sling swivels on a shotgun, so I had them taken off the only gun that had them, and have wished I hadn't ever since.

Chukars can be anywhere from top to bottom of this Washington canyon, but the rocky outcroppings are logical places.

There are a couple of shooting angles you don't run into much with other birds. One is the downhill flush with the bird taking off from well below you, and there's no set rule for how to take it. I've missed quite a number of those by pulling down as if the bird were a straightaway and having him simply disappear under the gun barrel on the downhill course. Then I've shot ridiculously high. There's another miss, almost the exact opposite, in which birds squirt out from under your feet, some distance down the slope, and go out over the canyon, either in level flight or bending only slightly downward. The lead in this case must be over the bird instead of under, but by the time I decide which kind of a shot I have it's usually too late. The answer is to be fairly slow in your shooting, establishing the bird's course before the gun is checked. That means a modified choke will be best for most of us.

A chukar takes off at moderate speed, and I think it goes about like a quail or a pheasant once it's under way. When you get a crossing shot with the bird going steeply downhill, you're dealing with teal speeds and it's hard to swing too far ahead. The shot from above and overhead has been very tough for me as I have trouble deciding just what direction the bird is going. I believe I hit that one better if I let the bird go over my head and then shoot it going away.

They're inconsistent on fairly level ground, sometimes towering quickly and sometimes speeding off pretty close to the ground. The towering bit comes when you've topped out a rise and the birds are coming back over you.

DOGS

The secret of chukar hunting with a dog is tight control, whether it's a poodle or a pointer. There are times when you must hold your dog quite close, even though you may like it to move out under some circumstances. When I'm in chukar country but hear or see no birds, I'd like for the dog to get out and work, no matter what breed it is. If it can point and hold birds, so much the better, but if it bumbles into some and scatters them I at least know where they are. Then, if the dog can be held very close you can use it to hunt down calling birds or those you've seen moving.

On a given day, chukars are likely to maintain about the same level on a slope, and careful hunters work just above the likely altitude.

On some occasions, I've seen a little bunch of chukars rise and fly for only a few yards, either because they were scared by a hawk or eagle or because they simply wanted to change positions for feeding purposes, but it's seldom you can walk right into such a bunch without help. If I can get over there and get a dog on them without letting it out of hand, I'm in a good position, even though they have moved a hundred yards in the interim. If the dog runs away from you you're just as well off without it.

CHUKAR HISTORY

We didn't hear much about chukar hunting until the 1950's, though there have been some in America for a long while and skimpy records show introductions as early as 1893. There are a number of varieties of red-legged partridges, native all the way from Spain and Holland to Inner Mongolia, and although several subspecies have been tried over various parts of the country it appears that the Indian bird furnished the basic stock for most of the American populations. From 1932 on, some 800,000 birds were released. The shooting really got under way in 1951, and they've been hunted recently over about 100,000 square miles in Arizona, California, Colorado, Idaho, Montana, Nevada, Oregon, Utah, Wyoming, and British Columbia as well as in Hawaii. Incidentally, they say there are a few in Baja California and they have found a home in New Zealand.

There's considerable curiosity about chukar, very few hazy fables due to their brief presence in this country, and not too much literature on the subject. *The Chukar Partridge*, Biological Bulletin No. 4 of the Nevada Department of Fish and Game, published in 1970 and compiled by Glen C. Christensen, is an excellent job and is an updating of work Christensen completed in 1954.

Wild chukars are hard to keep track of, even for biologists. This is no garden plot bird; it is said actually to feed routinely over a square mile of lumpy country. It's been tough to find nests until after the hatch, for example. A chukar nest is a simple depression with a little lining and probably contains about fifteen eggs, possibly at the base of brush or in a tumble of rock. Chukar pair off in spring and are largely monogamous, but it's very difficult to tell a cock from a hen (the cock should be larger and heavier), and how much cooperation there is in nesting and caring for the young is hard to say.

No matter how carefully the introductions have been arranged, it has been difficult to say just which were successful and which failed. All the management people can say is that they now have good populations of chukars in certain areas. As in Asia, the chukars are likely to be pretty high in America, showing up at 12,000 feet in the White Mountains of California and Nevada. However, they live below sea level in Death Valley.

They can take very hot weather and pretty cold weather but suffer in heavy snow, and that will force them to low elevations. Much of the early-season chukar hunting is about water sources, and that's the easiest, but when it rains the birds scatter .

The combination of chukars and cheatgrass is not accidental, as the grass (an exotic, as is the chukar) provides a large share of the chukar feed. Cheatgrass thrives along with sage and rabbit brush and is noted for taking over overgrazed terrain. It becomes very dry in summer, and cheatgrass fires are quite common, but the flame is close to the ground, the burn cools quickly, and apparently chukars survive such fires without difficulty. Young chukars are insect eaters, as are most upland youngsters.

Natural predators include hawks, eagles, and owls. Snakes sometimes raid nests, and coyotes, bobcats, and foxes take a few birds, but the chukar is a durable citizen and seems to take care of himself as long as the habitat is satisfactory.

There are stories of Asiatic tribesmen killing chukars with whips while riding their ponies over the rough country. After the first flush, some members of the chukar family evidently don't fly much. The ones I've hunted were capable of several strong flights, although I can see how a hard-riding expert might get into the midst of a covey before it could take off.

In Asia the chukar is domesticated and kept as a fighting cock in some areas. Most of the successful introductions in America came from game-farm stocks, and the chukar has been satisfactory as a game-preserve target in terrain quite different from its preferred wild range.

We can use more chukar hunters. So far the shooting has been only on fringes of chukar habitat. In starkly rugged terrain like the Salmon River canyon of Idaho there's hardly anyone who wants to try the sheer cliffs and their gabby residents. No matter how liberal the seasons or limits, most of the American chukars go untouched.

Along the precipitous banks of the Owyhee Reservoir in eastern Oregon we listened to chukars calling from half a dozen points at once. One of them decided to go down to water and swept dizzily off a rocky cliff to disappear somewhere below us.

"We can't get to 'em," McGowan said. "And if we could we couldn't find one if we killed it."

CHAPTER VII

Doves and Pigeons

Dove hunting is primarily a shooting sport. Most of the thousands who shoot them each year do so without much knowledge of the bird's habits, and as long as they know where they fly there isn't much incentive toward nature study. Most dove shooting requires no equipment except a gun and shells, and since it's often a social sport, much of the "hunting" is done by telephone.

"'Dove hunter' is the wrong term," says one expert I know. "I prefer to refer to them as 'licensees.'"

In dove shooting, more shells are expended per human energy unit than in any other game pursuit I know. It is sometimes a question who is the laziest—the shooter who stands up and waits or the one who carries a chair with him. Not all the hunting is like that, but much of it is.

Reputation of the mourning dove, the most popular of the dove targets, varies enormously. I have heard it called the most difficult shotgun target of all, and I have heard it scorned as unworthy of a wasted shell because it goes so slowly in easily predicted flight. As with other birds, this is a matter of where and how the bird is hunted, and I suspect that both descriptions are completely true at times. I do know that a lot of doves are missed, many of them by excellent wing shots. My favorite dove story concerns a sportsman named Bill Miller, who lives in Pittsburg, Kansas.

Bill can shoot a shotgun but doesn't claim to be a champ, and he is one of those modest fellows who is a perpetual student of his shooting, or whatever else he does. Bill went dove shooting on a very windy day and found the doves were flying freely across a field he'd selected. On one side were some tall trees, and the wind angle left a protected area there, so Bill took up a position where he could shoot birds sliding in and looking for a landing. He was sharp that day and felt warm all over at the way he dropped game with hardly a miss—the neat gun mount, the quick, easy swing, and the little puff of feathers as the dove folded.

Out in midfield the wind was whistling at some 30 or 40 miles an hour, and after Bill had only two birds to go for his limit he decided to try the tough ones, so he walked out there and found another stand within range of the doves that came riding down the blast.

"I don't like to be a quitter," he said, "but I had to go back to the trees because I ran out of shells."

This is the whole story of dove shooting.

I know how most of the best dove shooters have been developed, and there is hardly any other form of game shooting that permits so much practice. The way some of these hotshots came up is not strictly legal, but none of them are languishing behind bars for it and I don't doubt that it will be continued in many quarters.

This happens on those big communal dove shoots where some twenty or thirty shooters surround a good dove field. Some of them are casual hunters who don't get out very often and go along for the picnic and to take home a limit of birds. They are greeted with open arms by the neighborhood hotshots, who figure twenty shooters should mean twenty limits of birds, no matter who does the shooting. So the hangers-on sit around and bust a cap now and then while some of the good shots pile up a score of as many as fifty or sixty birds sometimes. A few years of that and a dove shooter has had almost as much practice as an old-time market hunter, so he gets very good indeed. There are also some expeditions to Central America or other southerly points where the supply of whitewings is virtually unlimited and your main problem is how many cases

Mourning doves are among the most popular of American game birds, feeding largely on the ground but spending much time in trees.

of shells you can get down there with. I am not saying that these bags have much of an effect on the overall dove population.

The dove is one of the more renewable of game birds and the annual mortality is very high. The assumption is that the shooter's share comes out of this total, which undoubtedly runs 70 percent or more. The fragility of the dove is easily demonstrated at any spot they are watched closely. We have a considerable number that we observe in a baited area of our backyard, sometimes as many as eight or ten birds there at once. Through the year we find quite a number of dead and dying ones. It would take a veterinary to learn what kills them, but they die without a mark on them.

GUNS AND SHOOTING

Most dove and pigeon shooting is a pass proposition, and sometimes the gunner is presented with a long series of chances at about the same range and with the birds flying in almost exactly the same direction. Such circumstances lead to long runs of hits and long runs of misses. As in some forms of clay-target shooting, the expert can sometimes miss more consistently than the novice, simply because he is doing exactly the same thing wrong on each shot, whereas the beginner is so erratic that he'll scratch down a few birds even when shooting poorly.

Dove flight is less consistent than that of most upland birds, not only because of a great change of pace but because the bird is generally traveling instead of flushing and is likely to be high enough to be affected greatly by the wind. Most of the doves and pigeons have something of a twisting flight, sometimes erratic enough to carry the bird completely out of a pattern, and when shooting starts they will veer violently. Doves coming into a field where they expect to feed or rest may hover and go so slowly that hardly any lead is necessary. I have shot ridiculously ahead of birds that were almost hanging still in the air and looking for a spot to alight. Up there against the sky there is no reference point, and if previous targets happened to be going pretty fast it's easy to have too much swing. Nevertheless, most of the misses are behind, as with nearly all other game.

There isn't much secret about a mourning dove's normal traveling speed when there's no wind and no shot on its tail. Many times I have noted them flying parallel to a road and have stayed even with them at about 35 miles an hour. I am guessing that they can make about 45 in a hurry, and this turns into something like 60 miles an hour with a good tailwind. The mathematics of lead gets pretty complicated with all of those variables, especially since they will occasionally hang motionless for a few seconds while hovering against a breeze.

Waterhole shooting can be the easiest if you shoot just as they drop in to the bank on a very small pond, or "tank," as a stock pond is called in the West. The procedure is usually a fairly swift glide until the bird is just a few feet above the ground, when it will brake and flutter down. There isn't much excuse for missing it in those last few feet, and it's much like shooting ducks over decoys after they're actually committed and coming down. Nevertheless, I took a little time to get used to it and missed too many the first time I tried. Most of the waterhole shooting isn't that easy. Usually it's a case of intercepting the flight some distance from the water when they're going at average traveling speeds, or possibly gliding downward.

Some of the tougher dove shooting is over dove fields where every arrival gets shot at. After being missed a few times, even the densest bird will decide something is wrong, and it will be driving and twisting as it decides to leave the area. Decoyed birds will sometimes hover, but most decoys are simply for the purpose of swinging a flight closer to the guns. Where birds are moving through scattered trees and intending to alight, they can be going quite slowly and at easily established ranges.

Improved cylinder or modified bores are best for most shooters, although experts can do very well with full-choked guns. One of the best gunners I know uses a trap gun for some of his shooting if the birds are wild, and he makes plenty of kills at 40 yards or a little more. Sometimes he takes two guns—an open-bored gun for close chances and the trap gun for the long ones. On other occasions, he uses a double, bored improved cylinder and modified. Skeet boring will handle doves only at very close range as the target is quite small.

I believe No. 7½ shot is most popular for doves the country over. Velocity isn't important, but you need plenty of shot to find the bird. Some careful handloaders make up 12-gauge loads with 1¼ ounces of shot but with a light powder charge to avoid recoil. It's pattern density they're after. For pass shooting, an ounce of shot in a 20-gauge is about minimal, and I can kill more birds by going whole hog with the 1¼-ounce 3-inch magnum.

If you're going to use a skeet or cylinder gun, I'd recommend No. 8 shot. For anything else, I fail to see need for anything smaller than No. 7½. You can kill a lot of doves with No. 6, but that will require a tightly bored gun. No one could call a dove a "tough" bird and it has a light structure, but they'll often glide a considerable distance, even after a fatal hit. Heavy shot can be dangerous on a crowded dove field, where everyone should wear glasses anyway and "sprinklings" are common.

I have noticed that some of the lads with hot dove reputations shoot very fast, being interested in the percentage of birds they stop rather than number of shells per bird. I have suspected that they see where a miss goes and change the lead instantly, reading the bird's actions as they swing. Many good dove shooters use semi-autos or pumps with adjustable choke devices, and whatever you may say about hunters who never change the nozzle, these guys *do* make adjustments.

Any discourse of dove hunting comes around to jump shooting, which is very easy if you can get close enough to the birds before the flush. Unless the cover is pretty high, doves tend to get up fairly wide and the shots are rather long. I have tried to use pointing dogs, but doves seldom play that game satisfactorily; they certainly aren't mesmerized by canine presence.

So we come around to the number of shells expended per bird. Forgetting the easy shots at targets fluttering into trees or gliding down to water, and taking them as they come over fields where there are probably several gunners at work, I'll say that one bird for three shells is pretty good shooting, day in and day out. When I have killed a limit of twelve doves with a box of twenty-five shells, I feel I have had a highly successful day, and it doesn't happen often. I do feel that dove shooting is inclined to run very hot and cold, dependent on whether you've solved a flight pattern or not.

I have seen some pretty fancy exhibitions by shooters who had been shooting regularly and were getting along toward the end of the season. On one occasion I managed a run of five birds with five shells in finishing out a limit and went over to brag to Buddy Nordmann, who is one of the best wing shots I know, shining especially on wide angles. Buddy congratulated me, knowing such a score was quite an event in my rather ragged career, and announced good-naturedly that he'd settle down and try to beat me, so I smugly sat down next to a frozen orange tree and watched. Buddy stepped back so his green camouflage suit merged into another frozen-out tree, held his old Model 12 trap gun at the ready, and eyed the sky intently. Taking them as they came at ranges over 35 yards (it's a rather tight-shooting gun), he proceeded to kill seven straight and missed the eighth when he got his feet tangled in trying for an awkward double behind him. Seven straight dove kills is no excuse for a neighborhood barbecue, but to announce you're going to do something like that and go ahead with a skeptical friend watching is pretty fair country dove shooting.

One of the main hazards of dove shooting for the average upland gunner is the fact that you have plenty of time to think about it before you miss, so few shooters can resist the overpowering temptation to cheek their guns and track the incoming birds. That leads to swing-stopping, head-lifting, and a lot of other things. Worst of all, it becomes a matter of mathematical leading, something best left to a very, very few master marksmen. On doves, I use a swing-through, although I'm somewhat ahead when I pull the trigger—still

A Labrador retrieves a dove to Buddy Nordmann during an afternoon shoot in an open field.

gaining on the bird in the most common form of wing shooting. Nordmann is very deliberate with his trapgun, lining up with care, "stringing out all those sights and ribs and things," as he says, before he actually goes for his lead. On close-in birds, however, when he's using an open gun, he's one of those free-swingers who follows through like a golfer.

I was entranced by the operations of a Southern dove shooter I watched in the middle of a dove field, well away from the majority of the shooters, who were strung around the borders. He had a ditch to hide in and most of his targets were really splitting the breeze. As a bird would appear he'd watch it intently with his old hump-backed automatic across his knees. As it approached shotgun range, he'd stand up in a low crouch, the gun still down low. Then as the bird reached the point he'd chosen, he'd straighten quickly and swing his gun hard and fast as if the birds were inches from escape. His score was excellent, and he wasn't doing the dramatics for effect. He knew he could hit them better by not dawdling. Perhaps his moves were a little exaggerated, but most of us will do much better on doves if we leave the gun down until we're ready to shoot. Incidentally, the same methods are essential in pass-shooting ducks, and your average duck hunter is likely to make most upland gunners look bad on doves.

SOME METHODS

Any dove or pigeon changes dramatically as the hunting season wears on and it's had a few escapes. The doves that come to our baited spot in the backyard are rather tame until after the season has been open a few days, then take off almost like sharptails. In some of the early operations, mourning doves don't pay much

Charles Nordmann of Florida shoots incoming mourning doves at the edge of a known roosting area in late afternoon. Camouflage is useful for dove shooting, although true blinds are seldom built.

attention to men with guns and might even come within range if they stand in the middle of 40 acres of grass. Later on, the hiding becomes more important. Camouflaged clothing is a great help, but very few dove hunters build intricate blinds, and most of them just stand against something that will break their outlines. I am confident the doves can see them most of the time but either don't recognize them or feel the plainer something shows the more dangerous it is. Where doves are coming in to roost or rest in trees they seem to be concentrating on landing spots and little else.

After being shot at or witnessing some shooting, birds tend to fly in the open and away from fencerows and bordering brush. This is a case when a few decoys on a fence or in a low tree might swing something your way. Most dove shoots are during the afternoon, morning shooting being illegal in some states, and it's logical to expect birds to come in about three or four o'clock for feeding, but doves are frequently ahead of schedule, and if they're not very hungry are likely to land in trees. One of the deadliest kinds of shooting is in scattered trees surrounded, or nearly surrounded, by open feeding areas. They'll come coasting into the trees and flutter along slowly looking for a place to perch and rest awhile, and the shooting can be easy. Later in the day, all arrivals may be in a hurry to eat and then go to roost, so they'll bore right into the field. Birds leaving after feeding aren't likely to fool around either, especially if it's late. Fields that are shot too frequently are abandoned by the birds, and some of the sharper operators keep close check to see just when it's time to renew a bombardment.

The standard pattern for doves is an early-morning feeding period, then rest during the middle of the day, with an afternoon feeding period and a visit to water before going to roost. Several things can change the schedule. For example, if food is plentiful the afternoon feeding can be very brief, a matter of only fifteen minutes or so, after which the doves might head for water early and simply loaf around until nearly time to go on the roost. Thus there may be good pass shooting near a waterhole, even in mid-afternoon. Under other circumstances, the arrivals would be too late for legal shooting.

In much of the northern range, early-season shooting is much simpler than that which comes later. Resident birds will have well-defined patterns of feeding and roosting, but once they move south and are replaced by migrants, the picture may be completely different. This is one of the factors that cause a good dove field suddenly to go stale. Residents that have been using it have been replaced by migrants having other ideas. Farther south, the birds may be less definite in their movements but the same thing happens to some degree.

Dove roosts are usually small and brushy trees. I have heard of birds crowding by the hundreds into a very small area, but most roosts are fairly scattered, several birds to each tree. This is in keeping with the rather loose flocking tendencies of mourning doves. The flock is not a close-knit group, and when flushed, a dozen birds may go in several directions, although there is a tendency for pairs to stick together, even when the mating season is not near. Migrating doves will often travel in large flocks, but they're scattered and there are numerous dropouts. There seems to be no group discipline, and migration is generally in short stages.

The roosts can provide productive shooting, even during midday, for birds often rest in the same places they roost, and it is possible to jump-shoot them where trees are thick enough. Two or three hunters can do better at that, for they'll usually go out of a tree on the opposite side from a single hunter and it's possible to drive them to someone else.

DOVE HABITS

Mourning doves or "turtle doves" (*Zenaidura macroura*) winter over most of the lower states and summer as far north as southern Alaska. Although the typical nest will contain only two eggs, there will be more than one nesting a year, possibly two in the North and several in the South. That's a safeguard of dove populations, and it isn't known whether one strain of birds stays put the year around while others migrate or if the thing is even more confusing than that. On some shooting grounds you'll have resident birds, migrating birds on their way somewhere else, and still others that have settled in for the winter, having come from farther north. Add to that a few birds who have been farther south and decided to move back up for one reason or another and the complexity begins to show. That's why shooting is so unpredictable, except in the early season when nearly all of the birds are natives. Even so, the south-ward movement may start very early in the fall.

Dove nests are fairly low in brushy trees, and they don't take much pains with them. Somebody else's abandoned nest is all right too. The females lay a couple of eggs, and both birds hatch them out by sitting in relays, feed them for a while with "pigeon milk," a regurgitated liquid, put them on their own, and make plans for another family. They breed somewhere in every month of the year. The whole works, from the male's first engaging coo until the scraggly youngsters hop off the limb, takes only a month. Then it starts over again. Maybe six broods in one year in the South.

The dove courting display takes place unnoticed by most people who live among them. Males are slightly larger, with more irides-cence in their neck feathers, and do a little strutting after the fashion of barnyard pigeons. They then take courting flights, going up fairly high and gliding downward in circles. The mournful cry that gives the bird its name is produced by the courting males, and its effect on humanity varies widely, causing some listeners to be-come quite sad. I like to hear them, having been raised where they were thick, and feeling it's a restful sound. The word "ven-triloquial" is overworked concerning bird sounds, but it sure fits the dove's cry. To me, it always seems to be farther away than it is.

Since mourning doves are migratory, they come under the frame-work of federal law, each state being allowed a certain number of hunting days if desired. A number of states still classify the dove as a songbird, primarily in the East. The continual argument over whether doves should be shot or not makes it impossible to guess just what states will or won't open seasons in a given year, and some of the maps are out of date. In any event it is not a matter of protection of the species as a whole. It has been proved that doves do just as well under controlled shooting as under complete legal protection. Their natural defense in hunter enthusiasm and discouragement is highly effective. When the doves are scarce or have moved out, hunting stops, law or no law. The dove is a favor-ite subject of the anti-hunter, even more popular than the quail, and its association with peace and love has done nothing to help the sportsman's case.

Doves are seed eaters and partial to many farm crops, eating corn, wheat, and sorghums. Bristlegrass is listed as a favorite crop content, and there is a wide variety of weed seeds on the menu, including doveweed and pigweed. Although baiting a dove field is illegal, planting dove fields is approved practice, and brown top millet is a favorite crop. The managed dove field is a rather recent practice of state conservation agencies. Appropriate crops are planted and public shoots are scheduled and supervised. Brown top millet is one of the more popular crops. The dove is not much on scratching or tree feeding. Doves and pigeons drink without tipping their heads backward, drawing the water up from a stationary position.

WHITEWINGS AND OTHERS

Whitewinged doves are a little larger than the mourning dove, have a bold section of white on their wings, and lack the long sharp tail so distinctive in flight. They fly less erratically, and their wings don't whistle like the mourning dove's. The mourner's wing whistle has been compared to that of the golden-eye but isn't nearly so loud.

Whitewings afford plenty of shooting in the very southern part of the United States, in Texas, New Mexico, Arizona, and California. They're also in Nevada. That seems to be the northern part of their range, and many of the big whitewing shoots are south of the border. The whitewings range clear into South America, and their choice of food is about the same as the mourning dove's. At times they are found in flocks of mourning doves and they occasionally stray wildly, even showing up in Florida on rare occasions. The whitewing (Zenaida asiatica) is divided into two subspecies, the Eastern being somewhat smaller and probably the one occasionally bagged east of Texas. At times the whitewings have been thick enough to damage crops, but the population goes up and down.

Bandtailed pigeons have open seasons in some parts of the West and live in oak and pine woods. They are best known along the Pacific Coast and have a reputation for very swift flying. They're larger than the domestic pigeon, which sometimes goes by the classier name of rock dove.

The domestic pigeon or blue rock is a European import that may sometime be widely recognized as a really difficult game bird in the feral state. Years ago I was talking to the late Ernie Simmons of shotgun-specialty fame and found him bubbling with enthusiasm over some pigeons he'd been shooting in the Idaho mountains.

"Plain, ordinary domestic pigeons gone wild," he grinned.

It was the first I'd heard of "rock doves" in the mountains. Sometime later I saw them flying about at dizzy heights on Rocky Mountain cliffs over a trout stream. Some of them are in truly impossible places, but I learned of some pretty wild shooting in a few spots. One trapshooter told me that he and his friends worked in pairs on some of the cliffs, and he showed me how it was done. The cliff he chose was vertical for the most part but there was a slope of talus coming down from the lower section. The idea is to climb as high as you can get on the talus with your shotgun, get your feet braced, and signal to your buddy down in the canyon. He cuts loose with a high-powered rifle, smashing the bullet into the cliff high up. The pigeons loafing and sightseeing in the crevices and caves near the top come clattering out to see what's going on, usually diving down in that sizzling sweep common to the tribe, and the poor guy on the slide rock is supposed to shoot them. You can use the same pigeon repeatedly in this sort of operation.

I have found barn- and bridge-dwelling pigeons almost as hard to hit. One of my more humiliating pigeon experiences came from an effort at trimming the barn population back on the farm. There was a large flock using the place and making a terrible mess in the hay mow, going in where the hay rope entered at the roof peak. The barn was exactly 40 feet high and I thought it would be sporty shooting to have someone chase the pigeons out through that little opening while I stood on the ground with my trusty pumpgun and cut them down. Everything worked according to plan except the execution part.

They'd dive out of that hole and hurtle toward the ground in gathering flying speed, with me industriously working the pumpgun and spraying empties one way as fast as I sprayed shot the other. My success was almost nil until I conceived the dirty trick of waiting until they had gone as close to the ground as they were going and were pulling up again. So I walked out away from the barn a little to be in good range and things worked better. I don't recall nailing but one bird as they did their dive.

These are the same pigeons used in competitive live bird shoots, a sport that is illegal in much of the United States but flourishes in Europe and Mexico. There are two systems. One formula calls for the birds to be placed in traps, and they are released just as a jet of compressed air gives them an initial boost. It's a row of traps, their tops level with the ground, and the shooter doesn't know which one is to give forth the bird. When it comes out, he has two shots with which to drop it inside a low fence. Some of the shots are mighty easy, and some are danged near impossible. The other system involves a thrower who flings the bird high into the air at command, and he and the bird cooperate in trying to fool the shooter. By pulling feathers from the bird's wing, the thrower makes some erratic targets. He usually takes out the tail feathers to keep

Ordinary "domestic" pigeons are used in live pigeon shoot, being released from ground-level traps. The same bird lives in the wild state in cliff areas of the West and makes a difficult target, especially on windy days.

the bird from braking his flight as he is thrown. All of this can be pretty expensive, even if you don't gamble.

There are numerous tropical pigeons I've never seen, some of them easy to hit and some extremely tough game, I understand. The white-crowned pigeon, fruit pigeon, or Cuban pigeon is generally a fairly slow flyer where I've watched it. It can be found in the Florida Keys but is not hunted there. The red-billed pigeon shows up occasionally along the lower Rio Grande River in southern Texas, but if I've seen that one I didn't recognize him.

The two pigeons native to a wide band of the United States were the band-tail and the passenger pigeon, now extinct. The passenger pigeon deserves a little comment, primarily because hunters have been blamed for destroying it. Its loss was partly because of commercial hunting and netting and because of destruction of nests for the squabs, which were considered a table delicacy, and the passenger went from flocks that "darkened the sun" to nothing in a short while.

In the first place, sports hunting didn't destroy the passenger pigeon. In the second place, it wasn't really a game bird, having a slavish addiction to flock movement. It nested in droves, traveled in droves, and roosted in droves. I have read that if you'd find one of those endless flocks flying cross-country and bending its course a little to avoid a pole you could cut down the pole and the thousands of following birds would continue to make that little swerve for hours. Whether that's true or not, I don't know, but the stories of blind shooting into solid masses of birds don't sound like sport. It was simply a slaughter, and the overharvest shouldn't be blamed on sports hunters. The near loss of the buffalo is a similar case. The plains bison had little of the qualifications of a game animal. As the passenger pigeons flocked, the bison herded.

CHAPTER VIII

Ruffed Grouse

"THEY MUST BE a different species of bird," my friend said in a tone I'd never heard him use before, and sounding as if he were trying to change a bird's feathers by sheer will. He was an Easterner, a fine wing shot, an owner of bird dogs, and seemingly highly reasonable on most subjects.

We'd been hunting sage grouse, but the subject was ruffed grouse, and I'd been telling him of the ruffs I'd found in western Canada, some of which refused to fly from small trees and one of which had watched me walk by from a distance of 6 feet, perched in plain sight on a fallen log. A startled look at my buddy's stricken countenance and I realized that I had crudely encroached upon a sacred subject, so I said the only gentlemanly thing:

"Oh, I suppose so. They just look a lot alike. The natives up there call them willow grouse."

Both he and I knew we were talking about the king of gamebirds as found in wilderness country, but the subject was closed. It was not the first time I have approached the subject of ruffed grouse too lightly, for I first met my ruffed grouse at the back door—or more precisely, on the side of a Western mountain where they were

*Frank Woolner, New England ruffed grouse authority, examines three
birds in Massachusetts. (Photo: Frank Woolner)*

simply somewhat different birds found among blue grouse and a
short walk from pheasant cover. To be a real ruffed-grouse man in
my opinion you must be raised with them—in the East.

The ruff is king, and having achieved its station through heredity,
its reign is no more disputed than that of other monarchs ruling
by divine right. Its only challenger is the bobwhite quail, a gentlemanly bird with respect for fine dogs, but the bobwhite can be
raised on game farms and sometimes becomes democratic through
sheer numbers. And although the ruff can be a backwoods bumpkin
at times such vagaries are not discussed in court.

The tradition of the American ruffed grouse has been abuilding
for three hundred years and has grown mainly in the Northeast,
where the ruff may not be as plentiful as elsewhere but is sought
by the cream of upland hunters with fine guns, tireless legs, and

love. Perhaps their greatest tribute to the bird is their year-round attention to its welfare and numbers. They also write endlessly of it, buy each other's books, and refuse to compare it with any other game. An outsider like me might enjoy poking a little fun at their devotion, but I am engrossed in almost any ruffed-grouse literature I find, having read Frank Woolner's *Grouse and Grouse Hunting* three times, and envy them their lifetime contact with the bird. Their attitude is one of unabashed sentimentality (rife among many upland gunners anyway), and it would be pleasant to be one of their cult. My principal object of gunnery sentimentality is the Wilson's snipe, in which I seem to be nearly alone, and if the ruffed-grouse shooters will be nice to me I will be nice to them.

There is no single trait that makes the Eastern ruffed grouse the king, rather it is a combination of appealing features. A ruffed grouse makes a roar when it flushes, but so does a bobwhite quail. A ruffed grouse flies erratically through heavy cover, but I doubt if it can beat a valley quail at that. A ruffed grouse flies swiftly at times, but probably not as fast as a downhill chukar. It drums a haunting fanfare to spring, but this is less bizarre than the prairie chicken's communal booming. It lives in a beautiful land, and although a ptarmigan's wind-scrubbed peak might be more spectacular, perhaps this is the key to the whole thing, for in the East it is a land of traditions, of succeeding cultures, of the abandoned stone fence and the gone-wild apple orchards. So it can be the king, with its combination of all these things, and may more of its regal mien attach to its Western kin in years to come.

MASTER OF COVER

The ruffed grouse *(Bonasa umbellus)* is a resident of the borders, as are many upland birds, but it is primarily a wilderness species, seldom having much of a bent for grain or garden. Apples are something else, but the grouse could get along without them as it did before the pilgrims arrived.

Grouse hunting is made challenging because of the bird's use of dense cover for protection, and although it has fairly rapid acceleration in takeoff, it is its ability to put obstacles between it and the gun that makes it an extremely tough target. There is little doubt that this is deliberate rather than accidental, and although some may swear otherwise, the trick was probably developed to escape birds of prey rather than No. 8 shot.

The ruff has short, rounded wings that can make a great deal of noise as it takes off, a racket that may fluster predators, including shotgunners. The roar of the takeoff, which is often accompanied by a boil of leaves from the forest floor and violent whipping of bush tops, is highly disconcerting for beginning shooters, but it gives me more opportunity than the ghostly shadows that slide ahead of me in some covers. The grouse may adopt the sneaking glide repeatedly in some areas. I don't know, but I suspect this is more common where there hasn't been much gunning pressure. The explosive takeoff is more likely with wilder birds, and especially those that have been approached quite closely before flushing.

The sneaky, silent escape often isn't seen at all, and that's its object. Sometimes it happens behind a hunter who has walked past a close-holding bird, and very often it is a ground-skimming tactic where cover is scarce. It isn't as easy a shot as it sounds, and it is one of my toughest, for I never can believe (until after the miss) that the bird isn't going to tower at any instant and I shoot over him. In some of the primitive hunting areas, one of these escapes gives a dog user an excellent chance for another flush as the ground skimmer doesn't often go far. However, he is likely to run away from a walking hunter. I have had such birds fly no more than 30 yards, dive into a clump of rose bushes, and disappear forever.

In many western "partridge" spots, the birds have a habit of the double flush—first hopping into a tree, possibly not far from the ground, and then doing either a noisy or silent getaway from the perch. If it's the silent, ground-hugging flight it can still be very fast, for the bird gets a quick start in diving from the limb, even if it doesn't drive hard enough for the traditional thunder. I recall one such trickster on a Rockies mountainside. My dog pointed at a clump of juniper and three grouse came out. Two of them disappeared in some unaccountable fashion and the third simply hopped up into a head-high spruce tree and sat there in plain sight, its topknot stretched in warning that it was going to fly as soon as it could decide on a route.

Before we go further, I may as well confess that a bird jumping downward from any tree is my most difficult shot, one that has resulted in many funny remarks on the part of my friends. There is one hunting companion who says he will jump out of trees all day and break his fall with an umbrella, giving me all the shooting I want at a dollar a shot. I am not that bad.

Anyway, the grouse in the tree decided to fly and came right at me, veered off at surprising speed, and skimmed over a patch of ground-hugging juniper to disappear in the shade of the forest. I fired twice and looked carefully for a dead bird where he entered the shadows, but neither I nor the dog was very confident. The bird had flown no more than three feet high at any time. We then moved on for a few yards and the bird flushed again, no more than 50 yards from the original jump, going silently very near the ground, and this time I spilled it into a clump of juniper, but I wasn't sure until the dog found him.

I've seen this ground-hugging flight quite frequently when two gunners are walking a little distance apart, or when dogs are operating up ahead and the bird accidentally flies very near me. This has happened most often where there was a rather skimpy undergrowth with scattered bushes or juniper. In most cases, the other hunter hasn't seen the bird. Frequently the dogs are working it but haven't been able to pin it. I've seen the origin of such a sneak several times, and one of the most interesting was while mule-deer hunting in the edge of a logged-over area, where I was following an old logging road. I saw a ruff sitting on a stump only a few feet away and watched it from the tail of my eye as I trudged on through the snow. After I'd passed it by about 15 feet or so, it slipped off the log in an owl-like flight, crossed the road, and sailed into some bushes well up a hillside. I think the silent flight is more common than we ordinarily believe.

To the embarrassment of its admirers, the ruffed grouse can be stupidly tame in country where it is not hunted much, and the stories of adults killed with sticks and beheaded with .22 pistols are true. It lacks dignity, but the shotgunning under such circumstances can be just as difficult as where the birds are educated. It may be hard to convince a New England grouser that he can miss a bird that sits and watches until he drives it from its perch with a stick, but if the brush is thick such ruffs can be well-nigh impossible, and a wing shot's swing simply is not grooved for birds spearing downward in the willows or upward through pine branches.

In the latter case, the birds may be headed for the top of a mighty tree where nobody is going to potshoot it, flush it, or even find it. They're tough enough for shotgunners in the back country, even though they are sometimes easy victims for snipers.

The most impossible grouse shooting I have ever done has been in willow draws with a few alders and brambles thrown in. Under such circumstances I have had birds flush within 5 feet and still be unable to get my gun into action. I would say nobody could kill ruffed grouse under such conditions, but I have seen it done by some specialists who could somehow manage enough room to get their guns pointed for quick shots at very close range. Of course they are able to swipe away brush with a practiced left arm, cheek their guns simultaneously with their right, and get off quick shots at the instant the left hand touches the fore end. Athletes have an advantage here, and there's a premium on short, light guns. The ideal gun for such scratchy work is a sawed-off weapon, and it might as well be a singleshot, but I don't think anyone is going to spend the whole day under such cover handicap, and that kind of gun wouldn't be quite so handy if things opened up a little.

Ruffs are not fast runners, but they're persistent at it and would rather walk than fly most of the time. Many years ago I was on an elk hunt and had been hauled by four-wheel-drive to a very high ridge at dawn with the scheme of walking downhill for several miles, and at one point found myself confronted by very dense brush between aspen patches. It was so steep there that I didn't want to walk around it, so I stooped over and began to slip along some sort of game trail with foliage knitted overhead. I had to continue my crouch, and after a few yards found I was following three ruffed grouse who had no intention of flying. They were about 8 feet ahead of me for some distance and paced along without much effort, but when I speeded up they gave evidence of haste and finally appeared to be tired of their running. They spread their wings, partly for balance, I suppose, bristled their feathers in alarm, and scuttled along like barnyard chickens. Finally they got off the trail but never tried to fly. I think the cover was too thick for a takeoff.

This was pretty early in the season, late September, and the birds were undoubtedly young ones. Many Northern and Western grouse seasons open a bit too early, and birds of a late hatch are neither strong flyers nor wise enough to fly when they should. They are often caught off base in situations that more experienced birds would avoid. When pointing dogs catch grouse, I think it is nearly always young birds that aren't really mature enough for gunning. As mentioned elsewhere, once in British Columbia I took my Brittany into grouse cover immediately following a ptarmigan hunt. After the nerve-wracking ptarmigan, his manners were badly frayed and he was quite willing to charge a bird that was clumsy in take-off. His first point was in a wide-open farm clearing spotted with brushpiles. Several grouse flushed, obviously a family covey, and one of them was somewhat hampered by brush. He caught it and injured it so that I had to put it in the bag. Lamenting this event, which was hard on both grouse and dog, I moved into nearby forest and immediately found more birds, probably part of the same bunch. He picked up another grouse that became tangled in a fallen treetop. That one wasn't injured and I released it.

Before indicting game management that permits such early seasons, remember there is very little serious grouse hunting in that country, that the supply is plentiful in most years, and that game managers try to have the grouse season open during nearly all big-game seasons. More grouse are sniped for camp meat with rifles or .410 shotguns than are shot in the air, and I doubt that the hunter's take has the slightest effect on the population. In much of the West the ruff is listed as part of the "mountain grouse" roster which includes blue grouse and spruce grouse. That is often the first game open in September, and if the season isn't opened early there is hardly any harvest at all. You seldom see a late-season shotgunner in the high mountains.

I am sure that all the mountain grouse lose prestige because a large percentage of the birds are too young to be strong flyers when the seasons first open. There are plenty of birds in much of that country, but it is elementary hunting compared to that of the East. I think the birds are just as hard to hit, once they mature, but Western hunting for grouse usually lacks the finesse employed where the birds are a beloved tradition. Grouse dogs are almost unheard-of in primitive areas.

There are some spots in the Northwest where ruffed grouse are hunted along with pheasants, especially where the ravines are choked with willows and spotted with conifers and aspen groves.

These areas may border mature forests, but not necessarily, and one grouse area I have hunted is located farther from heavy timber than any ruff is likely to fly. It is a series of tiny creeks, each lined by brush and trees, and the brushy strips are from 20 to 50 yards wide. Bordering land is cultivated or in pasture, and once a dog points a bird in such cover you'd think its jig was up, but it isn't so at all. Such ruffs are very hard to come by. It's a place where the "double flush" is routine, the birds hopping into low limbs with the approach of hunters or dogs, and when they make their second flight they whip through the brushtops. I don't recall ever seeing one make the towering turn that gives a gunner an open chance, however brief. Since a flight is seldom more than 75 yards, it would seem they could be followed up and pointed again with deadly results. A bird may be pointed two or three different times, but eventually it alights where it can't be found. On my last trip to that place there were three beautiful points and several flushes, but we never fired a shot at a grouse. We shot some pheasants.

The grouse is a short-flyer. It would need wind and terrain help to make it for a mile, and tests over water have shown many of them can't cut it for more than 200 yards on their first flush. Jump one several times in succession and it might be capable of only very short hops, but it's very affinity for the ground and vegetation makes it a tough quarry.

On my very first ruffed-grouse hunt I went with Ben Williams in southwestern Montana. Ben was young, tough, and eager, taking some boxing and football spirit into his grouse chasing. He had a pair of excellent grouse dogs, and he took me to a slope that had nurtured a few grouse each fall for as long as Ben had known of it. It was September, and the grouse lived in a little peninsula of aspen, conifers, willows, and alders that poked down a mountainside into hayfields. We had been hunting for only a few minutes when a dog pointed and a ruff whirred off uphill out of range, and a few minutes later Ben felled one in a typical grouser's sudden but controlled swing as it topped some willows. Other birds moved ahead of us and the dogs were looking up into trees.

"We'll go on up to the edge of heavy timber and chase 'em back down the hill," Ben promised. "They won't go 100 yards."

Although I hadn't pulled a trigger yet, this sounded like pretty easy business. I was feeling sorry for the poor things that were obviously doomed to fly back and forth on that hillside while we carried on a day of shotgun attrition. But it didn't work out that way. They went back down the hill all right. One of them flew out of a tall pine in a drive that brought a frantic miss. Although the birds flew back downhill and then back up again, their numbers dwindled as each bird found a spot where it wasn't disturbed by man or dog, and after several tours of the area we could fly no more birds. I had missed some grouse and killed one that had bulleted across an open space. I believe Ben had three.

Then as our hunt was ending, I stepped out into a freshly mowed hayfield and surprised some ruffs standing in the open. At the time I thought there must have been seventy-five or eighty, but as I look back I believe three is a more accurate estimate. One roared for the brush and I nicked it enough that a dog retrieved it. Another flew across an open neck of hayfield to give me a perfect chance for a double, so I was very careful and shot behind it as it made a power turn, sweeping upward toward a tall pine, and then sloped off into brush.

The birds at the edge had been eating grasshoppers, and nearly all of our birds had crops stuffed with the chilled hoppers of September. Although insects are a staple of very young birds, adults aren't supposed to be big on grasshoppers. But the ruff eats a lot of things, and nearly a thousand different forms of food have been catalogued from grouse crops in a single area. Between Alaska and Georgia, the total would be staggering.

There is another reason for a grouse to leave cover and walk into an open field—the necessity for takeoff room, and I have seen them leave nearly impenetrable stuff under the pressure of moving hunters, walking out to where their wings would work. Then when they finally flushed they would go right back into the thick stuff, but headed into a new area where hunters had passed or were unlikely to penetrate. It's common with pheasants and quail, but seldom mentioned in connection with ruffs.

I am not quite satisfied with explanations that the Eastern ruffed grouse is wilder because it is shot at, for most of the fall kill is birds of the year. Perhaps it is a matter of selective breeding, with tame birds being eliminated early. I do know that grouse get wild very quickly after a few shots and humbly confess that I've had better luck hitting the ready flushers than I have the sneaky types that sift off through the branches as silently as possible. I won't go along with gunners who say the wilderness birds are much easier to bag than the explosive ruffs, although I confess it adds nothing to a bird's image to throw rocks at it. I know one hard-hunted area where most of the birds go up like rockets, but at least you can count on their flying instead of ducking out of sight while you're still trying to put your gun on them.

There are all sorts of color phases, but no matter how we try to break up the ruffed-grouse family there's so much similarity between a Washington bird and a Missouri bird that we have to lump them together. The Latin that separates them has little effect on their silhouettes or flight. I have killed brown and pearl-gray birds in the same streak of aspens and have heard much of cherry-red ruffs. These color phases, they tell me, indicate no separate strain and may, in fact, be found in the same brood. There are areas of pale or dark grouse, however, separated geographically.

DOGS

There are differences of opinion about the speed at which a grouse dog should operate, some believing a fast dog is more likely to pin birds on the ground and others preferring a dog that works more cautiously. In any event, the grouse dog must stay close to the gun. A bell is almost standard equipment, and I don't think it scares birds. I feel that one of the chief objectives in grouse-dog training is teaching it to pinch in for close cover and open up a little when there's room to move in. That's only common sense, and some dogs have it to perfection.

I also think visible birdiness is especially important with grouse dogs, whether pointers or flushers, for grouse flushes are unpredictable as to time or place and it is a wonderful help to be ready when something really happens. Dogs that work with little outward sign of excitement in the presence of game can foul you up, especially when undergrowth gives infrequent or indistinct view of your helper. As in other hunting, long experience is the key to a good grouse dog—more important here because grouse are marked "special handling," and only experience can teach the procedures for working a skittish bird that prefers walking to flying but won't run very fast, and is sometimes inclined to feel a high perch will solve everything. In the cover where birds hop up into low branches in what I call the double flush, it is essential that the dog understand the bird hasn't left when it makes its first brief flight. Some good pointing dogs will sight-point after a bird flies into a tall bush or a tree. If they can't see or smell the bird they'll point the tree. A few will bark at a treed grouse, whether in frustration or in an effort at calling help, I wouldn't know.

Like other experts, the grouse dog is of no particular breed, although I suspect the English setter may be most popular. There have been strains of English pointers that worked the "pat" to perfection, some of them guarded jealously lest there be some vagrant infiltration of racehorse field-trial blood. The Brittany has come on strong lately. At one time it was the Gordon and the English setter, and all of the Germans will do the job, but it is the individual dog and not the pedigree that must be adapted to grouse.

Flushing breeds that work under tight control can be excellent grouse dogs, and although there are hunters who prefer to kick out their own birds without help, there seem to be no dog haters when a bird is down and lost. Where cripples are concerned, the ruff can be hard to find, and their protective coloration is excellent. Any good grouse dog should be a master at hunting dead, particularly since so much of the cover is thick. I think a bell is a great help, not only in telling just where the dog is working, but in giving warning when it catches a scent.

A good grouse dog can have a long career, for as it loses its steam with age, that shortcoming is overcome by sagacity. There are birds that can be handled by speed, point, and instinct—but the grouse requires something more, and some of the closer man-dog relationships are formed in ruffed-grouse coverts.

GUNS AND SHOOTING

Short, light, and fast, the ideal grouse gun can be handled easily in one fist while the other folds back the willows. It need not throw a heavy charge of shot, for the king is a comparatively fragile bird. Shooting is likely to be quick chances, making it necessary to carry the gun at the ready through much of a long autumn day, so light weight is even more helpful in grouse gunning than in other upland fields. Even though a shooter may be physically capable of mounting and firing an 8-pound cannon with great speed, he simply cannot remain comfortably ready with it for long periods of time, no mater how big his biceps. If he gets tired, he invariably finds his gun in the wrong position when the feathered fury blows up.

There are many double guns used for ruffed grouse, simply because they are traditional guns and grouse hunting is likely to be a traditional sport. But in addition to that, the double, whether over-under or side-by-side, is much shorter overall for its barrel length and is often made to very light weight. Now if you want a custom job I suspect it would be difficult to match the 5-pound 11-ounce 12-gauge used by the aforementioned Frank Woolner of Massachusetts. His is one of the no-longer-built Model 59 Winchester automatics with the glass barrel. It was light to begin with, and Woolner's is trimmed down in both length and weight. On grouse, I understand, he uses a cylinder barrel.

If you can get it light enough, there is much merit in the gas-operated automatic, simply because of its very light recoil which enables you to split that instant of getting back on a target if the first round misses. The only disadvantage of the ultralight gun is a difficulty in swinging it smoothly on wide-angle shots. My own pet for thick grouse coverts is a 20-gauge Sauer double that weighs 5¾ pounds, bored improved cylinder and modified. I may get the improved barrel opened up to skeet or cylinder but will probably leave the modified tube as it is. On straightaways and near straightaways, I can move pretty fast with that one, but I have a tendency to stop my swing on right angles. I simply mount the gun, find I am getting too far ahead, and then watch the bird leave after stopping my move entirely. The answer is to practice more with it, for nobody is likely to get enough shots at ruffs to become expert, and the solution will have to be clay targets.

While more experienced shooters than I look for as wide a pattern as possible, I think a cool and canny marksman might do well with a somewhat tighter second barrel on a double. Oh, I agree with the skeet pattern for the first shot, but there have been many times when a bird appeared briefly in an open spot some distance away. I even tried to count those occasions one fall and thought I could have used something tighter than the skeet boring I was using. But this is nitpicking, and I am the first to confess that I seldom hit any bird that disappears and then shows again at some 35 or 40 yards.

I believe the most popular ruff shot is No. 7½, with No. 8 about as good a choice. For open guns and closed brush, you need lots of pellets, and there are a few believers in No. 9. Although the range is short and the bird reasonably fragile, I'll want as much as an ounce of shot and preferably a little more. For gunners who adopt ultralight shotguns and want plenty of shot there are some hand-loads that employ somewhat more shot and less powder than factory loadings. You don't need much velocity, but you can use a dense pattern if you shoot through branches. I don't think 1¼ ounces is too much shot, although that may kick too much for users of ultralight guns with standard powder charges. It's not range but density you're after, for vegetation can soak up much of your charge.

The ruffed-grouse marksman seldom burns much powder in the field, and he is satisfied with fewer kills than most hunters—so he usually practices on something else and seems to be a better-than-average marksman, being a serious operator. The shooting must be quick and executed at an unexpected moment much of the time.

When the ruff goes, it is seldom from exactly where you expected, even if a dog has pointed, and if you are walking up your own

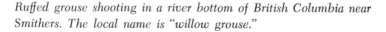

Ruffed grouse shooting in a river bottom of British Columbia near Smithers. The local name is "willow grouse."

game it is usually a complete surprise, a battering of wings, an eddy of undergrowth, and a blur that you can't see clearly for a moment. Then there is the clear view as it seems to hang motionless, although its wings are a haze, and you seem to move in molasses when even 6 pounds of honed steel and polished walnut becomes an unmanageable bludgeon. But it becomes a streak of brown and the gun finally moves, unseen and hardly felt until it bucks against your shoulder and you are standing still to watch twigs and fall leaves come down where your charge has gone, all in soft autumn sun, and you cannot tell where the bird went until you see the few feathers floating there above the briars, and you know your prize is on the ground below them.

I suppose that's why there is something special about real grouse hunters.

GROUSE HABITS AND HISTORY

Ruffed grouse have about the same range they've had since the country was first settled. They live across Canada, staying as far north as Hudson Bay, with their range going up into Alaska almost to the Arctic Circle. In the East, their territory follows the Appalachians down into northern Georgia. They are found in the Great Lakes states and down to southern Illinois and Missouri. In the West, they are plentiful in the northern Rockies with some in the Black Hills, and they occupy the coastal forests as far south as northern California. They have not taken to the Southwest, even where altitude and forest would seem to fit their requirements.

Ruffed grouse can be raised in captivity, but the operation has not been successful enough to make widespread introductions feasible. Game-management people feel they'll maintain their own populations if habitat is right, and there are few areas where gunning pressure alters the situations much. As hunting increases, the birds become wilder and the hunters become discouraged, the usual built-in balance. Again we come to the figure of something like a 70 percent turnover annually, guns or no guns. There are few "old" grouse, and the one that fools a hunter year after year is really a line of descendants that occupy the same spot, simply because it is a good spot for grouse. Very few wild birds are more than two years old, the biologists say.

It appears that erratic fluctuations of grouse numbers occur in the North more than in the southerly ranges. For hundreds of years, observers have announced that the birds have been shot out or destroyed by predators, but they come back if there are places for them to nest and feed. There are learned announcements about "cycles," but the true cycle is dependent upon consistent time periods, and the booms and busts of ruffed-grouse numbers have followed no time schedule. Some fluctuations have been explained but most of them have not, and no one knows if it's something inside the grouse that culls them or something from the outside. Undoubtedly, very wet nesting and hatching seasons can reduce the population and overly severe winters can be harmful. Over-predation has usually been of a local nature.

Male grouse drum for romantic attention in the spring, the sound carrying for considerable distance—an ethereal booming that sounds like a well-muffled gasoline motor with some unique characteristics of cadence, beginning rather slowly and climaxing with "explosions" that run together. After endless expert photography and study, it is well accepted now that the noise comes from the cock merely beating the air with his wings at high speed, forming a noisy vacuum. He finds an elevated spot, most frequently a large log, sits back on his stern, and flails mightily to produce the sound that has entranced outdoorsmen and poets for centuries. It is difficult to tell just where the sound comes from, partly because it is tossed about by timber and hills. Most of the drumming is done in spring, but there are other concerts in fall, evidently because a bird simply likes the weather.

Since the cock usually does his drumming on a log, it was for-merely thought that he was actually beating on it. It was then believed he thumped his wings against his sides or that he was striking his wings together behind him, but the vacuum theory is holding up better now.

The drumming attracks a hen to the general area, and courtship finds the cock in alternate fits of strutting dominance and abject worship. Cocks will fight each other vigorously. Most of the mating is monogamous, and the cock stays with the same hen through the nesting but leaves her when the chicks are hatched. The average clutch of eleven eggs is hatched in about seventeen days, and the nests are simple affairs, usually on the ground, and John Madson points out that the preference is for a solid backing, possibly against a tree or the base of a bush. As the time for hatching nears, the hen becomes very devoted and is sometimes hard to drive away. She hovers her young, causes them to freeze with a signal, and resorts to the crippled-bird deception or outright attack when they are in danger.

The young chicks live largely on insects, as do many other young gamebirds. The family group may be intact into early fall, and sometimes at the opening of early hunting seasons. Fall is the period of "crazy flight," a time when young birds are likely to kill themselves in collisions with all sorts of objects, including windows. The unguided flights have been blamed on fermented fruit and various plant poisons, but it is more generally accepted as simply a dramatic fall breakup of the family group. It's concluded after the leaves have fallen. A bird found with healed scars and carrying pieces of sticks imbedded in its body may well have gotten them during the crazy flights, but a grouse closely pursued by a predator may fly wildly at any time.

After the fall breakup, ruffs may be found singly, in pairs, or in loose coveys. It appears that some singles remain alone for long periods, and the range is not wide if food is satisfactory. Where they have not been hunted, individual birds will frequently be seen for several consecutive days, standing in almost exactly the same spot at almost any time of day—and if not disturbed they seem to accept visitors without fear as long as no one comes too close. There are cases in which grouse have become pets. I have had a wild grouse bristle and threaten me, and this in late fall when there was no possibility of small chicks. The differences between hens and cocks are not instantly noted. Males tend to be larger, and the black band on the end of the broad tail is likely to be continuous in the cock and somewhat broken near the center in the hens.

There are highly efficient grouse predators, headed by the great horned owl and the goshawk (the name came from "grouse hawk"), but they are seldom plentiful enough to overharvest a population. Foxes are grouse killers, as are bobcats and coyotes, and a variety of wild creatures would accept very young birds or eggs as targets of opportunity, but if predation is a strong factor in periods of low population, it has not been satisfactorily documented. Ruffed-grouse tactics in escaping winged predators, or even shotguns, can be described as violent. Snow is protection from predators, for they bury themselves there in extremely cold weather. Although they may have tunneled for some distance, they will sometimes burst almost straight up when alarmed.

Partridge are residents of the edge of the forest, a simple statement of a complex situation. They do not prefer climax forest, which is inclined to have little floor covering, but where there is mature forest there are natural borders, as where hardwoods or conifers break into swamp or creek bed. Those areas have always been with us, and that's where the grouse were before the Pilgrims started hacking at the trees. Then, with much of the East chopped into a pattern of small farms hemmed by stone or rails, we came to

A mixed bag of ruffed grouse and woodcock, often found in the same coverts in New England. Gun is a customized Winchester 59, used by Frank Woolner and even lighter than the original glass-barreled model. (Photo: Frank Woolner)

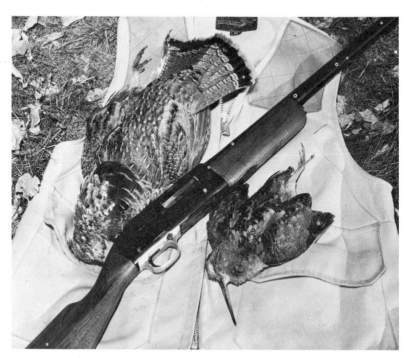

the heydey of the Eastern pat, we think. There were miles of forest border where there had been rods of it before, the bushes thrived, and the farmers planted apple trees that gave forth buds and fruit, both of which the grouse loved. There were times when they loved apple trees too much and bounties were offered.

Market hunting had little effect on those grouse. They fed many of the settlers and followed the forest borders as the axes went west. When the hill farms were abandoned, as many of them were at frequent intervals for a variety of economic reasons, the years as the farms "went back" were best of all, but when the forest moved in too far the grouse numbers decreased. Where the land was easily worked and highly fertile, as it was in much of the Midwest, the little fields gave way to broad ones, the fenceline brush was cleared, and the droning tractors are still rolling over what was once grouse habitat.

The Eastern hill farms became unprofitable as the twentieth century came on, and by midcentury there were millions of abandoned farm acres through New England and the Middle Atlantic States—it happened in Wisconsin, Minnesota, and Michigan too—finally growing back until the ruffed-grouse habitat was reduced again, the same story as with quail, deer, and turkey.

Some years ago, I met a wide-eyed grouse hunter who had made a trip to Alberta, north of Edmonton, where little farms and settlements were being cut out of native forest. He had never seen so many ruffed grouse in his life. All you had to do, he said, was walk the edges of the clearings, preferably those that had been there for a couple of years, and the ruffs would rumble into the trees. It was, of course, a near duplicate of the days when New England was first cleared for homes. Then later, I slogged along a clearing in western British Columbia, marching around the old piles of slash, and saw a dozen ruffs plunge into the forest. I had caught up with the saw and the partridge.

It is the forest fire and the power saw that can make grouse habitat, but their management is not only difficult, it is much debated. Even among ardent conservationists, there is disagreement, for it is a many-sided crusade. If selective cutting is employed, only part of the timber is felled at any one time, meaning that much of the effect of climax or mature forest remains and there is no time when large areas of new growth will provide grouse cover and food. If clean cutting (complete clearing of large areas of timber) is employed, there are the dangers of erosion of exposed soil, flooding, and the excessive warming of streams, but as new growth comes on, grouse and other game will prosper. But plant the entire area to seedlings that come on in a "doghair" growth and the habitat is ruined again after a few years.

Grouse feed on one of the longest menus of the wild. They eat almost all sorts of berries in season, and an individual can be stuffed with wild grapes, snowberries or juniper berries, or a hundred other kinds. They thrive on tender shoots and tree buds in the spring. They eat catkins and twigs in winter, like ferns and nuts, and will stuff with insects at times. Perhaps this is what makes them self-sufficient over so wide an area.

Grouse have "snowshoes," small protrusions on their toes that are really part of their skin and that become longer in winter. Some of their habitat is in fairly dry country, but on the Pacific slopes they face some of the wettest parts of the United States.

They live between civilization and the wilderness and can endure both.

CHAPTER IX

Woodcock and Snipe

IT WAS AN INTERESTING QUOTE, and I am sorry I cannot give the speaker's name. Believe me, however, he is a well-known New England gunner with an honest love for woodcock. I had asked him for his opinion of the bird and he looked furtively over his shoulder.

"I think the woodcock is one of the most fascinating creatures I have ever hunted," he said. "It's too bad it isn't a gamebird." This involves us with definitions of gamebirds and leads to the observation that none of our great gamebirds earns its reputation without its favorite environment. The ruffed grouse would not be game if it did not have its forest obstacles, the chukar is not particularly tough when separated from arid mountains, and the sharptail couldn't start its wind-splitting flights just a little too far away if it weren't where it could see you coming.

Describe a woodcock as a rather slow riser, explain that it has weak legs, and describe its flight speed as 15 miles an hour, as some observers have, and you come up with something that needs help to become game of satisfactory difficulty. The answer comes in a choice of thickets that allow the timberdoodle to fly away with its ghostly whistle of wings while hunters strain their eyes and their ears to find just where it is. Catch it on a grassy hillside (it can happen) with a pointing dog's nose almost over it and it is barely a gamebird at all.

I am not quite sold on the 15-mile-an-hour flight speed, but it is a reference point and classes the woodcock as one of the slower fliers. I don't doubt that it can keep airborne at that speed for those are broad wings and I have seen it pick its way through the higher branches as if it could stop and go into reverse at any moment. On the other hand, it can bore through its well-known escape routes between alder clumps with a broken-field abandon that indicates it *must* be going faster than 15 miles an hour, for nothing that slow can be missed so far with a familiar shotgun. No, sometimes it is a gamebird, even though I understand the expert's reluctance to classify it as one.

Listed speeds of gamebirds are a help to shooters, but saying a woodcock flies 15 miles an hour is like saying an automobile goes 40 miles an hour. The timberdoodle shifts gears repeatedly as it negotiates obstacles in its escapes. They are very easy woodcock shots, and there are some impossible ones.

THE WOODCOCK—UPLAND CLOWN

In the dryer parts of its range the woodcock (*Pilohela minor*) is likely to live with ruffed grouse or quail; in the damper parts of woodcock country it is likely to be next door to the jacksnipe or Wilson's snipe, which it superficially resembles. Primarily a worm eater, the woodcock must have earth to accept its probing beak, a wondrous instrument that flexes out near the tip. That means the earth must be moist and cannot be frozen, so it lives a bit precariously. Its parts are highly specialized and when put together turn out as a sort of caricaure, with a snipe's beak, a quail's breast, and flimsy legs that no one would want. Its eyes are those of a lost waif, located partly on top of its head; its nostrils are ahead of its eyes and against the base of its beak, where they apparently serve as part of a delicate worm-warning system. When it probes for worms it inserts its bill far down into the earth where it can actually grasp a worm with the flexible end, and sometimes it remains for some time with the beak inserted, evidently using its sensitive worm-

A bag of woodcock. Gun is open-bored over-under and vest is ideal for the hard work of brush travel. (Photo: Frank Woolner)

listening equipment. It also eats bugs and seeds, but they are a minor part of its diet.

The doodle must have worms and lots of them. In productive surroundings it is believed to consume twice its weight daily. It cannot fast for long periods like some birds, and many woodcock have been lost in severe freezes when the food supply was suddenly cut off. Perhaps because of its owl-like eyes, it is a twilight operator, feeding after other birds are roosting. Conversely, it can be captured at night with long-handled net and light, the system used by researchers who have banded thousands in migration studies.

Grits Gresham, Louisiana marksman, told me he tries to decide as soon as possible whether a woodcock is going through or over the cover. The worst time to shoot, Grits explains, is when a bird has just decided to tower to clear something high and is going up while you shoot where it's been. If the trees or brush are thick enough, there's no doubt about what the bird is going to do, so you wait for it to complete its towering act and level off, the same sort of shot some grouse shooters watch for. The catchy situation comes when the bird heads toward trees with open avenues between trunks and branches. Sometimes it goes through them and sometimes it goes over them, and if you have room to wait for it to commit itself you might have an easy shot one way or the other. My own system is to fire just before it towers, and I get the interesting view of a bird going almost straight up over my gun barrel while I try to get collected for a second shot.

There are gunners who think woodcock fly much faster than they do, simply because the escapees are often running an obstacle course and everything seems to happen fast, but the woodcock can do much better than 15 miles an hour, believe me. Now and then a bird will make a very short flight through treetops, dropping back to earth after a few yards, and on such abbreviated trips it seems to go quite slowly. The next one, possibly jumped in an open place, will whistle into the sky, level off 50 feet up, and leave like a mourning dove. One of the very best shotgunners I know lives on the thin edge of woodcock range and has never killed one, reporting that he has missed eight straight when they happened to go up during other hunting. He tries too hard, of course, and his woodcock make off behind a mental block.

Even the migration of the woodcock is mysterious and different from that of other birds. Woodcock live and breed over much of the eastern United States, mainly east of the Mississippi, and are found in southern Canada. The western border of their range runs through Minnesota, Iowa, Missouri, Oklahoma, and Texas, and over the southern part of the range the resident birds are greatly overlapped by migrants from the North. There are occasional strays over much of the West.

It travels great distances, but the woodcock is no canvasback and flies fairly close to the ground. Many birds are killed in collisions with buildings, wires, and poles. When weather is unfavorable they will congregate in great numbers to await favorable winds, especially if a navigational obstacle is blocking their way. Most famous of these stopovers is at Cape May, New Jersey, a spot where birds will wait for a tail wind before crossing the water south of there. Some of the most productive shooting of all is had by hunters who keep a close watch on the migrational routes and schedules, for a

Frank Woolner with a customized autoloader and the reason why it was shortened and lightened. (Photo: Frank Woolner)

low-going addict of short flights is vulnerable. The woodcock keeps to the unobstructed way, and migratory flocks are found more in valleys that run north and south than those running east and west, simply a matter of avoiding mountain crossings.

Migration seems to be mainly in hours of poor light, certainly at dusk, but it is believed the birds go as individuals and that any flocking is simply a matter of accident as they are bunched by natural contours of their route. Essentially, the woodcock is a solitary bird. Several go up at about the same time on rare occasions, but they do not go as a covey.

The females are considerably larger than the males, fly a bit more heavily, and cause unscientific hunters to believe there is a difference in the sizes of resident and migratory birds. The males have a reputation for migrating southward later than the hens and being harder to hit. Migrations are in stops and starts, and cover that may be dotted with resting timberdoodles today may be void of them tomorrow. Migratory or not, a given woodcock that runs into a charge of No. 8 is likely to be replaced immediately by another bird in almost exactly the same spot, often within only a few days, a ghostly process unexplained by topnotch hunters. It is, of course, good cover and probably a good place to feed, but it may be the same as acres of other cover as far as the hunter can tell. Still, the little timberdoodle's ghost goes up with his softly whistling wings, just as hard to hit as his predecessor—and the succession may continue through the years at the right season.

Ruffed-grouse hunters of the Northeast are likely to be woodcock hunters too, and it is in the East the woodcock receives due homage. It is accepted less in the Midwest and almost ignored in the South, a complex vagary of human attitude. I can understand how the ruffed grouse might get little attention in the West, where hunters are mainly riflemen and there is a wide variety of upland birds anyway—but the South is full of shotgunners, and in much of their country they hunt little except quail although the woodcock may be plentiful. Except for some of the crowded stopovers like those in New Jersey, I am sure the busiest woodcock shooting in the country is in Louisiana, Alabama, and Mississippi. Some of the quail gunners don't even know what they are, confusing them with snipe or ignoring them completely.

Woodcock hunters can quickly learn the signs. Wherever the woodcock feeds it leaves its white chalk marks, a plenitude of droppings, and it makes innumerable probe holes in its endless quest for worms. Where there is little ground cover, they are simply round holes in soft earth. Where there is a mat of leaves or dead grass, the bird rummages about so that there is considerable disturbance. Where there is a blanket of pine needles, it sometimes turns up areas that look as if gray squirrels had been hunting nuts. Although it looks like an inflated snipe and is a relative, the woodcock is many generations removed from the shorebird clan and doesn't care to wade. Although often found near water, it's on somewhat higher ground than shorebirds are usually found.

There is a routine carefully catalogued in the East. Although its feeding is done mostly in alder thickets and fairly thick, moist cover, it may spend much of the time resting on hardwood hillsides where it takes the sun on chilly days. That doesn't mean it never feeds in broad daylight, but simply that it may leave its best feeding spots to rest, and it does its most active worming at dawn and early evening. Experts try both the feeding grounds and some of the higher slopes before announcing the woodcock have moved.

Dan Holland, in writing about woodcock in his *Upland Game Hunter's Bible*, tells of seeing woodcock apparently leave for good after being flushed in late afternoon. The birds simply kept on flying instead of making the short flights and abrupt pitch-ins usually expected of them. Evidently Mr. Holland's birds just decided that was as good a time as any to get serious about migrating, already being in the air and all.

While the more northerly migrations of woodcock may sweep certain areas clear of birds and pile up the travelers at some other spot, the southerly regions of woodcock land have even more perplexing movements. Even though they have arrived at the region where they can be expected to winter, woodcock are likely to take to their wings and go back up north a little way if weather is unseasonably warm. I have arrived at a Southern site that was full of birds the week before, only to be told sadly that they had "gone back up into Arkansas," or that I should try just a little farther north. In one case, 100 miles of northward travel put me into birds aplenty.

Wherever it is hunted, the woodcock is likely to be a close holder, and many a hunter hears wings whistle behind him somewhere and knows he may have walked within 4 feet of a squatted bird, only to have it sneak out after he had gone. It is possible to have a bird take off at your feet, shoot at it, and have dogs working all over the place, and still have a second or third timberdoodle leave from somewhere around your boot soles. The bird has some of the most efficient coloration in nature, becoming a part of dead leaves, twigs, and grass stems. Often a bird holds tightly where there is very little cover, and its legs are not made for smashing through anything really heavy. All of this doesn't mean that they won't flush wild, but they do have a reputation for tight holding and will sit almost eye to eye with a pointing dog.

The male woodcock presents a strange mating ritual in spring, usually in evening dusk. After strutting about and making buzzing sounds, he takes off and spirals to considerable height, probably 300 feet or more, and then plunges down to his takeoff point, making musical sounds on the way down. More struttting and buzzing, and the act begins again, serving to attract the hen to him. Woodcock lay four eggs in a slight depression, and the main feature of the youngster's defense is an ability to freeze and stay put. The myth that hens can carry their young in the air is pretty well exploded.

This is a bird with traditions, traditions probably born in Europe, where a similar but somewhat larger woodcock has been a gunning mainstay for centuries. The woodcock is very plentiful in the East and Northeast, and that is the seat of American gunning traditions and history.

WOODCOCK DOGS

Woodcock dogs are usually slow and methodical operators. I'm reluctant to say that woodcock don't put out much scent because I can't smell a turkey either, but it's commonly believed they are a bit hard for dogs to corner. Part of this is probably due to the fact that there's usually only one woodcock to find instead of a covey. A single woodcock that isn't actively feeding probably puts

Grits Gresham, Louisiana writer and television personality, follows the woodcock hunter's ritual of looking about for the bird's logical escape route while his dog points.

out very little scent, and when you find traces of one that has been moving about in a thicket, the trail can be complicated enough that dogs will sometimes simply go off and leave it after some unproductive searching. A woodcock isn't going to take out and leg it for a mile or so across hill and dale but it will go trundling around a thicket like a toy bird with its spring winding down.

Bob Anderson of Ponchatoula, Louisiana, had some excellent woodcock dogs, which he ran with noisy bells and which showed remarkable patience in their woodcock hunting. They'd move briskly about the branch country and then settle down to sniffing out one small thicket where a bird had obviously been walking around, either because it was disturbed by the dogs or because it had been feeding in there. Sometimes some judicious bush kicking would get results, but there were times when we'd simply give up and leave, never knowing whether woodcock had sneaked out or not. That part isn't as simple as it sounds.

There was one case when two of Bob's dogs worked a small area very thoroughly. It included an open patch of grass with a couple of saplings in the center and a fringe of bushy cover around it. There were pine woods a little farther back from the 30-foot amphitheater. As I watched, I would guess the dogs must have crossed that little open place half a dozen times but gave more attention to the edges of it—then they left and we assumed the bird had flown unseen, but before Bob and I could get more than a few steps away, a third dog that hadn't been in on the earlier search came loping into the little clearing, became very birdy, and pointed staunchly. The woodcock was there, all right, and Bob got it. It had been right in the open area. All gamebirds do this sort of thing occasionally, but the woodcock is a professional.

Apparently the little will-o'-the-wisp of the alders and oaks has an odor very different from other gamebirds, and many dogs will not point a woodcock without special training, evidently disbelieving any hunter wants something that smells so oddly. And once a bird is down, many pointing dogs won't retrieve it. Although experience is an important qualification of any canine specialist, it's especially necessary with woodcock. But there is the exception that points woodcock immediately, as if that strange odor was what it had been looking for all its life, and then retrieves a timberdoodle as if it were the most natural thing in the world.

I believe the English setter is best known as a woodcock hunter, with the English pointer a close second. Brittanies are good, and the hunting style of conventionally bred German shorthairs should be almost perfect. Close-working flushing dogs are fine, but remember woodcock mix with quail in the South and with ruffed grouse in the North.

WOODCOCK GUNS AND SHOOTING

Woodcock guns should be light and open. I suppose there are cases when you can make really long shots, but the nature of cover makes them a bit unusual. In a double, improved cylinder and modified are a good combination, and I believe improved cylinder is the best choice for a repeater. Short barrels help in the brush.

No. 8 shot is about ideal, although No. 9 and No. 7½ will do. Anything that takes an ounce of shot should be enough. If there is a bird that can be hunted humanely with a .410 the timberdoodle just may be it, because it's usually shot at close range, isn't particularly hard to put down, and usually doesn't give tempting long chances. Still, anybody who gets a bit hungry for meat is likely to stretch the little gun. Only strong-willed veterans should dare to use it.

Timberdoodle marksmen are quick shooters and spend more time looking up at the brushtops and tree patterns than at the grass, for one of the secrets of a good score is figuring where the bird is going to go when it goes. Woodcock are noted for flying for daylight, and the chances are the largest patch of sky is where your bird will go when you hear its wings. I have seen Bob Anderson study the pattern of foliage for some time before walking in to his pointing dogs—and in most cases he was facing in the right direction when the bird flushed. Woodcock are not easily seen early in their flights unless light is good, for their camouflage works in the air as well as on the ground. They are not brush smashers like ruffed grouse, but they will drive through tips of upper branches.

THE WILSON SNIPE

Shooters laugh at jacksnipe, but they miss them so badly the joke tends to backfire. I don't want people making fun of snipe.

It is the Wilson snipe *(Capella gallinago delicata)*, truly a shore-bird, but fitting in with upland game, for it is hunted as upland game. It's a relative of the woodcock, but the snipe likes to stand in water, has somewhat longer legs, and is the only one of the many shorebirds that is legal game unless you list the rails and gallinules. The woodcock took to higher ground centuries ago.

In a few attics there are dusty snipe decoys, some of them crude but others masterpieces of carving, relics of the old shorebird days, which ended just before World War II. Seasons were closed on shorebirds then, but the snipe season was reopened in 1953, largely for a new generation of gunners who had little appreciation of it, and decoy hunting for snipe is a very rare sport today. The old decoys bring high prices with antique dealers now.

In the days of market hunting, the snipe was better known than it is now, and I have always thought it strange so small a bird should be profitable in a day when much larger birds were plentiful. The old market hunters may have been more efficient, but few hunters bag a snipe today without an average expenditure of more

The Wilson snipe or jacksnipe is easily outweighed by three of the shells needed to bring him down—and one for three is a fairly good score.

than its weight in ammunition. The snipe is the smallest of the common gamebirds, and since it is a table delicacy, the size may contribute to its gourmet value.

Nesting all the way to the Arctic Circle, snipe are migratory and appear in all of the contiguous states as well as Alaska. I have found more snipe shooters in the Southeast than elsewhere, and there are many shotgunners who don't know what they are. I have watched them straggle past a goose blind in northern Canada when my companions didn't recognize them. But there is no area where snipe are major game, and most snipe hunting seems to come incidentally on an off day for ducks. There are marshes or bogs that have snipe the year round, and there are waystations on their southern migrations where they are thick today and gone tomorrow.

Every hunter should have a bird to feel sentimental about, and the snipe is mine, I guess. Although I will flounder after them, wild-eyed and sweating, when more sensible shooters retire to the boat or car, there are certain places and conditions in which I don't want to shoot snipe. For example, I have a scraggly duck blind on a spring creek in Montana, a spot where the mallards slide in ahead of the freezes that close most other waters. For ten years I have carried my decoys along the shore of that creek, and there is one stretch where the mud is just the right consistency, with just the right gleaming water film on top. It is a stretch about 75 yards long and my blind sits at one end of it. Contingents of snipe, obviously stopping off on their way south, drop into the little flat all fall, stay for a few days, and leave again. Shooting them is perfectly legal and not necessarily easy. On one walk along the 75 yards, I put up thirty-one snipe, and on several occasions I have slipped a bunch of snipe loads into my coat, carefully separated from the duck ammunition, but I have never fired a shot with them. I finally quit carrying snipe loads.

Let 'em get down South and settled in their favorite bogs there and I'll run 'em ragged! What difference does it make where I shoot at them? I don't know. It certainly is no conservation measure, for the snipe can take care of themselves where I'm concerned. I guess it's just the awe of a spindle-legged clown that may have come all the way from Alaska and is still going.

Most of the snipe's preferred range is low, boggy ground where the earth is soft enough for worm probing, and the droppings are

V. M. Gowdy examines a limit of jacksnipe. A boat is a good means of reaching the birds, even though they are bagged while walking the marsh.

similar to the chalk marks of woodcock although not so copious. They eat a variety of insects, many worms, some very small fishes and fresh-water snails, and bits of marsh vegetation. Snipe can be found in both fresh and brackish marshland.

One of the obstacles to acceptance of the snipe as a major shot-gunning target is the hoary prank in which a scared kid is taken into a marsh at night, carrying a lantern and a burlap sack with which to catch snipe to be driven to him by other members of the party. The others go on home and leave the unfortunate with a thousand spooky marsh noises. The "snipe hunt" has been practiced some and talked about a great deal for a hundred years, and it is sometimes difficult to convince otherwise rational people that there really is such a thing as a snipe and that there really is such a thing as a snipe hunt with guns.

The toughest snipe shooting I've ever had was on a broad flat of short grass with just the right amount of water to attract birds. The grass was only ankle-high, and snipe could see you from the time you started loading your gun. The average rise was at 20-odd yards, and there were enough birds to be confusing as they went off at all angles. It required quick shooting and considerable aplomb, and it was on that trip I missed nineteen snipe straight. It is much easier when there is taller grass so that you can get closer to the bird before it flushes. Scattered clumps of switchgrass often leave open patches of mud for the snipe to feed but still conceal you from it—part of the time.

When they have not been hunted, snipe will do some foolish things, often dropping back to earth a few yards from where they flushed. On other occasions a bird will fly up until it is a speck in the sky, travel a mile or two, and then come back to where it started. Before they've dodged a few charges, snipe will often fly very low over a hunter out of curiosity, may even swing about him in a circle within easy range and flying slowly—but after the guns have cracked a few times, don't expect these maneuvers, even though inexperienced hunters will tell you they're typical.

Snipe flight appears inept, as if it were flying with only one wing at a time, but the speed is considerable and the snipe is one bird that swings enough in its darting course to fly out of a pattern of shot. They frequently tour about the marsh in ragged and disorganized flocks, with single birds occasionally peeling off on missions of their own, apparently dissatisfied with the group flight plan. When flushed, a snipe usually skims the ground as closely as possible at first and generally makes a scratchy call, described as "scaipe!" Others believe the term is "escape" and some say that once you hear that it's too late to shoot. That isn't correct, but one of the hardest things about snipe hunting is seeing them early in their flight, as the takeoff is fairly quiet except for the call, which doesn't always come.

Birds that are pushed from a favored spot are likely to return in the evening, and I have had good shooting from a makeshift blind as they circled for landing places, generally coming in by singles and pairs.

Hunting pressure makes birds steadily wilder, even though it may not cause them to abandon good areas. After several days of shooting in areas open enough for birds to see men, they may get so wild that you're wasting your time and it is possible to walk for hours, putting up dozens of birds, without a single one within range. Another fellow and I had located a number of snipe on a small island, perhaps 100 yards across, and had one good shoot there with birds reluctant to leave. We got there by outboard boat and were eager for another trip. We had a few shots that second time but it wasn't as good as before. On our third trip we saw a cloud of specks over the island while we were still offshore. The snipe had left—all of them. Generally, they don't all leave when a flock goes up, though, and there are a few sleepers that don't believe in the general alarm. A snipe doesn't even trust another snipe.

SNIPE DOGS

Except for retrieving duties, I'd rather hunt snipe without a dog. Flushing dogs can put them up and pointing dogs can find them, but those are not the problems. I believe there are very few snipe that don't flush when a hunter walks by within range. There may be some specific kinds of cover where they will hold too tightly to be flown, but I haven't found it. I've repeatedly hunted back over my trail to see what I missed, and usually it isn't much.

A retriever might find an occasional cripple but is seldom needed for dead birds. If you'll forego the chances for other shots while getting your kill, you can find a snipe in surprisingly shaggy vegetation. Just mark where you stood to fire, keep your eye glued to some sort of landmark near where the bird fell, and look closely. I'm not noted for super vision, but I've lost very, very few dead snipe, and those fell in strange places, usually in deep water. A crippled snipe seldom hides much.

I've had pointing dogs that did their part well, but the snipe flies when it's ready, whether your dog is holding or not, and most of them go up before I'm in range. Dogs have scared off more than they've held.

SNIPE GUNS AND SHOOTING

Pattern density is all-important in snipe shooting, and I have concluded I can kill more and kill them cleaner with No. 9 shot than with anything else. It takes only a few pellets to drop a snipe,

The toughest snipe shooting occurs on wet flats like this where the grass is very short. Here a shooter takes advantage of a treasured opportunity when a bird swings over him for a better look.

and they can be light, but the silhouette is very small, especially from the rear. By the time the bird is far enough away that No. 8 or No. 7 is needed for penetration, the pattern becomes so skimpy that the birds can fly through it. For me, at least, No. 9 was best by far in a pretty careful check.

Since a snipe is not often protected by foliage, he can be shot at fairly long range if you can hit him. The answer would seem to be a duck gun with No. 8, but it hasn't worked too well for me or for better shots. The dense center of a full-choke pattern is so small it is hard to put on a swiveling snipe, and the sketchy edges of full-choke charges are too thin to score consistently.

If you can find them in fairly high cover where they rise close to the gun, an improved cylinder with at least an ounce of No. 9 is perfect. Unless they have peeled back and are going past the gun in the other direction, few snipe are killed at the extremely close ranges possible with quail. The bird generally has moved a few feet before it is seen, it usually flushes a bit ahead, and it makes its most violent swerves as it takes off. By the time your gun has been adjusted to all of this, the chances are it'll be more than 20 yards away, no matter how you do it. Shooting them over short grass, I found the average kill was at about 28 yards, hurry as I would. I was turning down shots I estimated at more than 35 yards. I have very rarely killed a snipe at 40 yards, and a 37-yarder is a long one.

The straightaway is tough, because it offers you only a tiny silhouette and it swings violently from side to side. I have heard veterans say that you could time the swerves and catch it at the outside of its swing as it starts back, but I can't do that. Perhaps it could be worked if I had enough birds that would fly just the same way until I got the hang of it. The full-choke user will do better to wait until the bird has stopped its initial darting, for it settles down a little after that and flies steadily—for a snipe. It is easier to hit them at an angle where the side-to-side motion is not a factor, and there's a lot more bird to shoot at too.

If there's much breeze, a snipe will take off into it, even though it turns almost instantly. When you can walk downwind, you'll sight the birds much more quickly, catching a glimpse of the white underside as it turns up to catch the wind. I find I bag more birds if I devote my attention to the area immediately ahead of me, carry my gun at the ready with sweaty palms, and ignore derisive snipe cheeps to right or left—unless birds are scarce enough that each individual is an event. I come in from snipe hunts with aching legs that have dragged hip boots through miles of sinky bog, aching eyes that have stared for hours at grass and weeds the same color as snipe, and aching arms that have held a shotgun until my fingers will hardly open. It's wonderful.

Improved cylinder or modified seems to be the best choice choice for most snipe hunting, and I seldom get off more than two shots at each bird. Usually I fire only once, hit or miss, for by that time it's too far away. It's a simple matter of taking a little time for me to figure just what direction it's going in.

SNIPE LIFE

Although they spend most of their time over really wet ground, there are times when snipe get into woodcock territory, and sometimes even into places where the ground is quite dry. I assume the latter spots are used as resting places, and I have not found them there often. On one series of trips, I had much of my shooting along a strip of willows that bordered what looked like a good snipe marsh. The willows were high and dry, and I can't believe they were feeding there. On other days, most of the birds were out in the mud where they belonged.

Snipe hatch in damp areas, and the skimpy nest with four eggs seems in danger of being flooded sometimes. Sometimes the vegetation is fairly thick. Driven from a nest, females are reluctant to leave, and I have watched them sit on posts or other high points in order to watch men or dogs. One of the snipe mysteries is how they can see approaching hunters from thick cover when they are especially wild, and I believe they do considerable climbing to high points for a look around now and then.

The mating exhibition of the male snipe is almost the equal of the woodcock and involves dramatic soaring and diving. Aerobatics are performed at other seasons for no logical reason. Startle a snipe, even in hunting season, and it is likely to go to considerable altitude, fly in several directions at 500 feet in the air, and then dive toward earth with its wings drawn back so that the entire bird seems shaped like an arrowhead. Usually this performance is too far away for shooting, but on the few occasions when the dive has come close enough I missed. I am not programmed for shooting an object plunging straight downward in whistling speed. Just as it appears a snipe is about to pierce the earth's crust, it rocks back on its pointed wings and drops gently to earth on its slender legs, appearing surprised that it made it.

Snipe country will be one of the last areas to become crowded. Between the whining boats on the river or lake and the booming highway traffic, the snipe hunter can be a lonely walker on the bog.

CHAPTER X

Wilderness Grouse and Ptarmigan

S<small>EVEN FAT BLUE GROUSE</small> strolled about the base of a fir tree. Below them was a steep slope that swept down into a canyon we'd been in an hour before, and now we were on a rocky ridge, wind-swept almost completely clear of snow but carrying gnarled coni-fers, patches of grass, and some scraps of rotting timber.

The slope to the deep canyon was heavily timbered with matured forest but had wide and grassy parks where we had seen several mule deer on the way up. There were elk tracks on the ridge top, and the grouse haven had been located a week before when I was looking for deer. Now as we eyed the grouse we carried shot-guns. Farther back along the ridge our rifles had been cached at a fallen tree.

"This is ridiculous," Ben Williams had said. "We came up here to hunt grouse. Why carry this other stuff?"

Ben has always believed a big-game rifle is to be employed only when there are no birds available or when his wife, Bobbie, is in-sistent upon venison. I am sure he is prouder of a snipe than an elk.

We were 40 yards from the blue grouse and a little above them as they seemed to be working downhill a little, just off the backbone

The blue grouse, one of the largest of North American upland birds, is frequently hunted with .22 rifles. During hunting season, these are primarily high-mountain game.

of the ridge. We walked stealthily closer, and when we were about 25 yards away two or three of them eyed us curiously while the others rummaged about the ground for whatever blue grouse hunt on a windswept ridge in late fall. I looked at McGillicuddy and McGillicuddy looked at me, his eyes the size of saucers. McGillicuddy is a Brittany of vast logic and experience and belongs to Ben. Ben isn't competing in the cute-names-for-dogs sweepstakes, but McGillicuddy had to have a new designation a while back when Ben acquired other dogs that usurped his old call name, and it just came out like that, McGilly for short. McGilly considered seven burly blue grouse on nearly bare ground as some sort of hunting emergency. He was shivering a little.

We moved a little closer before we charged, and a bugle call couldn't have made it more dramatic. We ran with our shotguns pushed out as if they carried bayonets and the grouse thundered off in a ragged flush. One went into a tree, one dived down the slope, and one flew through the top of a bush. The gunfire volleyed and thundered, as the poet says. McGilly picked up one blue grouse (no one will ever know who killed it), and Ben and I tried to out-shout each other with alibies. Blue-grouse hunting isn't always that nutty, but it's generally nearly that bad. I go with Ben about once a year, but the nervous strain is almost too much for more than that.

After Ben had thrown sticks at the grouse in the tree and I had missed it when it swept down into the canyon we moved on down the ridge and skirted a little below a strip of rimrock, the top of which was only 20 feet above us. I happened to look up there, and for a split instant I saw the head of a grouse silhouetted as it peeked over. Then two birds zoomed down over our heads and a little to the front. Spat! Spat! went the two 20-gauges. Thump, thump, went the two grouse. After maudlin congratulations of each other, Ben and I decided we do much better when the birds surprise us.

Blue grouse (Dendragapus obscurus) are mainly high-country birds. Dusky and sooty grouse are accepted as subspecies, the dusky grouse living in the Rockies and the sooty being a Pacific range bird. They're big, considerably larger than the ruffed grouse, and lack the ruff's speed in takeoff unless they can dive downhill off a bluff or tree. Their wingbeat is slower than a ruff's but they're extremely noisy as they flush, momentarily scaring many a stalking deer hunter out of his wits.

Many years ago while hunting deer and elk with Bud Baker of Ennis, Montana, we came upon a flock of blues on a steep slope with big Douglas fir and grassy parks. They flew into the trees, where Bud began to pick them off by snipping their heads with his .270, explaining that blue grouse was better than venison and we *knew* where the blue grouse were and hadn't located any deer yet. I was greatly impressed with those birds and wondered if they might be good shotgun game. The following year I was back at the same spot with a shotgun and bagged a couple of grouse, but I can't say it was particularly sporty shooting—except that it was a long climb up to that place.

Most blue grouse are collected either at the very beginning of the season, which often comes before big-game season opens, or while the hunters are after big game and accept the blue grouse (or its relatives, Franklin or spruce grouse) as choice camp meat. It is a continual subject of discussion whether a grouse should be shot or not, since gunfire can make deer and elk decidedly suspicious. Red Monical says go ahead and shoot the grouse and doesn't consider it unsportsmanlike to nail them with his .257 Weatherby as long as it's a neat head shot. He reasons logically that such a shot is harder than hitting a deer. Of course the gimmick is to learn just how to hold with a rifle that is scope-sighted for 250 yards when the grouse is only 50 or 70 feet away. If you hold too low your bird disappears in a cloud of feathers.

The way to learn to shoot grouse with your big-game rifle, of course, is to practice on paper targets. Some handloaders build ammunition especially for grouse shooting and put in the mild loads after the birds are found. It isn't so noisy that way. In states where handguns are permitted on big-game expeditions, many hunters carry .22 pistols expressly for mountain grouse. When expressly after grouse they often use .22 rifles, and that can be considerable fun too. Rifle hunting for grouse has the blessing of most big-game states. My wife and I have hunted them with .22s in high forests, walking slowly through grouse country and hoping to sight them on the ground. If you go slowly you will frequently see the birds moving about on the ground, and although they will sometimes move into bushes as you approach they are not good hiders on the ground. The same tactics work when shotgunning, although there are occasions when the shooting can be almost too easy as a big bird takes off in the wide open at very close range. Of course it has the advantage of building you up to a nervous state as you get closer.

When you find them on the ground, blue grouse don't seem to flush at long range if there is any ground cover at all, tending to simply stroll out of your path. I suppose they can get much wilder if hunted hard, but most of the wild flushes I have seen have been from trees, where they're decidedly unpredictable.

The "double flush" is very common—the same as with ruffed grouse in primitive areas. The birds are walking around on the ground, and when they see or hear you coming they fly up into a nearby tree. Then when you get too close they'll frequently make a much longer flight, but a blue in a tree is unpredictable and will often behave in typical "fool hen" fashion, simply shifting position among the branches. A blue grouse in a 90-foot fir is mighty hard to locate, even after you see it go in there, and I've abandoned the search many times. It tends to sit on large limbs and sometimes quite close to the trunk.

You can usually count on blue grouse heading downhill when they make their long flights, and once they get started down a mountainside they may keep going for half a mile or more. When one of them passes you after getting up a full head of steam you'd better swing fast and follow through. It'll probably come out between a couple of tall conifers and be heading for another gap, so there may not be time for slide-rule marksmanship.

Blue grouse migrate in reverse. During late summer I've often found them at low altitude, feeding along trout streams in valleys and canyons. It is very easy to mistake the younger birds for ruffed grouse, as the summer habitat may be in heavy cover. As colder weather comes on they're found farther up the slope, and late fall usually finds them on the high ridges. Some of the best blue-grouse hunting Ben Williams and I have had was on a very high ridge in the Crazy Mountains of Montana. There's seldom heavy snow up there, as the wind cleans it off, and that spine is much better late in the season. Evidently the grouse are scattered widely in early fall. However, there are certain small areas that nearly always have a few, possibly family groups that haven't broken up. I'd guess that the bunching tendencies are about the same as those of ruffed grouse, and although I've often seen several together, even late in the season, they are likely to be loosely congregated over a quarter-mile of timber rather than within clucking distance of each other.

A light snow makes ideal conditions for hunting blues, as you can find their tracks easily enough, puttering trails that wander from bush to tree to fallen log. You know they aren't going to hike out of the county, so if you're persistent you'll either come on the birds or find where they took off. If they've flown, the chances are they'll be in a nearby tree, but it's uphill business to hunt birds in trees unless you've actually seen them go in.

I don't know if blue grouse are wilder than Franklin's grouse and spruce grouse or not, but they have the reputation of being better game birds. I suspect it's simply a matter of more blues being nearer civilization. The three varieties of wilderness grouse are very similar in habits.

In the Far North the spruce grouse *(Canachites canadensis)* is considered a fool hen of stolid stupidity, but that may be because it is even more of a wilderness dweller than the blue and seldom encounters man. The Franklin grouse is very closely related to the spruce hen, although confined to the West.

Evidently the spruce grouse often travels the bottom land in early fall the same as the blue grouse. In Alaska I found a bunch of young spruce grouse strolling about on a river trail, and they slid into very heavy weeds like a bunch of bobwhite quail. My dog pointed them and they then flushed and flew for the timber. I got a pair of them, feeling a little strange shooting spruce grouse with the weeds up to my armpits. I was glad to have a dog for the downed birds.

WILDERNESS-GROUSE DOGS

Not many bird dogs are used on back-country grouse, and I once thought a dog would be nothing but a nuisance, assuming the birds wouldn't hold on the ground anyway and that a dog would simply flush them wild. I have since concluded that a controlled dog can be a big help and have seen some good pointing on blue grouse. A close-in flushing dog helps too, but any dog that ranges far out is likely to tree the birds if it doesn't drive them off the mountain. Remember that mountain grouse aren't long on hiding on the ground and will get fidgety under a point.

One of my goofiest dog experiences occurred while looking for blue grouse on a mountain ridge. It was remote country and I was walking alone except for a Brittany wearing a bell. He'd needed a bell because earlier in the day we'd been prodding thick bottom brush for ruffed grouse.

The dog had somehow gotten misplaced and had circled around behind me. I was moving along just below the ridgetop and was perhaps 30 yards past a jumble of boulders that cropped out just a little above me. I'd missed the dog's bell for several minutes and then heard it coming in, the hard jangle of a galloping mutt who knows he's fouled up and is on the boss's trail. As the dog appeared in the timber behind me I caught a movement from the heap of boulders and saw a black bear's head and shoulders move up above them until the bear was posed like a fat sports fan in a box seat. It paid no attention to me but stared at the hurrying dog and his bell. The dog swept past the silent observer, whose head seemed almost to keep time to the jangling bell and turned as the oddity passed. After the dog had gone by I could swear the bear shook its head as if to say, "What'll they think of next?"—and it quietly sank from view. Some vagary of the mountain air currents had apparently prevented them from scenting each other, even at 20 feet.

When I tell that story to my friends I usually end up with the lame comment, "You'd have to be there to appreciate it," but the whole thing had a hilarious animated cartoon flavor I'll never forget.

WILDERNESS-GROUSE GUNS

If you hunt blues, Franklins, or spruce grouse with a shotgun, I'd keep it light, for it's rough walking and seems always to be uphill. They're big birds and I wouldn't use any gun with less than 1⅛ ounces of shot. I've used both No. 7½ and No. 6 shot and can't see much difference. If your gun is modified, the No. 6 might be better. If it's more open, I'd take the smaller size.

Mountain guns can be oddities. Perhaps the perfect weapon would be a drilling (combination rifle and shotgun). Such a choice would enable a grouse hunter to carry a deer caliber as well as a scattergun. They're not too popular in this country, although turkey hunters find them useful, generally with a light caliber such as .222 Remington in one barrel and 20-gauge or heavier in the shot tube. The typical turkey gun would be excellent if you want to shoot grouse in trees and .22 long rifle would be enough for sniping duties.

Shooting any bird on the ground or on a limb is a touchy subject with upland gunners addicted to wing shooting, but birds in tall trees at 8,000 feet can be a special case unless you're good with rocks and sticks. When using a .22 I prefer hollow-points unless you confine yourself to head shots, which is convenient if you have a scope. The logical spot for a body shot is at the butt of the wing as the bird sits, and a hollow-point there will kill cleanly without meat damage. That's where I aim with a pistol unless I'm quite close and can hit the head. Such operations may revolt some upland gunners, but I wouldn't knock it until I'd tried it.

A great many blue grouse are shot sitting with .410-gauge shotguns. That's a meat proposition.

WILDERNESS-GROUSE HABITS

The spruce grouse is found over most of Canada, much of Alaska, and in northern United States in the Northwest, along the Great Lakes area, and in New England. The blue grouse are in the West, mainly at fairly high altitudes, especially in the more southerly range.

All these birds are usually found in conifer forests or near them and depend largely on conifer leaves for food. There's a small amount of insect feeding in summer, and they'll eat berries in season. Population surveys are very difficult because of the remote areas of habitat, and there can be considerable disagreement about a current crop, even within a few miles. Management of such game has been largely a matter of setting season and limit. Although a great many of these birds are killed every year, they are not very seriously hunted. I don't know anyone who keeps dogs or vehicles just to hunt wilderness grouse.

All these are ground nesters, even though they spend much of their time in trees. The young birds are likely to be found in very brushy areas, including open slash and burns. Undoubtedly there are many exceptions, but I have usually found them near tall trees.

A Western game biologist and a National Park naturalist, both avid upland gunners, once came upon a bunch of blue grouse on the plains, miles from timber or even heavy brush. The hunters, who shall remain nameless, could not identify the birds at first, deciding they were sharptails, ruffed grouse, and then sage grouse, although they didn't look quite right. Finally, they decided they were blues (the season was closed on the other birds) and managed to save their reputation by killing a pair on the second flush. It is the only case I have heard of such birds being ten miles out in the plain and far from trees.

PTARMIGAN

The hunting status of ptarmigan is very similar to that of blue and spruce grouse, simply because it is found in rather remote

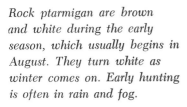

Rock ptarmigan are brown and white during the early season, which usually begins in August. They turn white as winter comes on. Early hunting is often in rain and fog.

sections. In the "lower states," ptarmigan are found only at very high altitude, and that's the white-tailed ptarmigan, the one that seeks the most inaccessible habitat of all.

There are three varieties, the willow, rock, and white-tailed. Although their ranges overlap considerably, it's generally the willow birds lower, then the rocks, and white-tailed highest of all. All of them live primarily above timberline, although they drop into brushier areas in cold weather. All of them are brown and white in summer, nearly completely white in winter. Few hunters know them apart and a biologist may have to look very closely.

In summer the willow ptarmigan stay much of the time in valleys and on moderate slopes, the rock ptarmigan are in hilly country, and the white-tailed birds are high in the mountains, often about rocky outcroppings. In winter the willow ptarmigan are found in willow thickets and in tall shrubs and scattered trees at timberline as well as in burns and muskeg below timberline. The rock ptarmigan then live in shrubby slopes at timberline and are often in windy areas where snow is shallow. The white-tailed birds continue to stay above timberline, evidently feeding on steep cliffs and wind-cleaned ridges.

The white-tailed ptarmigan is found in high mountains of Washington, Montana, Colorado, Wyoming, and New Mexico. The others are mainly in Canada and Alaska.

Buds and catkins make up a great deal of ptarmigan food, with dwarf birch buds heading the list of winter foods for rock ptarmigan. In spring and summer they take advantage of berries in season but eat very little animal food.

The ptarmigan is my choice of all game birds for eating, a rating that probably wouldn't suit those who have lived on them for long periods of time in the remote North. The wilderness grouse, blue and spruce, are almost as good and rate equally with the ruffed grouse in our oven. But then, that's a matter of individual preference. Some people don't like quail.

I sound like a broken record on this theme, but I have found ptarmigan too easy to be game in some circumstances and almost too tough for an overaged alpinist on other occasions. It is so common a paradox, especially with wilderness game, that it must be repeated over and over. The famous red grouse of Scotland is a race of willow ptarmigan.

When hunting rock ptarmigan (*Lagopus mutus*) north of Fairbanks, Alaska, we found coveys that walked about in plain sight, croaked amiably, and tried to stare down a pointing dog. When one got separated from his friends he almost walked over my feet getting back to them, muttering in a guttural monotone all the time. Others flew up out of range, and some flushed the way game birds are supposed to. In the air they're not particularly tough unless there's a high wind, when they have some of the erratic characteristics of doves and pigeons. In fact, their flight is very much like that of ordinary city-park pigeons in a hurry.

Many ptarmigan live on terrain best described as tundra, and although they are not addicted to careful hiding their coloration is sometimes highly protective. On some of those Alaskan hills a whole flock of ptarmigan can look exactly like an outcropping of blotchy rocks, and as long as they remain still you can walk past at pretty close range without seeing them. Many of the birds I have located have been moving about on the very top of a ridge. Sometimes they'll let you walk into range before flying, and the stories of ptar-

Diving off a mountain into rain and fog, a bunch of ptarmigan become difficult downhill targets in northern Alaska.

migan killed with sticks and stones are completely true. The stories of ptarmigan missed with both barrels as they dived off a precipice are also completely true.

Colonel Bob Carter, who has done considerable Alaska gunning, killed a lot of ptarmigan on the wing with a .22 rifle, but he is one of the country's top skeet competitors and did that where there were plenty of birds. Ptarmigan are important in the diet of many Alaskans, especially Indians and Eskimos who aren't particularly interested in sporty wing shooting.

I finally got an unfair start on the ptarmigan, having been given directions by Dr. Robert Weeden, recognized as a foremost authority on ptarmigan and then acting director of the Alaska Department of Fish and Game. He got me started where the supply seemed almost unlimited, but that came after several days of tough climbing during which I saw no game at all. I had followed directions of hunters who had found ptarmigan a year or two before, and the birds had simply moved. They do that, making unexplained migrations and abandoning territory that had been good country for years. They go in great loose flocks, sometimes funneling through mountain passes in such a way that the supply seems endless.

Dr. Weeden sent me first to Donnelly's Dome in central Alaska, a lonely little mountain that bulges out of a level plain within sight of snowy ranges but remote from them, and approached by an automobile highway. It looked easy, but like many Alaskan mountains, large or small, Donnelly's Dome has a base surrounded by a tangle of vegetation and something of a swamp. It took a while to get through that, and when we started up the dome's steep shoulders we met a wind that must have been blowing at least 40 miles an hour. As we neared the top it was much harder than that—hard enough to make me take special care with my footing in the rough places. When we found the ptarmigan they were on the very steep slope of short vegetation with small outcroppings of rock and miniature seeps. They went up wild, veered dramatically in the howling wind, and would disappear around a bulge of the mountain. That was tough shooting for anyone and made it hard to believe that sourdoughs kill ptarmigan with sticks or stones. It was only two days later in another area that I walked away from a whole hillside of ptarmigan, having shot all I wanted. Weeden had given me a choice of easy or tough hunting.

PTARMIGAN DOGS

Very few pointing dogs are used on ptarmigan. One Alaska resident who hunts lots of grouse with a setter told me that he had never put his dog on ptarmigan, and he was very curious as to how it worked out for me. For me, a pointing dog was a help but not necessary. One hunter told me that his pointer didn't point the birds but would run them up. They are a strain on a dog because they often walk around in plain sight. Mine didn't turn in a very showy performance and got to chasing them one day despite anything I could do or say. He recovered from that foolishness, but for a while I thought he was ruined. Game-management people often use dogs, sometimes retrievers, in their work. They capture nesting and brooding birds with nets.

PTARMIGAN GUNS

These birds are likely to be in wide-open country, and I suppose a modified choke would be about as good a choice as any. Sometimes a lot of very rugged climbing is involved, but there are occasions when you can drive to the birds in the family sedan. I have used No. 6 and No. 7½ shot in both 12-gauge and 20-gauge guns and see very little difference in results. The birds are about the size of plump pigeons and neither flimsy nor especially tough. Cripples are usually easy to recover unless they go over a cliff, and dead birds are easy to find everywhere I've hunted ptarmigan.

Mountain hunting is tough on guns, especially when it rains as much as it often does in Alaska. We camped in one spot where there was rain and fog for three days, finally soaking almost everything we owned, and guns required a lot of cleaning. Now that was for rock ptarmigan. Hunting white-tailed ptarmigan in Colorado would mean much more altitude and possibly more climbing.

CHAPTER XI

Prairie Grouse

TWO OF US PLODDED all day through a sea of sage, watched dozens of big sage chickens hammer their way into the air, and never had a shot. At first we tried to use a dog, but he couldn't make them hold close enough for us and finally decided chasing jackrabbits would be more fun, so we retired him and tried it alone. What birds we killed the following day were sheer accidents, grouse that were stumbled over before they happened to see us.

For birds with a reputation for clumsy stupidity, the sage hen changes its operations very quickly, so if you want easy hunting in an area of plentiful gunners, plan it for opening day. There are times when you will swear all sage-hen seasons should be closed, and there are other days when it seems no closed season is necessary at all.

SAGE GROUSE

The sage hen was part of the pioneer West, a giant grouse that fed wagon trains and homesteaders. Records don't show such things because it was no time for much naturalist foolishness, but

184

I strongly suspect there were areas and times of great plenty and others when the pickings were skimpy indeed. There were probably wagonmasters who reported all the sage chickens had been killed, and there were other times when it was possible for an industrious hunter to kill a hundred a day. This spotty population is a product of the grouse's habits of short migration, especially in the fall, and the gathering of enormous sage-grouse flocks can make it seem the supply is endless.

This is not to say that there haven't been times when the bird approached extinction. Only a few years ago there were biologists preparing to bid farewell to the sage hens and it appeared hunting would be stopped forever. Then the birds came back in a complex combination of land uses and legal protection. There are seasons now in much of the West, and unless land uses change drastically the sage grouse is probably here to stay. Some naturalists believe the late-summer hunting seasons are very hard on the birds, coming when juveniles are particularly vulnerable. Most seasons have been moved back a little later, but sage grouse are still among the first game hunted in the fall and they can be too easy.

I met my first sage grouse face to face while crawling on my stomach after a drifting herd of antelope. I'd been taking advantage

Typical prairie hunting country where wide-ranging dogs are a help. At midday the prairie birds are likely to concentrate in draws.

of a dry creek bed, and as I slipped up over the side of it to find just where I was from my pronghorns, I found myself being inspected by what appeared to be a 6-pound quail, an apparition that seemed to fit with the enormous sky, the purplish sweeps of sage, and a whitened steer's skull. The bird walked back deliberately and with dignity, looking back over its shoulder, but another one I hadn't seen flushed with a great beating of wings, scaring up a couple of its friends, and my herd of antelope slid off for half a mile to stop on a little knob with their rump hairs standing out like white powderpuffs. I abandoned that stalk and glared hopelessly at the original sage hen, which hadn't bothered to fly. Too tame to be game, I thought.

The days when it would be possible to kill a hundred sage grouse in a few hours have not necessarily gone forever. There have been two occasions when I've been in the midst of great, loose flocks that had apparently never been shot at, even though the season had been open for some time. In those cases I could certainly have killed a lot of birds without much effort and they must have been much as the wagon trains found them.

On the day before an antelope season opened in Montana, two of us were doing a little scouting and brought shotguns along. We planned to set up a truck camp in the midst of antelope country and be on hand for a daybreak chance at a big buck. We were driving along a trail when we saw a pair of sage grouse walking slowly off into the sage. That season was open, so I got out and walked toward them. They got up and others began to flush all about us, so without walking more than 50 feet we killed our limit, dressed our birds, and made camp by a nearby creek. I had no idea we were on the fringe of several square miles of sage hens until the following morning when Dan Bailey, another antelope hunter, met us. He had his shotgun too and was unable to resist a bird that he saw from the trail. I heard some shooting and found Dan and his Labrador had made short work of his limit of three birds. Thus far we had gone but a short stroll from the trail and two of us then took a somewhat longer walk, limiting out again within half an hour, and we decided we'd better get on with the antelope business.

All of this happened at the edge of an immense sage basin split by draws and creeks. As we hiked across it toward antelope we could see on hills three miles away, the sage grouse continued to

Dan Bailey collects a limit of sage hens in a brief time-out from antelope hunting. Close-working Lab can be a help and is frequently used in the West for sagebrush hunting.

flush, many of them within easy range, and I believe they were scattered over the entire bottom. We had stumbled upon a big concentration, and although it was not a particularly good sage-grouse year, at that time (early October) they were beginning to mass. A few days later they had moved enough that there were very few to be found in our antelope country.

There are some wild misconceptions about sage chickens, and probably the worst is that they are very slow walkers and don't actually slip away from man or dog. Another fallacy is that they are slow fliers. Slow and labored flushers they are; slow fliers they are not. Hunters who have seen only a few birds in rather restricted quarters (unwilling to leave good feeding and watering areas) have the mistaken idea that they make only short flights, whereas as nearly as I can estimate they are capable of longer flights than any other grouse or partridge. The sage grouse has a heavy, dark-meated breast, indicating a plentiful supply of blood for the big wings. When it gets way up there it can go, and don't you forget it.

And about that running, walking, and slipping—I had compiled a long list of mysterious sage-grouse disappearances before it dawned on me that they were simply running out of the country. When it wants to leave on the ground in a hurry, a sage grouse abandons its struttting stance, thrusts its head a little forward to make a low silhouette, and takes long and purposeful steps. Perhaps it can't scoot like a pheasant, but it'll go just as far, and the first time you see those shadows slipping up a hill a quarter-mile ahead of you they're always going faster than you expected. That's in thin grass and through sagebrush. It's too big a bird to make fast time in alfalfa or heavy weeds. The cocks go with more of a waddling gait; the hens seem more efficient. Conversely, the birds that make the funny twist and dipsy-dos when flying are the hens, while the roosters fly straight and level.

When considering walking or running sage grouse, think in terms of long distances. I believe I have seen them walk ahead of a gunner and dog for as much as 2 miles without flying, but I can't be positive for there aren't many landmarks in sagebrush country and the distances aren't in a straight line. When hunting sage hens with Max Stevenson, then a resident of Pennsylvania, we put up a single hen that wouldn't hold for our dog. It was too far away to shoot but I marked it very accurately, and I innocently believed that after flying a quarter-mile the bird would hold, so when the dog showed little interest in the new spot I got pretty cranky with him. He insisted on striking off over a hill, and Max followed him while I painstakingly kicked every sage bush within a 100-yard radius and told myself that the damned dog was trailing a jackrabbit.

Twenty minutes later I saw Max and the dog, little more than specks, topping out a hill a mile or so away, the sinking sun glinting from Max's pumpgun, still held optimistically at the ready. With dark coming on, I went back to our truck and drove in search of the wanderers. Max reported the dog had continued to trail and point for a mile or so and he'd finally sighted several birds going across an opening in the cover far ahead. Finally, two of them flushed wild after what we estimated at more than 2 miles of walking, but

Bill Browning collects a big sage grouse rooster. Even the old roosters are excellent table fare if properly prepared.

we never found the rest and they had evidently peeled out of the bunch one at a time and hidden in the sage. This is standard procedure for "smart" upland birds, but few hunters would concede the lead-headed sage grouse that much savvy.

In the country where Max and I chased the grouse there was almost endless sage for them to hide in. Corner them where they don't want to leave and they'll make some circuitous trips. Two of us working three dogs found a little bunch of less than a dozen birds in a small patch of tall sage surrounded by farmland. They'd been there almost every year, probably flying out to alfalfa fields and then coming back to the sage to rest and roost. We got a couple of birds on the first flush and the rest flew over a hill, where we followed them, hoping they wouldn't get out of the country. We jumped a single bird that I missed and then found the dogs working back around a hill toward where we'd come from. They pointed in exactly the same spot, and the whole bunch was there, less what we'd killed. It had been a matter of a quarter-mile flight, then a long walk around a hill back to the old stand.

Once sage hens get up high, it's seldom much use to attempt marking their flights. It's not unusual for them to get up more than 100 feet when planning a long trip, and they will sometimes get as high as 500 feet. Coveys seldom flush en masse, but there will be small groups that stick together in the air. On the eastern Idaho border I once saw five migrating sage grouse so high they were almost unrecognizable without binoculars, but I put the glasses on them and the hens gave themselves away with their quick, twisting turns in flight, giving the impression they get their wings out of synchronization momentarily. It was a wild sight—the big grouse against a sky of wind-torn clouds and the mountain peaks completely white with late fall snows. The last I saw of them they were specks over a ridge that was probably 9,000 feet high.

FINDING SAGE GROUSE

Stand on a hill overlooking grouse country and you can make some pretty accurate guesses as to where they'll be. They can go a long way for water but they'd rather not, and good resting places are in grass and sage draws within half a mile of water, possibly a lot nearer. When they're very close to water, they may walk to it, but if they're farther off they'll fly in. Generally they'll rest where the sage is a little thicker than elsewhere and probably down out of the wind if convenient, but they can feed in a blizzard if they want to. They have special nostril plugs.

I haven't had much luck at it, but some sage-grouse experts are faithful users of binoculars and spotting scopes in finding birds, studying large areas from an elevation, with special attention to trails and openings near fairly thick sagebrush. When they have young, the females assume sentrylike poses. There's often one member of an adult flock that stands in plain sight when no others are visible, and I've often heard that called a sentry. Perhaps it is, but most of them show a tendency to walk around when they'd never be noticed if they'd stand still. While one or two birds move about slowly, the rest of the bunch often stays tightly hidden, even after you've walked within range, and some of them don't fly until they've really been pushed. Since they seldom take off together, you wonder what good their sentry is, if that's its job.

The durable droppings are the most frequently sought sign of sage-grouse presence, and there are very large accumulations where they've roosted, appearing there in heaps of several dozen deposits. As a hunting friend of mine once remarked, sage-grouse droppings mean there once were grouse there, but it's quite possible they have long since gone to sage-hen heaven as the droppings themselves can stand months, even years, of harsh weather. There's something else that helps, however, and that's the very dark blobs of material that appear to have been discharged in a pool and then solidified. They last too, but not so long, and are called caecal droppings, not true "intestinal droppings," but coming from the caecal ducts at the juncture of the small and large intestines. I don't understand these blobs but I do know that they can indicate more recent traffic than ancient leavings of the other kind. Of course, truly fresh droppings of either sort indicate birds are still using the area.

Another checkpoint is the muddy waterhole where the big footprints of a sage grouse are unmistakable. Generally there are plenty of them, if any, and this is good enough information that you might actually want to hang around the place and see if birds are going to fly in. They might come for several miles. Generally, it's more productive to just keep on hunting in the vicinity with an eye for airborne birds that may come for water. I have found the grouse in a creek bottom at midday, evidently within a few inches of open water, but wouldn't say that's typical. They dislike thick cover of any kind if it's wet. Walking small creeks with willows and high weeds doesn't pay off very often, but has done so for me at least twice. I don't know why the birds were in that thick stuff. The mysterious "sage turkey" is surrounded by a great many "nontypical" stories, a surprising percentage of which are difficult to disprove.

SAGE-GROUSE HABITS AND HISTORY

Sage is basic in sage-grouse welfare, and where ranchers have destroyed it by spraying the sage grouse have almost disappeared. In much of their range they live with pronghorns; sometimes they warn antelopes by their takeoffs but I think the antelope usually see intruders first. When there's heavy snow, the browsing antelope often clear it off the sage, so the grouse can feed, and sagebrush is green the year round, a constant source of food supply, no matter how much it may be supplemented by grass shoots, alfalfa, or grasshoppers. I cannot say I've ever found them where they were not in daily contact with sage.

Among the sage-chicken fantasies is the report that they do not have gizzards, but like most of the other fables it has an element of truth, for the grouse's gizzard lacks the thick and muscular walls needed for macerating grain, and the birds are primarily leaf eaters. When a large flock begins serious operations on alfalfa they can crush a field down until it is a real loss to farmers. Some hunters have assumed sage grouse were grain eaters, simply because they have been killed in stubble, but most of the crops of such birds contain green leaves and shoots from young plants coming on between the stubble rows. Most of the stubble birds I've found tended to jump wild, but occasionally they'll try to hide, sometimes being too big to make a good job of it.

Such conjecture is highly unscientific, but I have always wondered why sage chickens were not destroyed by coyotes, since they take off so slowly and it would appear a patient little wolf could get near enough for a successful rush. Robert L. Patterson, author of the comprehensive book *The Sage Grouse of Wyoming*, says that badgers, ground squirrels, and magpies led the list of nest destroyers in his study area, but Mr. Patterson didn't have many coyotes. Golden eagles are native to much sage-grouse country. The motor car is a serious predator, for birds are attracted to grasses on highway shoulders.

The elaborate strutting displays of the cocks each spring has led to so much spectacular photography of the subject that some readers have the idea a sage grouse is always the pompous dude seen on the struttting grounds. A strutting cock is quite a sight, since he may weigh around 6 pounds or more. When they adopt a strutting area, each cock stakes out his own territory amid considerable bickering and some violence, and then each bird does his future strutting at that site for the edification of the hens, who don't participate

A minor disagreement about the retrieving of a sage grouse.
Females are likely to weigh three pounds. A full-grown cock might
weigh almost seven.

in any part of the show except the actual mating. Strutting grounds
are generally fairly open, and dawn is the prime time for the main
event. When they have completed their day's program, the birds
usually fly off in a group. The strutting may start as early as Janu-
ary, and the height of the season is probably sometime in April.
Most of the broods are hatched by early June. The nests are simply
depressions under bushes in most cases with an average of about
seven eggs.

Shooters make some choices in the field, most residents of sage-
chicken country preferring young birds since they aren't so tough.
This seeking for "young" birds assures that most of the bag will be
hens, for they're much smaller than the cocks, averaging about half
as heavy. There are many people of the West who simply will not
eat sage grouse, least of all an adult chicken. I'm at a loss about
this, for when we served several different kinds of upland game' at
a dinner, the majority of the guests picked sage grouse as the best
of all on two occasions. But there was one unconvinced Westerner

who wouldn't even taste it. He could tell by the size of the breast that he was being served a "damned sage buzzard."

There is one strange view, handed down for generations, that the sage grouse was a staple of people who couldn't get anything better, and there's a subconscious averision to it, an aversion I've found for venison in areas where families were once raised on it. Others say a sage hen is ugly.

Lewis and Clark reported the sage hen, and it was about one hundred years later, 1906, that the numbers were officially reported as decreasing rapidly. In the 1930's, with some biologists believing it was already too late, there were completely closed seasons over most of the West, but the birds came back enough that open seasons became widespread in the 1950's. Land practices contribute to the sage-hen supply, but there are cycles of population that remain unexplained.

It is a bird tied to the settlement and development of the West, at one time pickled in barrels as a staple of the pioneer family, and those who hunt it for sport begin to feel a part of the giant plain, the faraway buttes that shimmer in heat during early seasons, the prairie-dog towns with their yipping sentries, the furtive movements of coyotes, the high-turning golden eagles, and the ever-watching proghorns. This is not a bird of fence rows and barnyards, and as the hunter checks for landmarks, the only sign of man may be the dark cipher of a sheepherder's stone monument that will outlast the hunter and may have already outlived its builder.

SAGE-GROUSE DOGS AND GUNS

Bird dogs smell sage hens well, despite fables that they "can't work in sage." You can use one that gets out and scratches, for it's big country and visibility is usually good, but there's a special hazard about staunchness. Sage grouse usually get up raggedly, giving you plenty of time, but I've seen several dogs, especially one enthusiastic pointer, that came apart when a 6-pound grouse took off, and he proceeded to bounce the rest of the bunch. In a chain reaction, that single pointer once bounced roughly 40 acres of sage hens. Once you get into scattered flocks, dog control is the important thing.

John Gilpatrick of Montana uses a Lab to retrieve a sage grouse near Hilger. Low sage makes hunting difficult as birds flush wild.

Cripples are less problem than with most upland birds, as they frequently make no effort to hide. This isn't a hard-and-fast rule, for I've seen many of them that did find cover and stay put, but if you follow them up quickly very few get away. Although they can walk rapidly for a long way, I've found a running sage hen pretty easy for a man to catch. Nevertheless, things get pretty confusing with two or three shooters operating when a flock goes up in a scatter and after everybody has reloaded a time or two it's sometimes hard to tell who shot what and where.

Sage grouse are not hard to hit if within range, as their flight is pretty straight for shotgun purposes. Although the hens have a disturbing twist to their navigation, it isn't enough to carry one out of your pattern. They gain speed very slowly and are especially vulnerable as they rise, many of them laboring almost straight up for a while before leveling off. An easy one to miss is a riser that takes off skimming the sage tops, and it may put on considerable speed. I've heard they can get nearly 70 miles an hour under ideal conditions, probably with a tailwind and driving down a slope. I do know they go mighty fast under those circumstances, and you'll sometimes get such shots when they've been put up by other hunters. I know one good shot who has trouble with easy sage hens every year, and he believes they're so ponderous he can't make himself shoot ahead at all.

Although sage hens come down much more easily than pheasants or mallards, there's not much point in using shot smaller than No. 6, and I'd recommend a minimum of 1⅛ ounces of shot. 1¼ ounces of No. 6 is about right, and a modified barrel will do the job. Full choke can be used well by one who can shoot it, as it's nearly always open country and close risers can be waited out.

SHARPTAIL GROUSE

The sharptail (*Pedioecetes phasianellus*) seems to be more resourceful than the other plains grouse. It survived the pioneer days of the wholesale market hunting, the shifts in land use, and the arrival of the automobile as a hunting vehicle. For the most part, it seems to have withstood adversity better than the true prairie chicken or pinnated grouse, and certainly better than the heath hen, an Eastern version of prairie chicken that disappeared forever in the early 1930's.

I suspect the sharptail's strength lies mainly in its adaptability to a wider variety of food, a willingness to take to somewhat heavier cover than the prairie chicken goes for, and possibly a more aggressive disposition. Sharptails migrate to some extent, apparently moving to more suitable weather or feeding areas. There are resident flocks, of course, but I have seen spots that would be full of sharptails one week and completely barren of them the next—and there might be no more for a year. These movements are so irregular I doubt if anyone has made a very accurate survey of the routes. "Routes" may be the wrong word, as the wanderings seem to be at random at least part of the time.

Kelly almost becomes airborne in retrieving a sharptail grouse, the bird that had adapted to civilization better than the true prairie chicken.

The sharptail is simply known as "prairie chicken" in many plains areas and often lives with the pinnated grouse *(Tympanuchus cup-ido)*, but there are obvious differences in appearance. The sharptail is marked in spots or large flecks, and the prairie-chicken markings are dark bars. This difference shows up instantly on the breast and is less distinct on sides and back. The prairie chicken is sometimes known as a squaretail, whereas the sharptail gets its name from the pointed tail, which shows white in flight, and the overall appearance of the prairie chicken is darker.

Both species originally lived in native prairie grasses, and both adapted to grain farming to some extent, but the sharptail seemed to get along without the immense grass areas that disappeared with cultivation. The prairie chicken has been on the verge of extinction and the sharptail has hung on stronger. I have heard a sharptail will drive a prairie chicken or a pheasant from winter feed, but I've never seen it. The sharptail is not in danger of extinction and affords considerable shooting, although it has suffered from farming practices. In one area where the birds are much fewer than formerly, while the grain production hasn't changed much, one veteran rancher told me he felt the population went down when farmers quit using strawstacks. In the winter, he said, sharptails spent much time with the weather protection and ready waste grain of the stacks.

Sharptails can take a lot of weather, and not many U.S. hunters realize that their range extends to the Arctic Circle in Alaska. I am guessing that their ability to make short migrations can keep them operating on the fringe of boreal cold.

Like the sage grouse and the pinnated grouse or true prairie chicken, sharptail grouse have their early spring strutting or dancing grounds and the males go through similar maneuvers. It would be very difficult to tell males from females while hunting them. When flushed, most sharptails make a "cuk, cuk, cuk," in a monotone. It isn't the complex series of cackles delivered by a cock pheasant.

SHARPTAIL HUNTING

The sharptail is inconsistent in its behavior before the gun. The first one I ever saw was moved by a dog hunting below me in a brushy ravine bordered by hilly pastureland. This bird fluttered from the draw and landed on the ground, where its head and neck could be seen plainly above the grass, and it continued to look back toward where the dog was rustling through the cover. I had hunted for some time for my first sharptail and began a cautious approach, remembering with great clarity that I seldom hit a bird I can see before it flies. This one paid little attention to me, although I was in plain sight and only 30 yards away. It was more concerned with the mysterious sounds coming from the dog, and when it flew it came straight at me. If it had been a center hit I'd have blown it to fragments, but I was off enough that only a few shot struck it.

The most sharptails I have seen have been during two hunts in eastern Alberta. I hear more about the shooting in western Sas-

A bag of sharptail grouse is collected near an abandoned homestead in southern Alberta.

katchewan, but it's the same type of country as nearly as I can tell. Saskatchewan is a bit nearer large centers of population and has a larger area of sharptail habitat. Much of that Canadian country is used by bird-dog trainers during the summer, the younger sharptails holding well and polishing the skills of the fleet pointers that will spend the fall and winter on bobwhites in the South. But when the training season closes, most of them load their trucks and trailers and leave the maturing sharptails alone. The unpredictable and sometimes goofy performances of the "pintails" are likely to make hopeless neurotics of classic pointers.

I made my first Alberta sharptail hunt with what appeared to be a handicap in the form of Red Monical, who was in Alberta for geese and viewed my grouse fixation with kindly tolerance. We'd bagged the geese from meticulously constructed pits near Brooks

Sharptail grouse have learned to make the most of farm buildings with the shelter and scattered grain certain to be found there. These are in southern Alberta.

in southeastern Alberta, and even done some duck shooting in a stubblefield where mallards and pintails dropped carelessly in to black rag decoys. We'd parked our little camper at an abandoned farm while awaiting goose-shooting time, and a bunch of sharptails that lived about the place had flown to the barn roof in mild alarm and finally taken off for some distant brush clumps. There was a covey of Hungarian partridge there too, but those seasons weren't open.

Abandoned farms are a part of the Alberta landscape, the old buildings surviving well in that climate, the shelterbelts grown thick and tall in some cases and sheltering sharptails and Huns in howling prairie blizzards. The grain elevators are landmarks, often brightly colored, and standing idle except for those periods of hurry when the harvest comes in.

There is a tendency to stand at one of the decaying homesteads, shake your head sadly at the rusting farm machinery, and think of the dreams that may have faded there, but it may not have been a sad departure at all, and the man who built the slumping barn may now be rich and living in Calgary or Edmonton or in a giant ranch house. Agriculture has been ruthless in its patronage, and when the big tractors came the rolls of farmers were reduced both for better and for worse.

Red and I went farther north for our sharptail shooting, driving through enormous pastures and among great stubblefields, and camped at another abandoned farm, this time not far from Oyen. On the evening before season opening there were scattered sharptails flying into the grainfields for evening feeding, several bunches of Canada geese going out and back for late-afternoon gleaning, and small flocks of ducks on local missions. It was unseasonably hot for September. We started out at dawn the next day, marching resolutely into the fields of grass and rosebushes and wearing too much clothing, for the morning frost disappeared and the sun broiled us. We pushed a pair of coyotes from the first little ravine, and a whitetail buck slipped across a gap in the bushes. Our dog rummaged around the brush, and the first sharptail went up like a rocket so far away it was barely recognizable.

Then I somehow kicked one out at my feet and watched it drive through a notch in some tall stuff. Later I could not recall what position I'd had my gun in when it went up, but I never got on my bird until it was too late. Then we killed two individual singles that flew up fairly wild and watched several birds that refused to hold for the dog. At noon, we came back to the camper, a little confused and wondering if all of the sharptails in Alberta must be flushed one at a time from impenetrable rosebushes.

Oliver Glimsdale, a Fish and Wildlife officer I'd corresponded with, was waiting at our camp, a little surprised by our slender bag.

"I can't understand it," he said. "There's a whole bunch of grouse sitting on the railroad tracks over there."

That's what I keep telling you about sharptails. They're a little mixed up psychologically. We gulped some sandwiches, followed

Red Monical scores on sharptail grouse on a rosebush flat in Alberta.
When the birds rose wild, he went to a magnum duck gun.

Oliver's directions, and, sure enough, there was a bunch of sharptail grouse sitting on the railroad tracks. When we arrived they disappeared into the thick bushes and weeds, but we put up several of them and shot three. There are rusty railroad spurs running everywhere in that country, tying the big elevators to the main lines.

It was that afternoon when Red announced he needed his goose gun for those wild-flushers. It was a 3-inch, 12-gauge magnum, and when it pushed out 1⅞ ounces of No. 4 it made quite an impression. It was his business if he wanted to use a cannon, so I watched him put his bird gun away. As it worked out, the goose gun was a pretty good choice.

The small tree clumps are an important part of the rosebush pasturelands. In wet weather, there is water at each of them. During a dry fall such as we were having that year, there's no water, but the thick underbrush grows on the perimeter of the potholes and there are several good-sized trees too. Sharptails spend much of their resting time in these scattered patches of heavy color, probably using them as a roost too. It's possible to look at such a place with binoculars and even sight grouse strolling around on the bare ground where water would be in wet weather. It looks like a sure thing, but it doesn't always turn out that way.

You can walk right up to the little aspen-poplar grove, which may be 50 yards across, and hear the sharptails flying out of the other side. You can bust right through the brush and possibly put one up right under your nose. In any event, a dog isn't likely to be much good. There are some occasions when I've seen grouse leave such a setup while I was 100 yards away.

We'd approach one of the little groves, our dog birdy and excited, and Red would hunt a good spot to shoot from and hint that I should go into the scratchy tangle of underbrush beneath the trees. The dog and I would go in, and I'd hear some racket as the sharptails fought their way up through the brush; if they went in the right direction, Red would cut loose with his big gun at anything up to around 60 yards. After this had happened a couple of times and I was feeling sweatily put-upon, a pair of grouse swept across the bare spot at the middle of the little grove, the place where water would stand in wet weather, and I killed one of them with my open-bored bird gun. We had worked out a fairly satisfactory method of getting some shooting. Then our dog saved his threadbare reputation when I marked a sharptail that sailed for 300 yards and dropped into weeds at the top of a little knob. The dog got over there, pointed the bird, and held it like a woodcock to be kicked up from under his nose—so everybody was satisfied. Just why a single grouse should decide to play bobwhite I don't know. On a trip at the same season on the following year, the dog held a large percentage of the birds.

Knowing the birds tended to hole up at midday and feed morning and evening, we tried some jump shooting the following dawn, and Red stuck stubbornly to his weighty goose gun. I couldn't complain, for he collected a good bag of sharptails that went up at long range with little help from our dog, which earned his keep by finding dead birds in the brambles.

The early fall hunting has some bonuses in Alberta. There are Canada and snow geese if you'll take the trouble to find where they're working, the plentiful ducks haven't started south yet and are still wearing blotches of their summer plumage, and bunches of sandhill cranes make pictorial patterns at dawn and dusk. Some-

An early fall thunderstorm threatens a successful sharptail hunter in southern Canada.

times they fly over you at low altitude and make their wild call that sounds like a musical ratchet. A little later on they will form in businesslike migratory lines that appear to seam the entire sky.

Sharptail grouse will roost in trees, and when they're found in brushy ravines in grazing or farming country they'll often be found sitting well off the ground. If they haven't been worked over by hunters, they'll sometimes go for only a short distance on their first flush, but it isn't any weakness in the flight department, simply a matter of not being too badly scared. Large flocks often alight in grain stubble, but I've had poor luck in getting close enough and they tend to be pretty watchful. Under those circumstances, several hunters have an advantage, as they can work birds toward each other. Sharptails sometimes scatter wildly when flushed in large

The true prairie chicken or pinnated grouse has made something of a comeback after near extinction. These came from North Dakota.

numbers and frequently swing over shooters. Those aren't exactly easy shots, but they're frequently within good range, and I have seen them fly down an advancing line of hunters in easy shotgun distance, evidently reluctant to cross the line and not smart enough to gain more altitude.

PRAIRIE CHICKEN

The greater prairie chicken *(Tympanuchus cupido)* has habits similar to those of the sharptail, except that it is more wedded to grasslands, somewhat less attached to heavy brush, and less adaptable to changing land uses. There is a lesser prairie chicken that lives in a more southerly range for the most part.

It was the tall native grasses that accommodated millions of prairie chickens, and much of the early-day market hunting was directed at them, although the sharptails went to the stores too. From what I read and hear from old-timers, the prairie chicken of those days was quite vulnerable to a marching line of gunners and held well for dogs in the high grass. I haven't killed many prairie chickens, but I have found adult sharptails in tall grass where their performance before a dog would satisfy anyone, and in my limited prairie-chicken experience, I have found them likely to jump wild when sitting in bushes, but tight-holders at least part of the time in tall grass.

Somehow the prairie chicken has been a sentimental favorite of mine, for I grew up in southeastern Kansas on the edge of their range at a time when they were believed on the way out. Where I lived was only a few miles from where there were short open seasons, but a trek of 30 or 40 miles just to shoot at birds was considered poor economy on the farm, and I satisfied myself with my father's and grandfather's stories of the days before the Spanish American War when there had been plenty of chickens in Kansas and Missouri.

Prairie chickens stayed in the back of my mind, and when I got around to them a few years ago, I was a little surprised to find they had such a hallowed niche in my respect that I didn't really want to kill a limit of them. Sharptails were somehow different, but I held the true prairie chicken in some sort of separate category and felt it had enough adversity without my conniving. Even the sage hen lacked that kind of glamour for me. Okay, so I'm soft on prairie chickens.

But I was going to hunt them for a day, at least, and drove a very long way to South Dakota, where I was surprised to find they weren't so easy to come by, at least where I had planned to hunt. Pheasants and sharptails, yes. Prairie chicken were something else, and when half a dozen ranchers remarked they hadn't seen a real chicken in years I figured I'd picked the wrong spot.

It was noon of the second day when I talked to Ed Konip, standing surrounded by a small pack of crossbred coyote dogs. I'd found him by a series of rumors about his former guiding activities and his love for bird hunting.

"Now you don't want sharptails, do you?" Konip said. "You want real black prairie chickens."

Having explained what I wanted to quite a number of Dakotans,

I went over the thing again, complete with the description of barred breasts instead of speckled breasts. It wasn't necessary.

"Well," said Konip, "just take your dog down that little draw and into that brush. There ought to be a bunch there. There ought to be another bunch over that way."

He pointed to another draw that dived down into a larger ravine from the level grainfield, and the whole thing sounded too easy. Debie and I ate lunch, complained about the early fall heat and the persistent dust that settled over everything democratically, and then I took old Kelly and started into the draw. He panted manfully through the tall grass and the bushes and suddenly became birdy, then made a staunch point toward a pod of scrubby trees. Before I could move up, half a dozen birds, dark against the baked grass, flew out with irate cluckings, and three of them swung past me. I got the little 20-gauge into action faster than usual, and one of them thumped against the dusty bank of the ravine; another fell in taller grass. I quit while I was ahead.

Two of the birds went only 100 yards and sailed into a bank where grass was heavy. The dog followed and pinned them, but I never fired when they went up. I thanked Ed Konip, dressed my two birds by the Missouri River, and left South Dakota, for my hunting time had run out.

There are many other ways of hunting prairie chickens. Some hunters have found well-used fields where birds can actually be

Author brings in prairie chickens from a draw in North Dakota pastureland. True prairie chickens, like sharptailed grouse, often rest in low trees near water.

ambushed as they trade back and forth, and Jack Gowdy tells of doing that in the ancient coal-stripping pits of southeastern Kansas, a matter of hiding in the weathered and brushy mounds and waiting for chickens to come sliding over on their way to choice feeding spots.

Whether it's because they find the food more to their liking or because they can see their surroundings better, prairie chickens are likely to select mounds or knobs in prairie country. Their flushed flight is generally around a quarter-mile, although they can go much farther when really stirred up. They rise into the wind, so often a part of plains hunting.

The chicken nests in the grass with around a dozen olive-spotted eggs. Like the other prairie grouse, the prairie chicken stages communal ceremonies on booming and strutting grounds each spring, producing the booms from inflated air sacs on the neck. Only the cocks do the strutting and fighting.

PRAIRIE-GROUSE GUNS

I have killed plenty of sharptails with an open 20-gauge and No. 7½ shot, but there are times when a full-choke gun with No. 6 is much more practical, especially if you're not using a pointing dog. A duck gun will probably get more birds than a quail model if you can point it, for it's rare that the birds will fly behind anything except when they're living in the little tree groves. Both sharptails and prairie chickens fly fast enough, although neither is extremely fast on the takeoff. When they come out of bushes or small trees, they get going faster.

A double gun with choice of chokes is ideal if you're capable of choosing your barrel after the birds are in the air. The muzzle device on a repeater is a handy gadget, for it's likely a pattern of flight will be established on any given hunt, giving you a chance to make choking adjustments.

CHAPTER XII

Rabbits and Squirrels

A LARGE PERCENTAGE of Americans live within 100 yards of either rabbits or squirrels. A cottontail crosses our yard almost every evening, and there is a gray squirrel filching bird food 10 feet from my window right now. Such familiarity may build contempt for some who prefer more exotic game, but there are more rabbit and squirrel hunters than grouse or pheasant hunters. The cottontail is unquestioned Number One on the American game list, and the squirrel is well up there too.

Give the rabbit some weeds and give the squirrel some trees and they won't require much management. They can be killed by lousy shots with junk guns, but some rabbit and squirrel hunters are highly skilled sportsmen who have studied the game and know it well and are top marksmen with carefully chosen weapons. Except near large centers of population, hunting pressure is light, and both rabbits and squirrels are underharvested in much of their range. Their wildness matches the hunting pressure, and both can live within city limits or in the wilderness.

America's smallest big game is the gray squirrel, mainstay of hunting since the first settlers in eastern United States.

COTTONTAIL AND RELATIVES

Hunting cottontails may be fun when it's just sudden shooting at a bobbing white blob in a briar patch, but a little study of the things makes it better. Since a bunny will probably live out its days within the range of a sharply elevated .22 rifle, it's no great problem to find the right neighborhood. Narrowing the search down to the exact square foot and learning whether it's a good rabbit season or not will take a little investigation.

The East and the Middlewest have the most cottontail hunters, and the Eastern cottontail is best known of the tribe. The marsh rabbit is similar in appearance but darker in color and is found along the southern Atlantic Coast and as far west as Alabama. The swamp rabbit is somewhat larger and is found a little farther west. The brush rabbit is on the Pacific Coast, the desert cottontail and the mountain cottontail in the West and Southwest. There's a special brand of New England cottontail. All of them have similar habits but slightly different habitat. The big European hare has been introduced in the East.

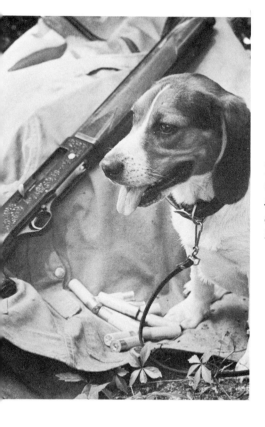

The beagle is a favorite of rabbit hunters, and there are some who aren't interested in collecting the bunnies—only in hearing the little hounds.

Like most of our upland birds, cottontails are residents of edge areas. Since most of their movement is at night, about the only ways of guessing the population are to beat the bushes or wait for a snow so you can check the tracks. Find a blackberry patch, a weedy fencerow, or a bit of marshy area next to grass, clover, field crops, or gardens, and there should be cottontails, barring one of their periodic low cycles. Find the right place and they can be moved with dogs, kicked up, or still-hunted by watching for sitting individuals. The last method takes the most skill, is probably least practiced, and places the least premium on marksmanship.

When there's no snow, this spotting system requires a lot of practice. A cottontail's form or "squat" is a sort of nest designed to accommodate only the rabbit. Generally it is designed so that the bunny actually sits on bare ground with the grass or weeds shaped about it so that it has good vision in one direction, usually to the downhill side. Evidently the rabbit thinks it can't be located from the other side, where there's usually heavy vegetation or brush. I don't know why it wants the bare ground under it. It doesn't care if it's wet, even in chilly weather, and it likes it close to water. There's no set way in which a rabbit rests in its form. Usually it sits hunched up with its ears flat and often with one eye almost in the center of the opening it uses to enter its hideout. Occasionally it sits with its nose pointed straight toward the opening. There are some forms constructed so that the rabbit lies well stretched out, almost at full length, with only its legs drawn under him. I go to all this detail to help anyone who wants to be a real hunter on a small scale. If you can spot rabbits consistently without snow, you should have no trouble with leopards, mountain sheep, or turkeys.

It doesn't take especially acute vision, but it takes concentration and the ability to look *through* the cover instead of at it. It is a business of looking for a rabbit's ears, or a fringe of rabbit fur. You won't get all-over views of rabbits in their forms.

Nearly all the true rabbit spotters do their shooting with .22 rifles or pistols. The range is generally extremely short, possibly no more than 10 feet, so the shooting requires no master marksman. Some of the better hunters of this type scorn any cartridge but the .22 short and aim only at the head.

I don't know of any better exercise for a hunter-naturalist. I got into this game through my father, who could spot well-hidden brown rabbits in brown grass after his eyes were too old to see the open sights on his pump rifle. All of us are tired, I'm sure, of the legends of keen-eyed woodsmen who can see things that escape mortal man, but I'll go so far as to say that he has often despaired of showing me a rabbit and has then told me where to shoot by pointing out a certain stick or a certain blade of grass. When I shot where he told me, out would roll a rabbit. I was pretty young, of course, but certainly old enough to have 20-20 vision. I was never good at this business but was surprised to find that I was much better than kids who had never hunted with my father. He never downrated other people's sport but didn't place much stock in the shotgun for rabbits.

If you want to do some cottontail sniping at longer ranges, use a rifle scope that gathers plenty of light, and move cautiously along river bottoms in late evening with dusk coming on. Keep in the open places and pay special attention to the areas right against the brush. Rabbits bent on evening feeding will hop out there first. Those can be fairly long shots, and you'll need long-rifle hollow-points, for the head business may not work out at those distances.

When it snows, the business of rabbit hunting is greatly simplified. Anyone who looks for rabbits in their forms has a big advantage then. Sometimes cottontails will be dug into soft snow until there's only a dark hole, but one eye is usually placed so that the resident can see out. If you can get afield on the morning after a snow that lasted until very late, trailing rabbits can be easy and productive. If they've had a day or two to bounce around in the snow there'll be so many tracks that trailing an individual is next to impossible. Rabbits do a lot of random hopping around on any night. When there's a fresh snow they seem bent on patting all of it down in the first few hours. The rabbit paths will indicate where game is thick, and where there are well-worn trails you'll find cottontails nearby, even though the trails may go on for miles. The individual rabbits don't travel so far, but their territories overlap and the animals that left the tracks may not even be acquaintances of the ones that made a section of the trail half a mile back. If you find a well-used path, there are likely to be daytime resting spots just a few yards to either side.

Some of the paths are so heavily used that they'll show up even when there is no snow and you can find rabbit droppings in them the year around. When there's heavy snow, the paths are essential, because cottontails can't travel well in snow more than 4 or 5 inches deep. I have long suspected that part of their post-snowstorm rambling is an instinctive effort to keep the trails open.

The small size of the rabbit's territory is the key to hunting it with beagles or bassets, for after being pushed by a trailing dog the rabbit will tend to circle back toward its starting place. Certainly it doesn't want to go very far into unfamiliar territory. In some of my earliest rabbit hunting I was amazed at the intelligence of a farm dog that seemed capable of circling the game back toward the hunter in almost every chase. Of course it is possible that some dogs do circle rabbits deliberately, but the bunny will come back on its own a good share of the time if left to its own devices. What passes for rabbit intelligence in avoiding pursuit is mainly familiarity with its surroundings. It has lived all its life in the same small range and knows every hideout in the place, including rockpiles, all sorts of abandoned dens built by other animals, and hollow trees and logs. Some of these sanctuaries have two or more exits so that it can get away while a dog or hunter is snooping about the hole where it went in. Apparently rabbits make frequent tours of these hideouts, even when not pressed, and with no intention of staying inside for long. I suppose it's just to refresh their memories and make sure the way is still clear. When I used to trap fur as a kid some of my best spots were old farm buildings with holes in their foundations, leading to big shelters under the rotting floors. Opossums, skunks, and civets lived under these old buildings, but my main difficulty was in keeping cottontails out of the traps. Evidently they were quite at home with the other residents, and they moved about more than the others. A cottontail seems to have little instinct for avoiding any kind of trap.

Once a rabbit gets into some sort of den or into a rockpile it may take a major excavation to get it out, and any hunter who goes rabbit digging may be simply destroying one of the features that has made the area attractive to bunnies. Might as well call off the dogs and try another rabbit.

Cottontails are quick but not particularly speedy on the straightaway, and many collies can outrun them. They don't have a lot of endurance, and a barefoot farm kid can run one down if he can keep it in the open long enough, which he seldom can. Given a little snow, a cottontail is easily caught if you can get it off a main-traveled trail. Fifty years ago, a heavy snow in some parts of the Midwest would set off a series of rabbit hunts with dogs, guns, and even clubs. Rabbits would be concentrated in draws and creek bottoms and could be killed by the dozens. At that time you could get a quarter for a rabbit and rabbit skins were bought by the pound, but I'm a little out of touch with that market. After one of those ideal periods for rabbit hunting, it might be slim hunting for the rest of the winter, but rabbits are famous for renewing their ranks and warm weather would bring them right back to plenty.

RABBIT GUNS AND SHOOTING

Almost any shotgun works for cottontails, and a bunny in the open is a pretty easy mark, but it's seldom in the open. It is its dodging that makes it hard to hit, and its dodging is simply a matter of working its way through the shrubbery. If it knows the country, as it usually does, it probably knows exactly where to land with every jump for the maximum speed through its personal labyrinth. A shotgunner doesn't do much swinging and quite a bit of stabbing with his gun muzzle. It's quite different from wing shooting.

After inept attempts with a .410 (even in those days it was considered a good gun for kids), I finally began to knock off running rabbits with an old Hopkins & Allen singleshot 12-gauge. It opened

Jackrabbits are used as practice targets by many big-game riflemen. In some areas they can become pests, but their cycles have deep lows as well as annoying highs.

with a bottom lever and I don't know if there was any choke or not, but there certainly wasn't much. Then, of course, I got a really good gun (full-choke) and my shooting got very bad.

For cottontails, low-brass shells with No. 6 shot are a pretty good choice. Anything smaller makes cleaning the game a mess. Most of the shooting is at reasonable range. If you're kicking them up they'll get out almost at your feet most of the time. Only when they're worked by dogs or sniped at dawn or dusk will bunnies tend to be long shots. A light gun has advantages, but there's seldom much climbing.

I've been talking about the business of actually bagging rabbits, but I'm fully aware there are many hunters who run rabbits with beagles or bassets with little intent of killing many or even any. Hound music is a different sport and a good one.

The Western jackrabbits aren't coveted as food, but they can be pests when they get out of hand and they are probably the best practice game for big-game hunters, being shot at long ranges and often while running. Nothing will develop an all-around rifleman much faster, and after shooting a few running jacks a hunter is likely to find moving deer, or even antelope, much easier than before. It can make you very humble, but when you see the dirt fly from your misses it's amazing how soon you begin to score. Many jackrabbits have been sold as feed for mink farms. Jackrabbit drives were common some years back when the population would get out of hand. Clubbing them was gory business but one way of keeping them under control.

Jackrabbits are hares, as are the snowshoes. One difference between hares and rabbits is that the hare's young are born furred and with their eyes open, while the rabbit young lack hair and are born with their eyes shut.

Jackrabbits have plenty of speed, and it usually takes a greyhound or whippet to catch one. Experienced farm dogs often make a great show of not seeing jackrabbits when they jump them, having been humiliated on previous occasions. I have checked jackrabbit speed many times on country roads, where they often run ahead of the car. Up to about 25 miles an hour a jack will keep both ears up and loaf along, but at nearly 30 it will drop an ear now and then. Above 30 it flattens them back and begins to dig. At 35 it prefers to abandon the race. That's generally tops.

RABBIT HABITS

Rabbits have few friends and they're food for almost all meat eaters, including coyotes and foxes. Bobcats are superior rabbit hunters, and weasels are highly efficient killers. Although all the rabbits and hares can do some kicking with their hind legs and females sometimes defend their young this way, the rabbit's specialty is retreat—agility in the cottontail and speed in the jack.

Although rabbit populations fluctuate wildly, there has been no danger of extinction, even after epidemics of tularemia, and rabbits are almost as prolific as the rabbit jokes indicate. A female starts planning her next family while attempting to raise a current one. Cottontails build ground nests about 5 inches deep, line them with fur, and keep them covered with a cap of grass and fur while the youngsters are too small to travel and eat greenery.

Jackrabbits are migratory to some extent, and I have seen droves of them moving slowly across prairie country, giving the impression that the supply is endless. Find a spot where there are numerous highway kills and you'll nearly always be in good rabbit country— temporarily. I once found thousands of rabbits in eastern Colorado and thought I had the mother lode for all jack hunting. Not knowing the traveling habits of jacks, I made a careful note of the exact spot and went back there with my rifle—ten years later—to learn the bumper crop had been gone for nine years. They were probably just moving through anyway.

Rabbits are among the most playful of animals. They'll stage impromptu games of tag, stop feeding for a short race, and cavort happily for no apparent reason. These antics are not necessarily related to breeding at all. I think the cottontails lead in such calisthenics, but others do it some.

The snowshoe or varying hare, which turns white in winter and lives in the northern United States and Canada, is one of the larger rabbits and one of the best to eat. It can be hunted with beagles and shotguns, although many of them are sniped by big-game hunters. Unlike the cottontails, which seem to prefer a civilized environment, the snowshoes are found in wilderness areas more than near farms or housing developments. They sometimes change their color too early in fall and appear as big ghostly bunnies in the tall timber. I have found them quite tame in primitive areas.

The color change, I understand, is keyed to the length of daylight rather than temperature. That's why a snowshoe may be caught in its ice-cream suit with the grass green and brown.

The marsh and swamp rabbits are not hunted much anywhere that I've found them. There's a lot of difference in their color, mostly darker than cottontails, and I know of one marsh where I've seen marsh bunnies almost as red as a fox. Elsewhere, they have been dark-brown—almost chocolate.

Rabbits are the last of the hunting in many places and should be highly valued. Glamorous they're not.

SQUIRRELS

Squirrels are the smallest big game, requiring some of the tactics of tiger hunting, and a woodlot containing gray squirrels is a capsule of the wilderness, even though it is within scent of kitchen odors and within sounds of front-porch conversation.

Some of the Eastern and Midwestern squirrel hunters are true woodsmen, although they walk no more than a quarter-mile on the average hunt. Southerners are not far behind them. Everybody knows that it is the squirrel hunters who supposedly make the best soldiers; it's been accepted since the Revolutionary War. In pioneer days there was something to it, for the "squirrel rifle" put a lot of meat on the table. It was a smallbore hairsplitter and deadly accurate for its time.

Unlike most of our upland game, the squirrels, especially the gray squirrel, are at home in mature forests. They say there was a time when a gray squirrel could make its way from Maine to Florida without ever leaving the treetops. I suspect there aren't nearly as many grays as there used to be, although they're amazingly plentiful in some sections. While turkey hunting in a backwoods hammock in the South last fall I found myself surrounded by so many noisy grays it would have been impossible to hear a turkey in hobnailed boots. Those hadn't been hunted, and a couple of the bolder ones hung head-down about 10 feet away and yelled at me until it became annoying instead of amusing. An irate squirrel is not exactly musical.

Camouflaged clothing and a big tree make a good setup for squirrel shooting. Concealment isn't as important as quiet.

That won't happen where they've been hunted hard, especially if someone has been using dogs and shotguns. Under such circumstances you can sometimes sit with your back to an oak until your neck stiffens and your eyes get bleary, and your only hope may be to see a tiny bump on a limb 40 yards away where an educated gray is taking a small peek to find out if you're still there. I am convinced the gray squirrels are more elusive than the bigger fox squirrels. I don't know about the little loud-mouthed red squirrels for I've never hunted them. They're hardly big enough to fry, and where I've found them they weren't afraid of me, having a vibrating vocabulary that would make the maddest gray squirrel draw a long breath. They say a red squirrel can whip any other kind, small as it is. Reds rob bird nests and are meat eaters to some extent.

One of the most pleasant ways of hunting gray or fox squirrels is simply moving through the woods very slowly and as quietly as possible in the hope that you'll find a squirrel on the ground and be able to nail it either as it makes for a tree or after it's in it. That's easily combined with another method. When you get into an area where you're sure there's plenty of game you can find a suitable place to watch some of the best trees and simply wait and look. Even if you don't use a squirrel call, you may attract the attention of curious individuals, or may not be noticed when they come out to feed. Strangely, a shot doesn't disturb them very much, and you may shoot two or more from the same stand. The ideal squirrel territory is one with den trees, usually partly dead and with holes in the trunks, and some kind of nut bearers. I've done most of my hunting in oaks, but hickorys or walnuts are just as good.

You can find where squirrels have buried or dug up nuts and where they've showered shell particles from a favorite feeding perch. Squirrel nests are a sure indication if they've been made from reasonably fresh materials. Squirrels will build nests for no particular reason, and the same female may house her family in a hollow tree and maintain one or more nests in the vicinity.

As with most other game, there are unexplained periods of intensive activity and other times when all is silent. This has been explained tentatively as a matter of barometric pressure or tidal movements. Often the rush hours and quiet times correspond to the activities of birds, but not always. Squirrels don't come out much during rainstorms, but I have known exceptions when they would feed busily while water ran off their fur and matted their tails. Early morning and late evening usually mean considerable activity, and I think morning is best.

One of the least subtle means of bagging squirrels is to go through the forest noisily, preferably with a dog or two, in the hope that the game will continue to run and jump after getting into a tree and give exciting shooting. Another thing happens when a squirrel is pushed very hard—sometimes it becomes so excited it loses its judgment and actually falls out of a treetop while traveling in small branches. It won't hurt it, as it breaks its fall with its legs and flattens out on its belly with a noisy plop, but it may be in considerable trouble if there are dogs on the ground. At best, it's in a good position to be bagged if someone is using a shotgun.

Once you've treed a squirrel there are some little tricks in sighting it. Its tail, invaluable as a rudder in the air and as a balance on the branches, sometimes does it dirt when it hides, for the tail is the one part it's a little careless about. A random sunbeam can shine through the long tail hairs and make a little halo visible far up in the tops. That doesn't mean the rest of the squirrel will be in a shootable position, but you know where it is and can wait for it to show itself. A squirrel sometimes hides in large forks, and there's little chance of getting a shot then unless it decides to take a little peek and show its head.

When it's plastered against a vertical trunk or a small limb, there are some ways of getting it into the open. You can simply wait quietly in hope it will reveal itself when it begins to wonder if you've left. You can slip around the base of the tree in hope of sneaking up on it. You can toss a stick or stone to the other side, hoping it will move toward you when it hears the noise. You can hang your coat on something and then sneak around, hoping it will turn back when it sights what you hope it thinks is you. You can send a dog around. Or you can hunt with someone else.

When sitting and watching for squirrels you can hear surprisingly small movements if there isn't much wind. You can hear teeth grating on a nut, feet moving on bark, or rustles of leaves on high or on the ground. Even the fragmentary dust of falling bark particles can indicate a moving squirrel somewhere up there. The main thing is to get into a comfortable position where you can see a good-sized area of squirrel country without having to move for a long while, and it's nice to have your gun where you can get it into action without dislocating your spine or getting up.

There are several squirrel calls, some operated by using a striker against the edge of a piece of wood, some that have rubber bulbs that give forth lifelike barks when struck against your hand. I have never worked these calls very long at a time, fearful that I'd foul up. Whether I have actually made my quarry think I was another squirrel or not I don't know, but the calls have made them come out into the open. Just a bark or two will arouse curiosity, which is an important part of a squirrel that hasn't been shot at. After it's had to take it on the lam with a gun booming behind him, a squirrel quickly loses that curiosity. You can sometimes get attention by making a rustling noise with a loose branch.

You can press your lips to your wrist and make an exaggerated kissing noise that sounds like one squirrel remark. You can crack

Some effective commercial squirrel calls. The one at left involves striking wood on wood. The others produce their sounds when tapped on another object.

two small stones together and make a sound like a squirrel bark. The squirrel's vocal efforts are many and varied. We've lived among them for twenty years in a grove of laurel oaks, and I still hear noises I'm not sure were made by squirrels until I watch and listen very carefully.

SQUIRREL GUNS AND DOGS

When I used to hunt burly fox squirrels in the Osage-orange hedges and small walnut trees of the Midwest I thought it was unfair to use a shotgun. The targets were big and comparatively slow and at close range, and I liked to hunt them with a target pistol or an open-sighted .22 rifle. Later I encountered gray squirrels leaping and plunging through the top branches of giant oaks and began to see the shotgun side of things. I still like a rifle for the grays but prefer a low-powered scope sight. If you're going to get them on the move in the tops you'll need a fast-firing repeater, preferably a semi-auto or pump, although I've used a lever-action pretty satisfactorily. The bolt-action I use for most squirrel hunting is a bit slow for that.

The one I've used most is an ancient Winchester Model 52 target .22 that has been cut down for the sake of convenience. It has a Bushnell 2½-power scope that was intended for big-game hunting. Most squirrel hunters use the inexpensive scopes made especially for light .22s. I don't think the extra accuracy of the old target rifle is necessary for most squirrel shooting, and it's pretty slow going into action, but I'm attached to it. I use hollow-point long-rifle ammunition, and although I admit I can spoil a little meat with a sloppy hold, there are many squirrels who have died in dens with .22 holes in them when solid bullets were used.

Quite a few big-game hunters load down their centerfire ammunition for squirrel hunting, using a bullet that's big enough to knock one down even without expansion. I knew one fellow who

Hunting from a stand is highly effective with a scope-sighted rifle. Here I use a modified old-model Winchester 52 target .22.

used a .300 Weatherby loaded down until it tossed a heavy bullet like a basketball. Unless you're a real handloader, that's a lot of trouble. In pistol hunting I've used long-rifle hollow-points and .38 wadcutters, both fired in handguns with target sights. A handgun scope would make it easier.

If there is a place for the .410 shotgun in game shooting it comes in squirrel operations, especially when the game is to be potted whether moving or sitting. I'd take a full-choke .410 with large shot, about the only excuse for using anything larger than No. 8 in the peewee scattergun. One sporting-goods dealer in the South tells me that he sells a lot of .410 ammunition with No. 4 shot for squirrel shooting. The merit of the .410? It's quieter than something more potent, a merit in civilized areas and of some advantage in keeping the woods quiet elsewhere. For most shotguns, No. 6 is about right. Small shot is a mess to remove from the carcasses.

A good squirrel dog will stay in fairly close and will follow a fresh squirrel trail, but if it's a cold-trailer it can be a nuisance, for it'll be "treeing" squirrels that have long since gone to sleep in a hollow tree. You're interested only in reasonably fresh trails. When this dog tracks or chases the subject to a tree it should look up into the tree whether it barks or not, and that's about all you can expect from a squirrel dog. Breed is unimportant, and a fox terrier can be as good as anything. A Great Dane might work just as well, but not any better. Some beagles are all right, but you don't want to be tied up with old trails.

SQUIRREL RANGES AND HABITS

The Eastern gray squirrel and the Eastern fox squirrel have nearly duplicate ranges, living over most of the eastern half of the contiguous states. The gray lives a little farther north, whereas the fox squirrel doesn't show up much north of the southern shores of the Great Lakes. In some parts of its range the fox squirrel is an overall grayish red, but in the South it may have dramatic markings of black and very light tan or gray. There are black ones in some sections.

The Western gray squirrel is a Pacific Coast resident. The red squirrels and chickarees are found in coniferous forests for the most part and are generally considered too small for game. There's a beautiful tassel-eared squirrel in the Southwest.

One of the chief differences in the habits of the gray and fox squirrels is the gray's insistence on sticking close to trees, whereas the fox squirrels will forage some distance into the open. Although both like corn and some other crops, the fox squirrel is the one most likely to be found several rows into the field. I consider the fox type much easier to bag and not nearly as resourceful as the gray. The fox is much larger.

Squirrels are hoarders and bury nuts by the thousands. I used to believe they then hunted their caches at random, but biologists tell us that they can unerringly dig up one of their treasures even when there are several inches of snow. Undoubtedly there are some thieves in the society.

The grays do considerable feuding among themselves, and some squirrel fights are noisy donnybrooks, usually occurring during mating season. An unreceptive female can be an ill-natured shrew and leads the males through some trying times. The litter of gray squirrels is generally about three, born hairless and tiny, often in a den tree. When they are still young, they are frequently moved by their mother to other dens or nests.

There are fabled migrations of great droves of squirrels, most of them having occurred a long while ago. There aren't enough squirrels now to make such a scene when they travel. Reasons for the movements can be a shortage of food in a given area, but sometimes they take off when there's a good mast crop and man has no explanation.

Squirrels have been pests in pioneer times and were killed by the thousand both for food and for control. Even today there are occasions when they are hard on crops. I've seen cornfields badly damaged by fox squirrels.

Most squirrel seasons are long and limits are generous. If you become a really good squirrel finder you should pick up lion or elephant hunting pretty quickly.

CHAPTER XIII

Turkeys

I KNOW A GOOD TURKEY HUNTER, and I expect to keep very close track of him, for they are very scarce. No matter how many times Milt Culp comes by the house to show me an especially big gobbler I shall always appear enthusiastic, however jealous, for he takes me along occasionally and I don't want to lose out.

A turkey hunter is a combination of squirrel hunter, goose hunter, undercover agent, and jungle sniper, doubled in spades. If he's really good at it he hunts turkeys the year round, even though he shoots them only during a very short season. Some of the best of the turkey-hunting tribe make a special effort at bagging an especially big gobbler and may pursue a particular one for years, both gobbler and hunter getting smarter as the seasons go by. When you find a turkey hunter who turns down completely legal specimens in hope of a really big one you have a graduated gumshoe, probably full of woodcraft and turkey thoughts. Maybe it's partly hereditary. Milt's father, Stanley, is a good turkey hunter too.

The wild turkey has staged a remarkable comeback. It was plentiful in pioneer times and found in quantity up until shortly after 1900, when it seemed to go into a decline over much of its range.

Often called the king of game birds, the wild turkey gobbler is the object of some of America's most skilled hunting and woodcraft.

It is still a touchy character for game managers, and they had plenty of problems in those days. In much of the South the land has been partitioned up into small farms and almost everybody was on the lookout for a turkey dinner. When the small farms began to give way to larger holdings and the human population began to concentrate in cities and housing developments, the turkey began to come back with an assist from enlightened game-management people.

Progress of the turkey is one of the brightest spots in the management picture. It is estimated that the population increased five-fold from 1952 to 1968, reaching a total of 500,000 birds. Wild turkeys are hard to count, so the current population is a bit uncertain. Florida claims the largest annual kill, although other Southern states report greater populations.

In the West the original wild turkey disappeared from some of its old haunts as well as being nurtured in areas where there may have been no turkeys at all in pioneer times. Seasons are becoming more generous, and many states have both a general fall and winter season and a spring gobbler season. A few of the fall and winter kills are by accident when hunters are after something else. The spring gobbler kills are on purpose and nearly always require careful hunting.

Still-hunting by moving carefully through the woods accounts for many birds, but most good turkey hunters are experts from a stand and can use a call. Stand-hunting works in both fall and spring seasons, but old gobblers seldom come to a call except during the spring season. "Roosting" turkeys involves finding where the birds will spend the night and being ready to go to work at dawn. Although they may be intercepted on their way to roost, it is usually too late in the evening to actually approach the roost tree for shooting.

A good site for a stand is usually located by finding turkey tracks or seeing birds move through the area, and it is likely the stand or blind will be located between roosting or resting areas and known feeding spots. You sneak to the stand as if it were already surrounded by suspicious gobblers. Evening and early morning are the best times. During spring seasons, hunting is sometimes permitted only in the morning.

Some stands are used year after year; more of them are impromptu selections. Being pretty green on the turkey business, I was very much surprised at the number of birds heard compared to the numbers actually seen or shot at, and that goes for both fall and spring hunting. When Milt stationed me in an open palmetto flat before dawn during spring gobbler season in Florida, I had the childish idea I'd probably get a shot at most of the birds I heard gobble, never stopping to think they could be heard for half a mile on a still morning. That stand had swamp and timber on three sides, but there was nothing heavy within less than 100 yards. It was a known crossover. Before sunup I heard a gobbler straight ahead of me, and knowing a turkey call, like a duck or goose call, can be used too much, I was very sparing with my yelper, possibly too sparing. Frankly, I lack confidence in my calling. The first gobbler never came any closer, but I heard gobbles from two other directions, nearly fell over when a wood duck skimmed past my hideout, and wished a fish crow would go away. It sat in a scrub pine within easy range and announced that something strange was going on. I heard half a day of turkey talk and never saw a one.

During a winter season, Milt steered me through an orange grove in late afternoon and showed me fresh tracks where a turkey had come out of a thick hammock and walked off into the grove. Then, with some disappointment, we found where it had hurried back into the brush, obviously having been moved at our approach. He stationed me at the point where the bird had gone in, hoping it might come back when things quieted down. That seemed to be the best place, so Milt went on for 200 yards and took up his own stand, facing into the timber. He was nearly trampled by a bunch of birds that came out an hour later and returned to the hammock when they detected something suspicious.

Then he slipped quietly back to me, moved me to near where he'd seen the birds, got us both comfortably concealed, and began calling. Within a few minutes the birds were back, one of them yelping repeatedly somewhere in the palmetto and tangled vine within easy range. Another walked steadily off at another angle, but before I even sighted one they had moved away. Probably they saw me as I wriggled about in my palmetto blind, trying to find an alert head sticking out of the underbrush. Under such circumstances the head is what you're most likely to see first, and that's what you're likely to shoot at. As dusk came on we listened for the brief whipping of wings that would mean birds were going up into their roosting trees, but the hammock was full of busy gray squirrels that kept up a continual rustling and crashing in palmettos and treetops. When we came back two evenings later we neither saw nor heard turkeys. Probably they had avoided the spot because of the disturbance we'd made. Veteran turkey hunters take such vicissitudes in stride, and Milt will probably be back there next year.

GUNS AND SHOOTING

There's no shooting in which there's more fussing about what gun and ammunition to use. Most turkeys are killed with shotguns, but there are times and places when a scope-sighted rifle is a better answer. The old .22 hornet is a ready-made turkey caliber, and the .222 Remington is a good one if loaded down to modest velocity or carefully pointed. I knew one marksman who did all his turkey hunting with a heavy target .22 rimfire and 15-power scope, shooting only for the head, but he had unlimited time for his hunting, was prepared to pass up chances that were too difficult, and spent days working out just the proper situation for the execution.

Most centerfire calibers can be used if loaded down. Solid bullets are sometimes used in .30-caliber rifles but are extremely dangerous in settled communities. Even when driven at high speed, a solid bullet may not do too much damage to the bird. The best spot for the rifleman is at the butt of the turkey's wing when viewed from the side, quite high on the breast from the front, and the back when viewed from the rear. Open-sighted rifles are difficult for turkey shooting, and if you can hit satisfactorily with open sights under the common conditions of poor lights and bird movement you'd probably be within shotgun range.

The turkey is the only upland bird that is considered fair game for the shotgun when it's on the ground or in a tree, and the choice

The drilling, a gun with both shotgun and rifle barrels, is favored by some turkey hunters who want both close-range and long-range coverage. This is a European model.

of loads is difficult to make. It's a matter of whether you expect to shoot into the body or into the head and neck. Heavy loads are needed in any event, and the 12-gauge is usually the best choice, although 16-gauge and magnum 20-gauge are fine if loaded as heavily as possible. A full choke serves best under most conditions.

For the standing shot most shotgunners feel the best hold is on the middle of the neck, or possibly where the neck meets the bird's shoulders. The idea is that the pattern will spread enough to get the head and possibly the base of the neck. If the gun shoots very tightly, No. 5 or No. 6 shot will be good, but there are many who believe in No. 7½ shot in a pattern that is almost certain to hit the head within reasonable range. Those who use the smaller shot usually shoot straight at the head. For body shots, No. 2 or No. 4 will be better.

Why a body shot? Well, there are cases when a bird is walked up and either flies or runs swiftly at rather long range. The ideal situation is to have the big shot in your gun while walking through turkey country, even though you exchange it for something much smaller when you are on a stand. There is a theory of using small shot on a stand only for the first cartridge, and having it backed up with heavy loads in case you have a crippled bird and no time for head shooting. There's an inclination toward repeaters for turkeys, as three shots may be needed in case of a nonfatal hit. It's a lot of bird and takes a lot of killing, and any game that has been hit should be shot at as long as there is the slightest chance of putting it down. Crippling losses are very high with turkeys.

A short barrel is handy in turkey cover, but few full chokes come that way, and most shooters think of duck and turkey guns together. A drilling type can be an excellent choice. If you use two shotgun barrels and a light rifle barrel you have nearly a perfect combination. Put a low-powered scope on it and there should be no complaints—if you can manage an occasional wing shot with the scope. Most "turkey guns" have a single shotgun barrel and a rifle barrel. Open sights take skill and good eyes in thick forest.

WILD AND TAME TURKEYS

A wild turkey lives mainly on the ground, although it uses trees for roosting and sometimes for feeding. Its appearance is a great deal like the tame turkey's except that it is more streamlined and lighter in the breast. Of course some of the domestics, long bred for the market, are low-slung waddlers. The domestic turkeys, developed from native wild birds, gradually acquired immunity to some of the poultry diseases, but the wild birds freely crossed with tame ones and were highly susceptible.

Many of the birds introduced to the wild had domestic blood, and instead of bolstering the wild population, they simply spread disease among it. These were some of the difficulties of early turkey management. For that matter, even the tame birds are hard to raise and likely to acquire disease from other poultry. Many strains of domestic turkeys are close enough to the wild ones to be a nuisance in some ways. When raised unconfined on farms or ranches, some of the domestic hens tend to hide their nests and are sometimes followed so that their eggs can be taken up and incubated free of predators. This is a touchy business, even with domestic turkeys.

HUNTING TURKEYS

A wild turkey is capable of incredible running speed in the open. It's hard to learn just how fast it can go, for when it approaches its running limit it'll take to the air, but I have seen them darting through grassy openings much faster than a pheasant can leg it. Twenty miles an hour? Probably more than that. Some say a turkey can outrun a racehorse, but I wouldn't go that far. I know a good sprinter who caught a winged bird, but the injury may have slowed it somewhat. He had to run it down.

Like much other game, wild turkeys can become so accustomed to car or boat traffic that they pay little attention to it. It's not unusual to see them feeding along the shoulders of superhighways, although they stick close to the cover. Hard as they are to approach on foot, I have moved right up to a flock by using an outboard boat along a canal. They were feeding along the dike and simply walked away when I stopped within 20 yards of them. Those were birds in an open hunting area. Baited turkeys can be brought very close for photography, but baiting (often pretty hard to prove) is illegal in most turkey hunting.

Milt Culp, who wrote a paper on the Florida turkey, says the Florida population is one of the largest in the eastern United States, living in flatwoods, scrub, and hammock terrain, broken up by cypress or hardwood ponds and swamps. There's plenty of saw palmetto, oak, and pine.

Wet weather in spring nesting time is a severe limiting factor of turkey populations, as the hen seems to make no particular effort at finding high ground and may nest in a depression or even on the very border of a cypress pond in the South. Young turkeys, wherever they are found, are extremely delicate and can be killed by excessive moisture.

A turkey family of hen and young is likely to stay together until the following mating season, and Milt believes temperature is a major factor in establishing the mating period. Gobblers have definite territories and defend them in violent fights, much more damaging than the showy sparring of some other gamebirds. The strutting and gobbling of the males is one of the more dramatic of nature's shows.

When undisturbed, turkeys often adopt a fairly rigid routine for the day's activities and may pass a given point within a few minutes of the same time each day for a considerable period. This goes for both flocks and lone gobblers. Feeding turkeys are not particularly quiet, do a great deal of scratching, and often make considerable conversation among themselves. They frequently tear up considerable areas of a forest floor in looking for acorns or other food. Once they have been alarmed, however, they can move away silently. They maintain a sentry system in nearly all their operations, one or more birds usually with head up and twisting neck.

There are two kinds of turkey flocks. One is made up of a hen and her brood of the year. The other kind is made up of gobblers, sometimes quite a number of them. Older gobblers are often loners, but not necessarily. It's commonly accepted that gobblers are more wary than hens. Young birds are more prone to come to a call, although some of the wisest old strutters will answer repeatedly with no intention of coming into range. When all else has failed, some gunners resort to a flapping noise such as beating a hat against a bush or pantleg, hoping to imitate two gobblers fighting. That sometimes works in spring.

When a band of turkeys is flushed it is quite likely that they will attempt to reassemble near the same point in an hour or more. That's the key to some of the best calling effort, and it is the separated flock that is most vulnerable to the call. The experts tell me that the flock is likely to answer, alright, but that they expect the "host" caller to join up with them and aren't inclined to move to it.

There are some strange comments about the effect of shooting, and when a bird is shot from a blind it is not unusual for other birds to stand around "putting" in apprehension but showing little tendency to leave. Gunfire is not particularly alarming to turkeys in many instances, but sight of the hunter may cause them to leave the country. They say that if you stay hidden after shooting a turkey, allowing others to leave without seeing you, they may be right back in the area the following day, or even sooner. I have seen this work once but had supposed it was unusual. Evidently not.

They have remarkable eyesight and will study a poorly hidden man under circumstances where a whitetail buck would walk right past him. Camouflage is important, and since there's nothing color-blind about a gobbler, the camouflage must be natural. The red camouflage used for deer hunting won't work. Some gunners go to the extent of blotching their faces as well as their shirts and pants. Shiny gun barrels are no help, and a very few camouflage their hardware. Sitting at the base of a big oak tree with a turkey call and carefully camouflaged can be a bit dangerous in heavily hunted country. For that matter, expert turkey finders make a great effort to find isolated grounds and will accept fewer turkeys if there are fewer hunters. Careful turkey seeking doesn't go well with human crowds.

Turkeys that are flushed strongly enough to fly can go a long way. Even over level ground they will go nearly a mile, and the flying birds are sad news to rough-country hunters as they can land on another mountain. Crossing a river is another favorite escape trick. To a moderate degree, turkeys walk up and fly down in the accepted upland pattern, and callers prefer to be above rather than below the birds.

They may roost in nearly the same place for several nights in succession, or for much longer, but there are times when they change the location each night. It is very common for them to roost over water, probably to discourage predators. In rainy or foggy weather they may stay on the roost for a long while after sunrise, and they dislike moving through wet bushes so they are often intercepted on roads or trails before things have dried off.

There's some mystery about their preference of habitat. If the wild turkey was as plentiful in pioneer days as is usually believed it stands to reason that the birds encountered by the pilgrims were living mainly in mature forests. Today, however, one of the tools of management is the forest opening, constructed with considerable effort and established as a desirable turkey feature. The turkeys prosper better where there are openings today. Perhaps they are somehow changed. Anyway, turkeys tend to wander about during midday, whether in the deep forest or at the edges of clearings. Encountered in the forest, they are likely to freeze instead of fly if it appears there's good chance of escaping detection.

It is often said that wild birds won't tolerate manmade noise, and they'd probably prefer not to have it, but I know of a bunch that hangs out where the ground is shaken regularly by passing trains, and they seem to tolerate tractors and trucks about farms. Of course it may be that there is simply no better place for them to go. It has been suggested that some of the more recent strains of game-farm turkeys have actually had a steadying effect on the tribe and might make them more tolerant of civilization. At this point it is obvious a large share of the wild birds have some ancestral blood from penned turkeys.

Since turkey tracks are very important in learning where to hunt, it's good to know what to look for. I'm not good at it myself, but I have learned that the easiest thing to find is the long imprint of a single toe in soft earth; then try to make out the rest of the outline. Where the ground is partly covered with leaves or grass, this looking for a partial track is much easier than wandering about hunting a textbook outline of a foot. On very hard ground the pattern of the bird's toenails will give a clue.

There are several types of turkey calls, and the most widely accepted is the "box call," sometimes a piece of chalked slate scraped across the edge of a thin-sided box and sometimes a loosely mounted lid that can be moved across the edges. Some of the best yelpers are simply a piece of slate scraped by a nearly vertical peg held in the hand. There is another yelper in the form of a membrane gadget that can be held in the back of the caller's mouth, and it has the advantage of leaving both hands free. I am skeptical of

Milt Culp with a Florida gobbler, the result of long hours of patience and stealth. Like most successful turkey hunters, Culp is an expert caller.

homemade calls unless they have been proved in the field, and a little error in tone is too much. Woodsmen who can call turkeys without mechanical aid do exist, but they're far between. The first and foremost rule of calling is to do it in moderation and not get carried away. There is a rule to "call a little less than the noisiest bird."

Under some circumstances, especially when the quarry is getting close, exact tones are very important. On the other hand, there are times when almost any loud noise will cause a mature gobbler to sound off in spring, whether he'll come closer or not. A crow call or owl hoot will often turn him on.

Regulations vary, and there have been changes in custom from time to time. Some states forbid the use of dogs in turkey hunting. Few turkeys will hold for a pointing dog, but there are times when a dog would be a great help in catching cripples. Turkey laws are important, and poaching is a real danger, according to management experts. They explain that once a man really learns the turkey-hunting game he is capable of killing large numbers of them. One unscrupulous turkey expert is more dangerous to the population than families of bobcats, probably the second most efficient predators.

Wild turkeys *(Meleagris gallopavo)* are scattered all over the map due to recent introductions. Pennsylvania and states to the south of that through Florida have had native populations of varying size through the years, and there have always been turkeys in the West and Midwest—in spots. The Merriam wild turkey is a Westerner. There are Eastern and Florida turkeys, the Florida model being a little darker in color, and there is a Rio Grande turkey.

At present the tribe seems to be increasing. Human development and management will establish the turkey's future.

CHAPTER XIV

Guns and Using Them

Upland shooting is more art than science and more mental than mechanical. There are many more good shots than there are good instructors, for very few expert shotgunners know how they do it.

Since shooting anything that moves rapidly involves a rather long series of reactions, it is easy to describe it in terms that are either too complicated or too simplified. Only a few gifted shooters can perform wonders, but anyone with fairly normal reactions can shoot game fairly well.

Skeet and trap shooters generally get a much quicker start than do field shooters, because there is usually competent instruction at hand and in two hours they can fire more shots at clay targets than the game-only shooter is likely to fire in two years. Some sort of clay-target practice is needed by every beginner, and nearly every veteran can profit by it too.

Some shooters have a hang-up about clay-target practice, clinging to the common belief that all true American boys acquire marksmanship automatically through some vague heritage from Davy Crockett, Buffalo Bill Cody, and Western films. This heritage evidently applies only to targets with hair or feathers, and many

Some ultra-light upland game guns, all weighing 6¼ pounds or less and all 20-gauge. Left to right: Sauer, Simmons Quails Fargo, Browning, and Franchi. The two center guns are chambered for 3-inch shells.

veteran hunters avoid clay targets for fear of appearing foolish at an unfamiliar game.

Upland guns are usually selected because of their appearance, reputations, and availability. Not one shooter in a thousand has coldbloodedly borrowed an armful of shotguns and fired them alternately at practice targets to find which he actually shoots best.

But the gun clubs are making quite a break in the haze of rumor and black magic that has long surrounded shotgunning. A few million clay targets have done a great deal to develop a more thoughtful attitude toward all kinds of gunning, and clay-target shooting is not expensive by the standards of other current amusements.

ACTIONS

Semi-automatics. The semi-automatic shotgun is most popular of all, mainly for the wrong reasons. An "automatic" is supposed to have firepower, and loud, fast shooting appeals to young hunters especially.

Autos are restricted to three shots for much hunting. A three-shot gun is indicted by many, who will say two chances are enough for anybody on any covey rise and that three shots are hoggish. I don't need but two shots on the rise, but there have been many times when a third was needed for a cripple, and I vote that three shots are better than two, unless you're a fast man with your loading hand and have automatic ejectors.

As to the speed of an auto. Its *practical* speed is pretty well matched by the expert pumpgunner, who flips the slide while he's getting on for another shot. If he's good, he can get off just about as many well-pointed shots as the auto operator. But here we get into the mental business again. Many shooters are sure they can concentrate better without having to run that slide through the back of their brains. One help is to think of slide operation as part of the shot just fired instead of as a preparation for the next.

One of the biggest selling points for the auto is its absorption of recoil in gas-operated models. Using a fairly heavy auto, a slightly built or recoil-sensitive gunner can shoot heavy loads he wouldn't consider with other types of action. The light recoil of gas-operated guns has made its point in skeet and trapshooting, where many butt-battered souls have turned to the semi-autos for long tournaments in which ability to withstand the pounding of hundreds of shots is necessary for any kind of win.

The automatic is not perfect, though. Some of us are bothered by the mechanical sounds that emerge from its innards. It throws away the empties—no great crime while actually shooting at game, but something of a nuisance for a handloader who shoots practice clays and would rather not scrounge his empties from the grit.

An auto is more likely to be put out of service by dirt or rust than a pumpgun. In my experience, an auto is the most likely action to fail, but since the auto is a mass-produced weapon and pretty simple in construction it can be handled by almost any competent gunsmith and fixed with little expense, almost as simply as the pumpgun. Although quality double guns are highly reliable, you're likely to have problems when they *do* break down. Not every gunsmith is happy to face a complex mechanism with an exotic foreign name.

Like the pumpgun, the auto has a long receiver and thus gets additional overall measurements for a given length of barrel. For some reason the shooting public cannot separate itself from the idea that long barrels are necessary for "hard" shooting guns. Except for riot and slug guns, most manufacturers don't build any barrels less than 26 inches long. So a 26-inch barrel on an auto or pump will give you a much longer gun than you get with the same length of barrel on a double or over-and-under. Since my own mental hangup is the short gun for upland shooting, I'm a little unhappy with pumps and autos, especially in the brush.

Long guns have their innings at trapshooting and wildfowling— anywhere a long swing is needed. They tend to be much slower for quick shooting at close range.

Pumpguns. The mass-produced pumpgun is an American institution. It is simply constructed, hard to break, and capable of long service, even with abuse. There are true pumpgunners who wouldn't consider any other gun, and there are some who have gone back to the pumps after ventures into very expensive custom doubles. Although the slide action is considered a crude and provincial tool by many European gunners, it is very difficult to argue with birds on the grass. I am cautious about betting against men with well-worn pumps.

You won't find loyalties to surpass those of the pumpers. Many years ago I was discussing such guns with the late Louis Montague, a well-known game shot, trapshooter, and live-pigeon marksman. The only two guns I ever saw him use were a fine Parker and a pigeon-grade Winchester Model 12 pump. Like other pumpgunners, he moved the slide in a blur.

"If you can hear the slide work between shots," said Monty, "he's no pumpgunner."

Louis Nordmann, a Florida game shot, keeps coming back to a Winchester Model 12 pumpgun when he thinks the going may be tough.

"I saw one of those things dropped overboard into salt water on

Friday afternoon," Nordmann says. "We wiped it off and shot it Saturday and Sunday, so I figured it was a pretty good choice for rough treatment."

This is no crusade for any particular make of pumpgun. Readily interchangeable barrels add to the versatility of either pump or automatic, as does the adjustable muzzle device or interchangeable muzzle tubes.

I do find the expense of having a pump action smoothed is a good investment. It's already done on most high-grade models, and a good gunsmith can do it for a few bucks on less exotic ones. Hard-working slides can be distracting.

Double-barreled shotguns. The double is the classic and traditional shotgun. For the upland gunner it can be made short and light, and it is socially acceptable in circles easily chilled by the presence of repeaters. It gives ready choice of two different chokes, and it is extremely safe because it can be opened and/or unloaded in an instant. Users of doubles tend to slide the shells out when approaching a fence, when about to sit down for lunch, or when getting into a hunting vehicle. Despite much pious safety talk, users of repeaters find unloading a lot of trouble and are often satisfied simply to remove the shell from the chamber and leave the magazine loaded. Loading and unloading repeaters is too much trouble for many tired hunters.

Double guns will digest lumpy handloads that refuse to work through autos or pumps. They are better sealed against dirt and wet, although once something does get inside a closely fitted double you may have a job of work on your hands.

Of late, the over-under seems to be much more popular than the side-by-side. For one thing, it gives a single sighting plane, important to a populace that grew up with rifles and pumpguns. The lower barrel kicks almost straight back with little upthrust—and since it is usually the more open barrel it is generally fired first and doesn't disturb the alignment for a second shot.

The arrangement of the barrels puts the fore-end at an ideal position. For the right-handed shooter, the left hand is extended at a level most natural to pointing, a feature that can be accomplished with other actions by using a thick beavertail fore-end. The importance of this left-hand location is a subject of argument, but suffice it to say that a beginning shooter devoid of prejudice is very likely to feel that the over-under is the best-feeling gun.

The over-under must be broken very far for loading and unloading, an inconvenience in blinds or in thick brush. This, of course, is more of a problem with a 12-gauge than with a 20-gauge since the big hull demands more room to come out of there.

Some of our best over-unders have very deep receivers, no problem in actual shooting but a rather awkward handful when the gun is carried for long distances. The deep receiver comes as a result of the stacked barrels *plus* locking lugs that are installed below the barrels. Some guns are made shallow by employing lugs at the rear end of the barrels rather than at the bottom. The bottom lugs leave the breech and extractors completely in the open as the gun is broken. The breech lugs are slightly in the way for loading, but this is real nitpicking.

The side-by-side is slightly simpler to construct but, like the high-grade over-under, the better ones require considerable hand-fitting. The side-by-side generally runs to a somewhat lighter weight. It is a relatively short-breaking piece and can be loaded and unloaded just a bit easier than the stacked models. There is a disadvantage in the recoil effect, for the side-by-side twists off a little one way or the other, the barrels being a bit off center.

There are learned reasons why you can't shoot as accurately with both barrels as with one, but in practical hunting use most of the theory tends to disappear. If I had to break it down I'd say that the broad outline of two barrels is actually a help in extremely quick gun handling, as with ruffed grouse in the willows. That broad black shadow in the foreground seems to move toward the bird almost automatically. On the other hand, with a dove crossing downwind at 40 yards, I feel a single sighting plane, and preferably a ribbed one, makes the pointing more precise.

Of course you can use a raised, ventilated rib with a side-by-side to approximate the effect of a single barrel. The raised rib is almost standard equipment on over-under guns. One complaint with the side-by-side is that it hides a large area *beneath* the barrels, a problem most often set forth by trapshooters.

Selective single triggers enable you to choose which barrel will fire first, but not many gunners are adroit enough to make the selection as the gun is mounted. Lining up the bird, sliding off the safety, and mounting the stock is about all most of us can handle for the moment. The matter of moving a trigger selector becomes one too many things, so most shooters leave the selector where it was when the bird flew. In any kind of pass shooting, as with snipe or doves, there's plenty of time to select, however.

Inventors had a long, tough time of it building selective single triggers that worked without doubling. Now there are a number of good ones, but some European builders are reluctant to install selective triggers, and if the maker lacks faith in his product, I sure wouldn't insist.

The nonselective single trigger, which fires the open barrel first in most installations, can be quite reliable, but I am not sold on it for some kinds of shooting. For quail or ruffed grouse it's fine, but there was the day I was working on some wide-flushing snipe and simply couldn't use my improved-cylinder barrel. In order to fire my modi-fied barrel with the nonselective trigger I'd load the tight barrel only, snap the hammer on the open barrel, and then operate with what amounted to a singleshot gun. That's the hard way.

One uncommon but practical system consists of a "single-double" trigger. As with ordinary single-triggered guns, you can fire both barrels by successive pulls on one trigger, but there are two trig-gers—one fires the open barrel first, the other leads off with the tight barrel.

I know several shooters who can't get along with recoil-operated, single-selective triggers. In order to ready the second barrel for firing the recoil of the first must be stopped firmly. A fellow who is likely to fire his first shot with the gun actually held away from his shoulder simply won't activate his second barrel. I know that's supposed to be poor form, but I've known several characters, gen-erally big husky guys, who don't always use their shoulders. It took quite a while for this to soak into my head, and I felt one buddy's new over-under was a factory mistake. He had failed to get off the second shot several times. Then came the day that he borrowed my over-under for some reason, a gun that had been through some 10,000 rounds without a miscue. It immediately failed him on the second shot, and I realized what he was doing. I've never had the trouble myself, for one of my many faults is hugging the stock too tightly. Some shotguns have mechanically actuated single triggers that do not depend on recoil, and others can be altered if you have trouble getting off the second one.

Many single-trigger guns employ a tang safety that can be moved left or right as it goes forward to select the barrel to be used. Most of them (it takes some doing) can be stalled in the middle so that neither barrel will fire. Some shooters have never done this in long careers of shooting. I believe I did it once. But don't forget what I said about shotgunnery being largely mental. Take my poor friend, Henry. Henry got a new over-under and shot very well with it for two or three years before he ever pushed the safety wrong and got it stuck in the middle. Once it happened it turned into an obsession and he then stuck the fool thing seven times in a row, so he finally gave up his gun. Sticking the safety was a subconscious wish of his, I guess.

Double triggers give instant barrel selection, and changing from one trigger to the other is a process easily learned and slowly forgotten. The main disadvantage of this traditional double-gun rig is that the trigger guard is very long and some shooters bruise their third finger on the guard when pulling the front trigger. Then other shooters (or maybe the same ones) bruise their forefingers on the front trigger when they pull the rear one.

The third-finger bruise is avoided by gripping the stock a little farther back and reaching well forward to use only the first pad of your trigger finger. The forefinger bruise can be avoided partly by using only the finger tip and partly by having the front trigger installed with a hinge so it will fold a little on contact. Although I like pistol grips and semi-pistol grips on most shotguns, I think the straight grip is best for the double-triggered gun.

Bolt-action shotguns. Bolt action works best with rifles and most serious wing shots wouldn't have it, but it is rugged, simple, and quite usable in a gun that is getting rough treatment. There is nothing about a bolt action that keeps a shotgun from shooting well, but it is slow to manipulate—too unhandy for most wing shooting.

Singleshots. Regardless of the action used, singles shooters are impractical for most upland gunning. A second shot may be unnecessary to put game in the bag, but it's a wonderful conservation aid in the case of a cripple. There is nothing wrong with the singleshot as a learning gun for clay targets.

GAUGES

The 12-gauge shotgun is the standard of most of the world now. The 16-gauge, long the favorite in continental Europe, is losing ground in America, and very few American firms sell it. The 20-gauge comes on strong, with a bundle of advantages over anything else, but is handicapped by the small hole in the muzzle. Evidently Americans like large holes in their barrels, for rhyme, reason, and ballistics will not convince most American shooters that the 20-gauge is not too small.

Trying desperately to hold my own with a battalion of experienced Southern dove gunners, I swung a 20-gauge with determination as the targets twisted in over a frozen orange grove. I came out a long way from being high gun, but I had a score that saved my face temporarily at least. I had 12 for 24, which is neither good nor bad, but I overheard a compliment that, for such company, was almost maudlin. "He killed those birds with a little old 20-gauge," said one of the shooters admiringly.

The fellow talking had, like almost everyone else, been shooting a 12-gauge gun with 1⅛ ounces of No. 7½ shot, a pretty standard dove load. The "little old 20-gauge" had been poking out 1¼ ounces of shot from its 3-inch hulls all afternoon, giving me an advantage instead of a handicap. For ego reasons I never explained this to my associates, but even if I had, it probably wouldn't have made much of an impression. Regardless of what came out of the muzzle it was still an undersized shotgun to them.

Once when I was doing my version of a scientific experiment and proving to myself that a small, light 20-gauge could do almost everything a big, heavy 12-gauge could do, I had a whole batch of pattern sheets strung around my feet when a doctor friend came by. He's a scientific type and was greatly interested in my experiments. He was evidently impressed by my conclusions about the 20-gauge with 3-inch chambers. It was wonderful, he said, that a handy little 6-pound 20-gauge could throw just as much shot and pattern it just as well as a 7½-pound 12-gauge he had been using. Next time he was going to get a 20-gauge.

The doctor left, his head full of pattern percentages and apparently buzzing with plans for a smaller, lighter shotgun. It was only two days later that another friend came by, a fellow who was just thinking of taking up shotgunnery and wanted to know what he should get for bird shooting. He'd just talked to the doctor. Now he was concerned with the action and make he should buy.

"Well, what did Doc advise?" I asked him, loving to hear of the impression I'd made with my experiments.

"Oh, Doc said it didn't make much difference about what action I got but be sure to get a 12-gauge."

It's that hard to convince anyone a small gun is as good as a big gun. The reverence for the 12-gauge comes from the days when it really did have a great deal more shot in it. It still has some advantages, although they're not the ones commonly attributed.

Unless you go to the short magnum load of 1½ ounces of shot or a 3-inch magnum with still more lead the 12-gauge has little advantage in range or pattern over the 20-gauge—or the 16-gauge for that matter. Most of these ultrapotent charges are for waterfowling, and they rarely find much use in the uplands except for turkeys, the odd long-range pheasant situation, and some cases in which prairie grouse are getting up wild. Many a shotgun expert has said the high-velocity 1¼-ounce load is all anybody really needs for anything. I won't go that far, but I could spend the rest of my shooting life in the uplands with nothing heavier and be happy. Both the 20-gauge and the 16-gauge will shoot that load.

At the moment, I think the main advantage of the 12-gauge is its wide variety of commercial loads. Many years ago when the cartridge situation seemed to be getting out of hand the ammunition companies boiled the list of loadings down to a minimum, especially in the case of the smaller gauges. There's a much better selection, at less cost per ounce of shot, in 12-gauge, and whenever someone comes out with an especially low-priced load it's usually for the 12-gauge.

There are some gaps in the loadings for the 20-gauge. I'd particularly like to see 1⅛ ounces of No. 8 as a near-perfect quail load for an open-bored gun. That's the "short-magnum" charge for the 20-gauge, and it isn't uncomfortable in my 5¾-pound side-by-side. Since 1⅛ ounces is the standard quail load for a 12-gauge, I can't see why it shouldn't be for sale in the 20-gauge. Although I get the flinches and a nervous tic as quickly as anyone else when shooting heavy loads at targets or pattern sheets, I find I can take quite a bit of jolt under hunting conditions without noticing, especially when it's unlikely I'll fire more than a box of shells in a session. I think most users of light, fast upland guns are needlessly shy of heavier loads.

For a long while the chief advantage of the 12-gauge was its superior patterning caused by a minimum of shot distortion. Before the development of plastic shot cups and sleeved wads, as the shot came through the barrel much of it was crushed against the steel and jammed out of shape. These weirdly shaped pellets went whistling over into Giles County and ruined the pattern. The smaller the barrel, the larger the percentage of pellets that rubbed the bore, so the 16-gauge had patterning disadvantages and the 20-gauge even more.

When the plastic shot cups and sleeved wads came along, much of the pellet distortion was eliminated. I don't say the smaller gauges pattern every bit as well as the 12-gauge, but I do say that the differences on the pattern board are hardly measurable. There is also a criticism that the smaller gauges throw a longer shot string, meaning that fewer pellets would strike a bird going at right angles, some arriving too soon and some arriving too late. Still, I have heard top shotgunners insist that the lengthened shot string is what most of us hit with and that it gives us an advantage on angle shots. These arguments are cutting things pretty fine, with both sides sounding pretty reasonable.

The larger gun with its bulkier receiver and larger barrel or barrels has some advantage for some shooters in quick pointing. To fit the larger receiver the stock is generally bulkier. Some of the ultralight and toylike smallbores are easily canted or tipped in mounting, whereas the 12-gauge may be so bulky there are few wrong places for it to go as it comes to your shoulder. This does not work for all shooters, but it does for some. Not all gunners like light shotguns, simply because they tend to stop swinging with them. I was on a lightweight kick for a long while where upland game was concerned. I feel now that my optimum weight for bird shooting is between 5½ and 6¾ pounds, but it might be different for many others who are better shots.

There never was anything wrong with the 16-gauge, but it's losing its popularity because of an overlap with the 20-gauge in ballistics and it is used very little in the clay-target games. Popularity of the 16-gauge has been a sectional thing, and there are practically none of them in some parts of the country. In the South they seem to retain their popularity. In the Northwest a few months ago I visited a large department store that was stuck with a big stock of 16-gauge shells and had put them on sale at about one-third the usual retail price. They still had trouble unloading them until the word got out and a couple of 16-gauge owners rushed in and bought a lifetime supply of ammunition.

The 28-gauge is getting pretty small, but its heaviest load of a full ounce of No. 8 is fine for quail or grouse. Even heavier hand-loads have been used, but it should be carried only by an expert in most hunting. The .410 is too small except for target shooting or potshooting of stationary game. I know there are marksmen who can do well with it, but they leave cripples unless they select their shots with great care. I do not doubt their marksmanship but I doubt their judgment. There's always the urge to stretch it just a little and the .410 doesn't bear stretching, so before hunting with a 28-gauge or a .410 you'd better search your soul and think in terms of 20-yard shots and an iron will.

CHOKES

Choke is simply the constriction of a shotgun barrel at or near the muzzle for the purpose of concentrating the charge of shot. For convenience of discussion, chokes are usually classified by the per-centage of a shot charge that is included in a 30-inch circle at 40 yards. Although many guns and loads were never intended for use at that range, the method is as good as any for classification.

To measure choke results you shoot at a paper or board at 40 yards and then enclose the thickest part of the pattern in a 30-inch circle. If you do this on a piece of paper it is easy to record the shot holes by marking each one as it is counted. Few shotgunners ever pattern their guns, and one friend of mine said never to do it. "When you see what it actually looks like and find all those holes in it, it'll ruin your whole life," he said.

Not all ballisticians classify chokes the same, but this scale is about typical:

Full choke: 65 percent or more
Improved-modified: 55-65 percent

Modified: 45-55 percent

Improved-cylinder: 35-45 percent

Cylinder or skeet: 25-35 percent

When you look at patterns made out past 35 yards you realize that most long-range kills involve very unlucky birds. I once had some cutouts made the size of a snipe body going straight away, intending to fit them into gaps in the pattern to demonstrate pattern weakness past 35 yards. I had to get more cutouts before I could fill the gaps in my first test pattern, and the thing got so ridiculous

A dramatic demonstration of the holes in a shotgun pattern. The black disks represents the vital area of a snipe or small quail going away from the gun and show how nineteen such birds could slip through a standard 12-gauge upland load of 1⅛ ounces of shot at 30 yards— if they were lucky. The result was fairly typical and the gun was bored improved cylinder.

I gave up. I sometimes wish all scatterguns carried a neon sign atop the receiver. Every time you shouldered it the sign would light up and state: "A shotgun is a short shooter."

Since they don't consider the fallibility of the shooter himself, most beginning shotgunners tend to lean toward tight chokes for everything. When I got my first 12-gauge pumpgun as a kid in Kansas it was natural to buy a 30-inch, full-choked barrel, hardly the thing for an occasional quail along Cow Creek or rabbits among the Osage-orange hedges. It wasn't much better over the little ponds where mallards dropped in at dusk, but it was a tight-shooting gun and I was happy with it until I tried an ancient Damascus-barreled double loaned me by Don Buck, a boyhood hunting companion. The old double proved to be a remarkably deadly and "hard-shooting" gun. It developed the real reason for my success with it was that it had no choke at all. Generally speaking, few gunners are capable of getting the most out of full-choked guns and should confine their shooting to ranges where more open bores are effective.

For most upland game the improved cylinder is about right, with modified choke as a close second choice, and the usual boring of an upland double is improved cylinder and modified. Real brush shooting is often easier with skeet borings or cylinder guns, intended for use out to about 30 yards with small shot. Large shot doesn't have much place with skeet guns, as it's just too scattered out where the game is.

But all guns have their little peculiarities, and each has distinctive patterning with various sizes and kinds of shots and wads. By fooling a little with pattern boards you will learn the best loads for a particular barrel. Most of us just take the word of the maker and go forth, even if our "modified" is throwing a full-choke pattern. Maybe it's more fun that way.

Improved cylinder and full choke are a handy combination for double and over-under guns, although not readily available in off-the-shelf models. When I first ordered one like that the comments were that it "should be fine for someone with very slow reactions." I make no claim to lightning responses, but that wasn't the idea.

The gun had double triggers and I could select instantly, a good idea in dove shooting and much open-country grouse gunning. For wide-jumping birds it's often good to have the improved cylinder for a hastily pointed try and then use the full choke as a follow-up.

I have found that a rising bird at around 25 yards is still a little close for a quick modified shot, just right for improved-cylinder. My second shot will come at around 35 or 40 yards in such a situation, and that's getting into full-choke country. If it's a really wide jump at around 30 yards the full choke is just right—that's handicap range for a trapshooter. The improved and full gun is a 12-gauge light-weight, a big bore primarily because I can use scatter or brush loads in the full barrel when all shooting becomes close. The brush loads available for the 20-gauge are not heavy enough to suit me. There is no such thing as an all-round double gun, but this one comes close.

Some muzzle devices for choke regulations are adjustable so that you simply turn the dial to the amount of scatter you want. Others are removable tubes, each of a different constriction.

The knob and extra weight of the adjustable devices are a nuisance to some shooters, while others swear they actually improve the pointing. That's a mental thing, of course, but one fine feature of the adjustable muzzle device is that it can be installed to make your barrel as short as you like, and most pump and auto barrels are overly long for upland gunning. If the knob bothers on a plain barrel, the addition of a ventilated rib can make it appear much less noticeable from the stock end. Some of the removable tubes come with recoil reducers that make a little extra noise but do use up some of the kick. They tend to be bulky. Some of the plain interchangeable tubes are flush with the barrel and don't show at all.

Whatever else you may think of adjustable muzzle devices, they've reached a stage of pretty accurate control. Having once owned an ancient model that left a spaniel-sized gap in the center of the pattern and assured that no properly pointed shot should be a hit, I decided to write an exposé of muzzle devices. I ordered a brand-new one, factory-installed, figuring that I'd have an interesting report, the theme of which was to be that each device must be calibrated by the owner as they couldn't be expected to follow the original markings. The whole project fell flat when the new gadget patterned exactly by the markings—and they were even patterns too.

Of course the number of shot in the 30-inch circle at 40 yards lacks a great deal of being the whole story. If there are big holes in the pattern, it's a poor one. Generally, not always, the more open chokes give a somewhat more even pattern, even though it spreads

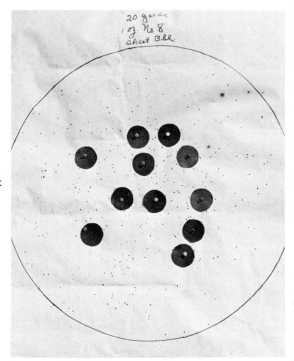

The center of the pattern of a 20-gauge skeet gun at 20 yards, using No. 8 shot, one-ounce load. Without using the outer edges of the 30-inch circle at all, it is possible to locate eleven disks in the center of the pattern, each disk representing the vital area of a straightaway snipe or small quail. The likelihood of the bodies being located exactly right for escape might be fairly remote but the obvious possibility is there.

out. Full-choke patterns can come out as tight bunches in the center of the circle but with the rest of the charge going all over the map, a case in which the shot count doesn't tell the story at all.

It's natural to think of the shot going out in a funnel shape, spreading evenly as it goes, and novices assume it's just as easy to hit at 50 yards with a full choke as it is at 25 yards with an improved cylinder. Of course the target is farther away, but you have all that shot spread, haven't you? Without going into all the variables, let's just say that long shots with a scattergun are harder than close ones—a lot harder.

It is not expensive to have a choke opened up by a skilled gunsmith, although that isn't advisable if the barrel has a chrome lining that must be cut through. If you're going to be persnickety about your choke you can buy it a little tighter than wanted and then have it changed to suit. I had a nice European double with the right barrel bored tighter than the left, originally intended to be used on incoming driven game. Since it was too tightly choked and the reverse of the usual American order of things, I had a gunsmith open up the right barrel a little at a time until it suited. It shoots good patterns. Building more choke into a barrel that's too open is a complex emergency process of uncertain results, but some additional choking can be acquired by recessing.

The logical rule is to use smaller shot in open guns, larger in those that are tightly choked. The open gun throws a wide pattern that will have too many holes with large shots, and it is not intended for use out where the penetration of very large pellets is needed.

SHOT SIZES

It's common to say that the nearest to all-round shot is No. 6. For open-bored upland guns I'd judge the nearest to an all-round size would be No. 7½, a little large for snipe and a little small for open-country pheasants but acceptable for all under the proper conditions. Some turkey hunters use it, planning on head shots only. No. 5 or No. 6 shot is best for the big sage grouse and long-range pheasants. No. 9 is my choice for snipe, and some choose it for bobwhite quail in skeet or cylinder guns, although No. 8 is more popular.

Shot velocity is seldom a problem at upland ranges, for at the distances most upland birds are shot there is enough penetration anyway. Ultralight shot charges are not sporty. With a given gun it is no harder to hit with a very light shot charge than with a full charge, but it is much easier to cripple. Under some circumstances it is possible to overkill at very close range, but it's better to have an occasional damaged bird at the table than to allow cripples to escape.

The brush or scatter load is primarily intended to provide open shot patterns with tightly choked guns. The cartridge is loaded with wad spacers between the various layers of shot or with longitudinal cards interlocked to spread the charge under pressure. The patterns are not as consistent as those with conventional shells but at short range they can be very effective. They are generally sold only in No. 8 shot, 1⅛ ounces in 12-gauge, an ounce in 16-gauge, and ⅞ ounce in 20-gauge.

GUN FIT

Few beginning shooters start out with custom-fitted guns, and unless a novice has unusual physical characteristics this is as it should be. Most American factory guns are a pretty good compromise as to stock measurements. After a little experience a shooter may have legitimate reason for wanting something changed.

The three most important measurements are length of stock, with about 14 inches being standard for a field gun; the drop at comb (top of forward part of stock), about 1⅜ inches; the drop at heel, about 2⅜ inches. The drop at comb is the distance it is below the line of sight. Drop at heel is the distance the top of the butt (in firing position) is below the line of sight. Another measurement is pitch down, secured by setting the top of the gun's receiver against a wall with the butt plate or recoil pad flat against the floor. The pitch is the distance the muzzle stands out from the wall in such a position. This is a tricky measurement, since the butt shape can alter it drastically with little effect upon the shooter.

Stock dimensions are important, and careless measurements produce some strange figures. Things get especially fuzzy in measuring the length of stock with a gun having double triggers. The usual stock measurement is really "length of pull" from the trigger to the butt.

Stock length is easily adjusted by a gunsmith if a recoil pad is to be used. Bad effects of a stock that is too short can include bruises on the jaw, which contacts the stock too far forward on the comb. A stock that's too short can allow fingers of the stock-gripping hand to strike your mouth during recoil. There is a tendencey to shoot high with a stock that's too short and low with one that's too long. The longer stock and the straighter stock tend to deliver less kick. A stock that's too long is hard to mount and will strike your clothing before it is settled into the shoulder notch. The straight stock (less drop from the line of sight) naturally shoots higher, as it tends to give the shooter a view of more of the top of his barrel or rib.

By and large, experienced shooters tend to use slightly straighter stocks as they gain experience, and I have known new shooters who went overboard in ordering new custom guns and ended up with excessive drop that they later tired of. A great deal of drop or "crooked stock" is needed by a shooter who has a long neck or steeply sloping shoulders. Most of us can go with little deviation from factory dimensions.

Custom guns frequently have "cast-off," which means the butt end of the stock is turned slightly away from the shooter, a gradual slope from the receiver to the buttplate. I have a gun with cast-off and I like it, but it is not extremely important. It is seldom found with off-the-shelf guns, for the boys at the factory don't know if the shooter will be right- or left-handed. Occasionally a shooter requires cast-on. Don't let this business worry you.

A hunter's anatomy seems to be a very adjustable thing, and we see 7-foot, 300-pound giants and short-armed youngsters using the same factory stocks. Some years ago a friend asked me to fill out the dimensions for an order of a custom Italian shotgun, and I did it—with flourishes. When it came everything was exactly as requested except that something had happened to the stock dimensions. Evidently our inches had gotten stirred up with some European millimeters and we had a stock so straight I had to hold what appeared to be a foot and a half under a clay target to break it. Same for my buddy, but Italy was a long way off and there was no stock genius handy so he took the thing hunting. After all, the engraving was pretty. He hit a few and missed a lot at first, but he got used to that stock and never did have it changed. He says he now holds under without thinking, and he's blue murder on a variety of upland game.

The very best way to see if a gun fits you is to face a mirror and try to throw the gun up so that it points at your aiming eye. If you need to do a great deal of adjusting to make it point where you want it, the chances are the gun doesn't fit. If it naturally points at your aiming eye as you mount it, it isn't too far off in measurements.

A professional gun fitter has you point the gun at his eye and then makes changes as he seets fit, often using a try gun, a shotgun mounted on a skeleton stock with a variety of adjustments. The other guy isn't always right, and you're the fellow who has to hit things. When a gun fitter comes forth with measurements a long way from what you like, you'd better go around again.

Your master eye is the one that takes charge when you try to line up your finger on an object while holding your arm extended. By shutting your eyes alternately you can quickly tell which one it is.

*A nearly ideal method of learning which gun is best for the individual.
Using three different shotguns, the shooter fires one shot at a time
with each, keeping track of his misses. After 100 shots in this manner,
many veteran shooters are surprised to find they've been using the
wrong gun. The one they like isn't always the best.*

If you shoot from the right shoulder and have a master left eye
you have a minor problem. If you can easily change to your left
shoulder, do it, but if that doesn't work the chances are you can
get by through squinting your left eye.

Shooting with both eyes open helps some, but I know some
excellent marksmen who shut one eye and many who squint one
eye a little, often doubtful whether they actually see through it or
not. I am inclined to discount the importance of having both
eyes open.

In battling through some pistol tournaments many years ago I
found that a double sight image bothered me a little, but I had

been so indoctrinated by the both-eyes-open school that I refused to close my left eye. Instead I squinted it very slightly, and I guess I threw it out of gear. At any rate the double image disappeared and I came to the very unscientific conclusion that my brain just wasn't getting a message from my open left eye. It was creepy business but shooters say funny things about what they see.

There is a "cripple stock" made by some custom stock builders so that you can shoot from your right shoulder and use your left eye for pointing. Very few shooters need that, but one who has lost the sight of one eye may find it a lifesaver.

GUN MOUNTING

An inexperienced shotgun user will check out a gun by lifting it to his shoulder and then putting his face against the stock and squirming around until he can look down the barrel or rib. A good shot will invariably pick out a target or imaginary target, push the gun muzzle at it, and then see just how the gun fits. He doesn't thrust his head forward extremely far, but he endeavors to meet the gun stock with it.

I have heard you should not move your head at all if the gun fits. I doubt that many good shots hold it perfectly still, most of them moving it forward just a little. If in this tirade I can convince a beginner that gun mounting is part of the shot instead of a separate operation, I'll be satisfied.

In shotgunning, the eye acts as a rear sight and the front bead or end of the barrel is simply pointed at the spot the shot is to go. Here is a point where advice from veterans can be harmful unless they have had teaching experience. Many of them will tell you they don't see the gun at all, and that they just look at the place they want their shot and pull the trigger. The fact is that they are not conscious of seeing the out-of-focus end of the barrel because, through long practice, it has become an automatic thing. A beginning shooter cannot help being conscious of the barrel or sight for a while. It gradually becomes less noticeable, and finally he has no more memory of seeing it than he has of pressing the accelerator when he wants to speed up his car. The final proof of this is that

Gun is brought back against the shoulder as the muzzles are aligned.
Safety is pushed off as gun comes up and trigger finger contacts
trigger as butt settles into shoulder notch. The slight forward thrust on
the way up allows for a stock that may be a little too long and
avoids catching clothing.

a good shot can hit *some* with a gun that doesn't fit him. He'd have
to line things up!

There are many combinations of sights and ribs intended to make
barrel pointing more natural. Although the eye should be focused
on the moving target, there is no doubt the appearance of the
barrel, rib, and sight or sights can be a help. The ventilated rib is
definitely preferred for long-range shooting. Most shooters see a
little more than the front bead; in other words, the barrel or rib
appears in a greatly foreshortened form but still shows a little.
There are some gunners who line up the barrel so that they see
nothing but the front sight over the receiver, but some of them still
prefer the rib because they feel it helps in the instant before everything is lined up.

The opposite of the ventilated rib is the sunken rib found on
some double guns, a rib that actually runs between the barrels at
the muzzles with the barrels bulging up above it; in effect, you are

Some British gun instructors recommend that the forefinger of the forend hand be used in pointing at the target as the gun is mounted.

An approved method of preparing to mount the shotgun. As muzzles are directed at the target, the butt will come up slightly ahead of the shoulder to avoid catching in the jacket.

looking down a groove instead of along a ridge. To me, this is an excellent short-range, quick-pointing arrangement but not as good as a high rib for long and more deliberate shots.

The ideal form for mounting a shotgun is to follow the target with the muzzle as the gun comes up, establishing the lead and swing speed at about the time the butt reaches the shoulder. Then the shot is fired promptly with little hesitation. I won't say it should go off just as the butt hits the shoulder, but I do say the shot should come pretty quickly. As the gun comes up, it should already be tracking the target properly and the shooter should be standing with his left foot slightly forward (for a right-handed shooter) and with the left knee slightly bent. Most of his weight is on the front foot with the other used to make corrections in the way his body points. The gun should be swung with body movements instead of arm movement.

This foot position is accepted by nearly all trap and skeet shooters and by nearly all hunters who practice on clay targets. The fact is, however, that a large percentage of them exaggerate the stance on live birds. I learned that in taking sequence photos of experienced shooters in action in the field. When the chips are down, the wings roaring, and the adrenalin pumping, some of these cool customers squat like Japanese wrestlers. I have pictures of myself looking somewhat like a linebacker instead of a gentleman sportsman. Does this exaggerated stance do any harm? I don't know. Of course it would be very tiring in extended target shooting.

The body swings a little from the knees up, quite a bit from the waist up. Shooters who swing the whole carcass have some difficulties when they try to shoot from a sitting position. Waist swingers get along better there. Anyway, don't try to do it with your arms, for that's when you get the gun away from your cheek and a miss is almost a certainty. The cheek must stay against the stock throughout the swing.

One school of gunning instruction places great emphasis on the finger-pointing theory, believing that the left hand can point accurately where the shot should go because it is easy to point your finger straight at a distant object without aiming. This is an English system but practiced by provincials too.

It's an excellent idea, whether practiced as the essential element of gun pointing or simply as an aid. The system practiced by the British often includes a long "reach" with the pointing hand. The left hand (for a right-hander) goes far out beneath the barrel or barrels and the forefinger actually points at the target from beneath the barrel (generally "barrels" in England). This reach goes clear past the small fore-end of many European guns, and the British instructors say that the fore-end is to hold the gun together and not for grabbing with the left hand. It is a shame for all that expensive checkering to go to waste, but I'll take them at their word. Some English shooters use a leather sleeve around the lower part of the barrels out where the left hand goes.

This system is followed in America to a great extent, except that you seldom see the left hand extended that far. Pumpgunners usually reach forward a little farther than others. The beavertail fore-end and the big slide on many pumpguns are intended to make the left hand point parallel to the route of the shot.

A pose widely recommended for awaiting driven game in Europe. Stock is tucked under upper arm only a short move from the shoulder. Left forefinger is extended. This position is not recommended when the gunner is walking as it would be easy to point it at a companion. High or low muzzle would be preferable under such circumstances. Gun shown here is a Webley & Scott.

In studying shotgunning it is impossible to ignore the British influence. At times I may seem to be kidding the English, and perhaps I am, but I have the utmost respect for their game shooting, even though some of their views about guns are rigidly conservative. Conservative? I am the guy who visited the Purdey headquarters in London, conversed for half an hour with one of their officials, and was never shown a gun. They could tell I wasn't a live one with four thousand bucks for a double.

The British system has evolved about driven game, and they are "gunning," not "hunting." Driven game comes from the beaters, approaching the guns from the front, crosses over the butts or blinds, and can be shot at both going and coming. It is essentially short-range shooting with light loads. At that business they evidently have no peers, and one American expert who has shot with

Fairly standard pose for taking a shot. Note that left arm is fairly well extended. Authorities vary as to position of right elbow, some feeling it should be higher than shown to help lock stock into position, but some expert shooters hold it even lower than illustrated. This is about average.

the British says they are the "fastest and best short-range shooters in the world in a controlled situation with driven game." This may sound like damning with faint praise, but it doesn't mean an Englishman can't be good at what they call "rough shooting" too. And remember they get off a lot more shots in a season of driven game than you will following a dog. I go into this because much shooting instruction comes from England, even though greatly modified by Americans.

Most gun mounting is achieved from a position roughly resembling the military port arms, with the gun held with the muzzle high and to the front, diagonally across the chest. No matter how he has been carrying his gun before the bird jumps, the shooter generally goes through that position as he mounts his gun. There is an exception if he is carrying his gun with the stock under his upper arm and the barrel pointing almost straight forward. This is an excellent hold if he is standing and waiting for game but dangerous if he's walking. In most mounts, as the barrel is aligned and the stock comes up to the shoulder and cheek the butt may scrape the clothing, and for that reason most upland gunners prefer fairly

The approved way of walking with the muzzle down while in the field. Gun can be mounted rapidly from this position, although most experienced shooters prefer the high muzzle when game is expected momentarily. Gun shown here is Winchester 101, 20-gauge.

smooth butts that won't catch on a coat or a shoulder pad. I believe it is just as easy to learn gun mounting so that the whole gun is pushed forward a little before being brought back to the shoulder, thus clearing the clothing.

One good carry for a walking gunner is with the muzzle pointed down and across the body in front. The stock is under the elbow. It is nearly as good for a quick mount as the high port carry. Many gunners carry guns at the balance in one hand and with the arm hanging straight down. With practice they learn to mount their guns quickly from this position, whichever hand is carrying it. Carrying a gun over the shoulder with the barrel up can be dangerous, for the muzzle can easily be pointed toward a companion. Carrying it "upside down" with the top of the receiver on the shoulder can make it quickly available, but this is touchy with a gun that has a tang safety, as it's easy for the safety to be worked off against the shoulder.

A Crazy Quail installation in which the man at the trap can face in any direction, sending clay targets to any point of the compass. The back half of the pit is built up for safety, but low targets can be thrown in the direction of the camera.

Holding a gun on the shoulder with the barrel pointed forward and grasping the barrel is a restful carry but dangerous unless the gun is empty, and getting it into action if it were loaded would require some calesthenics. A double gun can be carried open this way when no game is expected.

A large part of the quick shot's efficiency comes from being ready when the game flushes, and the way he carries his gun is much of that, although it isn't always the most comfortable carry. He often comes home with aching arms, but that's the price paid by many grouse shooters.

There's many a time when you find yourself seeming to move in cement as you try to get on a bird fast. After it's over you'll have forgotten where your gun was when you started to mount it, but those fumbling efforts usually come when the gun's "around your neck" as one shooter describes it.

In walking through brush, over rocks and logs, and in other uncomfortable places there are some shooters who are continually planning how they will fire if a shot comes up suddenly. Some of

A safe way of shouldering a loaded double gun when others are in the vicinity. If the gun is pushed farther up, however, with the right hand holding the butt, it is very easy for a tang safety to be pushed off accidentally. If the weapon is turned over so that the trigger guard is down, it is easy to point the muzzle at a companion.

them always put their left feet forward (right-handers) in crossing an obstruction. They push through brush with their left shoulders shielding the gun in case it is needed suddenly. Small things, but worthwhile if you take the utmost advantage of your abilities.

When a shot must be taken to the rear, most good shots turn on one foot and have the proper advance foot in position as they come around. There are others who believe it's easier to twist from the waist without coming all the way around with the feet. There are those who avoid shots nearly straight overhead, saying they can be taken a little earlier or a little later to avoid tying up the swinging muscles. Heavy charges can be painful when fired straight up. Perhaps the exact method is less important than the matter of practicing. A little dry firing will enable a shooter to find what seems the most practical method, and when the time comes he'll probably do it automatically.

The safety should be released as the shotgun comes up, and if you're familiar with your safety and its location I see no reason why

A controversial shooting stance, often recommended for incoming game. Many good shooters say that a bird should not be followed overhead like this as the shooter is likely to tie up and stop his swing. They recommend turning around and taking the shot as the bird goes away. One disadvantage of this position is that heavy loads can cause uncomfortable recoil almost straight down. The rear foot steers the body and receives more weight as the body comes back.

this should slow the shot in any way, as it is done during the mounting instead of before or after it. Many shooters release the safety as they approach a pointing dog or feel that a flush is imminent, but I don't like it. No matter how experienced they are there is always the possibility of a stumble. And I like to think of the hotshot quail popper I cross-questioned about his shooting procedures. What, I asked him, was his procedure as he approached his pointing dogs?

"I focus my eyes a little ahead of where I think the birds will jump," he said, "and I listen for that little click as my buddy pushes off his safety. If I hear that click before the birds go, I walk back-

ward very carefully and let him have the covey all to himself. I
don't want to walk up birds with anyone who isn't using his safety,
especially in country where there may be rattlesnakes, because I
have seen some of the goofy things a guy can do when he hears a
buzz at his feet. Then too, I know he is watching for birds, and how
do I know he isn't going to stumble and fall on his belly with his
gun pointing at *my* belly? I figure that safety is there for a reason."

The automatic safety (one that goes on automatically as the gun
is opened) is common on many doubles, and although it is roundly
cursed by many fine shooters I am sure it has prevented accidents.
If a shooter were confronted by some dangerous game I can see
why he might want a safety that stayed off while he reloaded to
avoid any slight chance of mistake, but when only an upland bird
is involved I think the automatic safety is worthwhile, even if it
prevents only a single accidental discharge in a hundred years.
Nevertheless, most of my guns have nonautomatic safeties. Nearly
all repeaters have them.

So you follow the bird with your muzzle as you shoulder the

*Stance for a quick shot, nearly to
the rear. Turning any farther will
tie the shooter up and probably
stop his swing. He would then do
better to move his right foot
and take a new stance as he
mounts his gun.*

gun; you push off the safety as it comes up; you push forward a little as the stock rises to reach the notch between your shoulder and neck so the butt won't catch in your clothing; you pull it back snugly; you drop the head just a little to make contact with the stock; you see the target over the barrel or rib; you establish your lead or hold; and you pull the trigger firmly. You practice these things for a few minutes daily at home until they become automatic. Even an old-timer should dry-fire a few now and then to see that he's still in his groove.

The proper place for the butt is on the muscle between the shoulder joint and the neck, but as a gun comes up in a hurry it is possible to nest the butt into the notch between the upper bicep and the shoulder. In firing position it is very near the proper spot, but it can lead to misses and bruising. Try to avoid it, but all of us fumble into that sometimes when in a rush, and a lot of birds have been dropped with the butt against the arm.

The recoil is going to have some effect on your balance, and you should thrust your weight forward just a little to meet it, but you needn't go very far forward if your feet are properly positioned. The greenhorn fencer's thrust that I have achieved in some unposed photos is completely unnecessary, however dramatic.

LEAD

Since a bird that isn't going straight away from you has a motion that continues while the shot is on its way, you have to shoot ahead of it. That's lead, the subject of more discussion and sneering remarks than any other phase of shotgunning.

There are three methods of lead: spot-shooting where the target is going to be and not moving the gun (snap shooting); establishing a set lead ahead of the target and holding it until the shot (sustained lead); and swinging past the target so that the muzzle is going faster than the bird and gaining on it. The last is called swinging through and is most popular of the upland game methods. In most situations it is the most practical, but many shooters occasionally use a combination of the swing-through and the sustained lead. In heavy brush most of us occasionally snap-shoot.

There are some special things to remember about shooting in heavy brush, and I have learned them from good brush shots. Although I am defeated by the brush more than by any other adversity, I can at least parrot the instructions and try to follow them myself.

First, you must shoot through brush as if it didn't exist. The vague shadow zipping along back of the branches or trees is just as large and goes no faster than it does in the wide open. Forget the intervening hazards and shoot the same as if they weren't there. Occasionally I do that and down comes the bird along with a shower of twigs, a few dry leaves, and heaven knows what else.

Most brush shooting is at close range and must be done rather fast. There are times when you can actually swing with the bird's shadow or the spot where you *think* he is and then fire at an open space just as he flies into it. One of my most common sins is to fire too fast before the gun is properly mounted, partly because I know I will have to hurry, and so I overdo it. When birds were fairly well in the open but very close to heavy foliage I have several times emptied my gun while there was still plenty of time for a more careful shot and then watched the game fly away in safety. There is usually more time than you think.

Another foolish brush shot comes when a bird flies straight at me and I miss it at a distance of 7 feet when all I need do is turn around and take it going away. After years of telling myself this is silly business, I still do it occasionally.

One secret of good brush shooting is a constant awareness of the route a flushed bird is likely to take. Sometimes it's pretty obvious, especially in the case of woodcock and quail. I have watched a good woodcock shooter stand for a long while studying the cover before approaching a pointing dog, and it can be almost spot-shooting with the gun on the hole before the timberdoodle gets there.

A Georgia quail shooter I know almost wiped out a covey of quail with a single shot. The dog had pointed and as the birds flushed he picked out a specific target and swung after it as it buzzed for a small opening in the brush. As he fired there was a shower of bodies, for the entire covey had chosen that 30-inch space for escape, a near limit of birds he hadn't even seen before shooting.

Many game birds are flushed from trees by thrown sticks or

An experiment in shooting vision. Shooter did almost as well when looking through gauze over his shooting glasses, indicating that critical vision may not be necessary, even though concentration is essential.

stones, but you will have to learn the shooting method from someone else. I have such an impressive list of misses under those circumstances I would rather not discuss it.

You can go deep into the mathematics of leading, but it is hard to apply your findings, for the right-angle shot is seldom a true right angle, the straightaway is seldom a true straightaway, and what looks like a 5-foot lead to me may look like a 10-foot lead to you. The swing-through minimizes all these variables. In theory, you swing faster on a faster target and thus minimize errors. It works, but it is art instead of science.

In a swing-through you generally come up behind the target, move past it, and fire. If you swing very fast and react fairly slowly you can pull the trigger as you come past the target. As the gun fires your mental picture will be the barrel aligned against the bird, even though it will have passed the bird before the discharge. I do it about that way, unless it is a near right angle requiring a very long lead, in which case I see considerable daylight between the bird and the barrel when I think I shoot. Some will say that is partly sustained lead, but I still call it a swing-through because I am still gaining on the target as I shoot.

Some better shots than I am throw the gun up ahead of the bird and go on from there, but unless I swing my muzzle *through* the target I am likely to be off course and shoot high or low. There are quite a number of ways of missing a pheasant.

A properly mounted gun should come up just a little below the bird to avoid blotting it out. Since upland game is likely to be rising, this gives you momentum in the right direction, but the move can be exaggerated. I had a long streak of misses on straightaways when I got into the habit of coming up too fast under them and shooting over. If your gun shoots a little high, as many shooters feel it should, your mistake is multiplied.

Blessed is the shooter who can analyze his own mistakes. At one time or another nearly everyone gets a habit of stopping his swing. He cannot see it happen, and the mind picture he has is the same he had when he was killing a dozen straight. He remembers where the muzzle was when he decided to pull the trigger, but instead of continuing the swing he simply stopped and didn't know it. The only remedy is to develop a follow-through and make yourself do it. There are all sorts of childish ways of making yourself continue. For example, when I've missed a few by apparently stopping my swing, I say "Push!" to myself just as the muzzle passes the bird, and with this moronic advice I continue to swing. To me it seems that I speed up, but I probably just continue the same speed of muzzle travel. A smooth swing is most desirable, but some good shots are pretty jerky. Some of them put the muzzle on the bird, ride with it for an instant, and then shove out ahead. Since all of these things happen pretty fast they are hard to observe.

Second only to the swing-stopper in misses is the head-lifter. Knowing the shot is about to be touched off and eager to watch his bird fall in a cloud of feathers, the shooter simply does his pointing and then lifts his head from the stock before he fires. He doesn't know it. When mysterious misses occur, try pushing your cheek extra hard against the stock for a few shots; then make yourself go through an exaggerated follow-through.

There is no need for a delicate squeeze of the trigger in shotgunning, a brisk pull serving the purpose. Some clay-target shooters are trigger slappers, but I don't believe many hunters use that

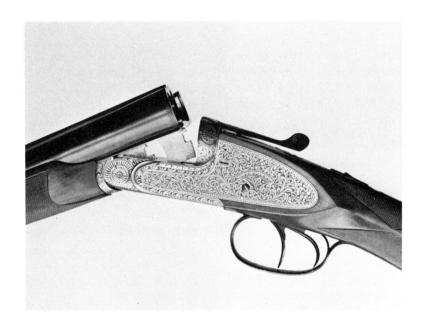

*A classic sidelock double, generally accepted as the most beautiful
of shotguns. Both boxlock and sidelock guns have their advantages, but
the sidelock, with its long plates, offers much more area for engraving
and appears more streamlined.*

method. The weight of trigger pull on a shotgun can vary widely
without being a serious handicap as long as it is fairly crisp. Even
an 8-pound pull (a 4-pounder is generally about right) won't handicap a game shot after a little practice with it. If you are engaged
in hundreds of shots at targets and riding on the edge of your
nerves anyway, a trigger pull can become important, but for twenty-
five shots or so I can hardly tell whether a scattergun has a light
or heavy pull unless it's truly excessive.

Lest you think I am a crude and insensitive shooter I'll report
that I am a real trigger nut when it comes to rifles and pistols, going
into quivering tantrums over a little creep in a rifle trigger or a few
ounces too much weight on a pistol. A shotgun trigger is pulled
decisively and quickly.

Straightaways are sometimes blown into fragments and sometimes missed by marksmen in a hurry. It should be the easiest shot.
The gun comes up while you're judging the true course of the bird,
and you must judge whether it's still rising or leveling off. Take a
little time with it if the distance will allow.

High incomers aren't encountered often enough by most shooters to make them expert. The idea is to swing up under the bird, blot it out with the muzzle, and continue swinging as you shoot. Weight can be shifted to the back foot. The difficult part is deciding whether to take the bird coming in or to turn and take it going away. There's a tendency to wait too long and tie yourself up in a back-bending exercise. This incomer seems impossible to many shooters, but once they get the hang of it they become very consistent. The skeet incomers are excellent practice for this and it is generally learned quickly.

High outgoers aren't tough, but the lead is *underneath* the bird, something a lot of us are slow to recognize. A friend of mine missed them all for years and then turned it into his most certain shot.

Very slight angles are the best subjects for snap or spot-shooting. If the bird goes just a little to the left you can shoot with a stationary gun just a little to that side.

Right angles and nearly right angles require full swings and follow-through. Since the bird is in range for a long while, there is a tendency to dally with this one and there's an urge to aim too carefully and stop the gun once it's out ahead. You can kill it only once, so go ahead and shoot. Very few birds are missed by too much lead in this situation.

"Flock shooting" is a cardinal sin, especially prevalent where big covies are encountered, and especially with small birds. The bobwhite covey with its muttering roar and sometimes coming up in what appears to be a tight formation is especially provocative, drawing hasty and poorly pointed shots at no particular bird. The good shot picks out a single bird, and if he is thinking in terms of two birds with a single shot he cooly selects two together but concentrates on one of the two. Hunters who want to break themselves of flock shooting can concentrate on birds at the very edge of a covey rise.

SAFETY IN THE FIELD

By the time they get into the field most shooters have heard the standard safety rules, but here are some special thoughts for the expert.

One of the chief dangers is in handling guns in and about automobiles. Many state laws prohibit any loaded gun in a vehicle, and it's considered loaded if there's a round in the magazine, even if there's none in the chamber. After unloading repeatedly to get into a vehicle it begins to seem like a lot of extra effort as the day wears on, and a lot of loaded guns ride in hunting rigs.

Gun familiarization is easily managed by a little dry handling before you go afield. I often see veteran hunters out with new guns they haven't bothered to check out.

Stumbling, falling, and dropping guns can kill old-timers as well as novices. I've often read that *all* gun accidents are a result of carelessness and can be avoided. Perhaps so, but there's an occasional mishap that seems to happen despite normal precaution. A very careful friend of mine started to set his over-under down on its butt with the muzzle pointed safely up and forward. It slipped through his glove and dropped into some large rocks. As it went down a rock struck the tang safety and pushed it off. The recoil pad struck hard and bounced the gun up so that another rock caught the trigger and fired the gun into the air. That's a nasty chain of circumstances. Of course he should have held the gun firmly and never let it drop, but that same accident could happen to many hunters who are considered careful.

Unloading for fence-crossing or entering vehicles is a risky process unless everyone deliberately holds his muzzle away from everybody else.

Hunting parties tend to get too large. I don't like to see more than two gunners walking up to pointing dogs. Some hunting couples go by the rule of having only one shooter walk in and the second hunter, well to one side, takes what's left after the flight pattern is established.

Some kinds of fast-running birds must be approached by the hunter at a fast walk or even at a run. It's easy for one shooter to get in front of another and between him and the birds. It's a time for special cool.

PRACTICE

Few of us can afford enough game shooting to become expert without some form of practice, but clay targets will fill the gap.

Trapshooting at River Ranch Acres, Florida, a Winchester-franchised shooting center. Trap is considered excellent basic training for upland game, although most trapshooters need a little field experience before their skill is applied to live birds.

The fundamentals of shotgun handling can be learned at trap and skeet, and almost any good skeet or trap marksman will do well afield—possibly not the first day or two but certainly with a little experience. Field shooters delight in luring hotshot target men into tough upland situations and then smirking at their discomfort. It wouldn't be so funny after a few days, because the target shooter has the basics and will get the trimmings quickly, but the test probably won't last that long, and so the field shooters have funny stories to last a lifetime. It's a dirty trick.

Skeet gives a good variety of target angles, and if it is shot with the gun unmounted before the bird is called for it is excellent practice, but there comes a time when it begins to lose its value to a field shooter. That's the time when he begins to achieve the carefully grooved swing and mechanical pointing of the skeet champion. It may take him a hundred rounds of skeet to reach this point, but

Russ Howard, manager of the Winchester shooting center at Remuda Ranch near Naples, Florida, inks a high incoming target. Note that Howard, a famous skeet shot, is following through with his muzzle after firing and is now pointing far above the point of break. He fires with left foot only slightly advanced and keeps his head down after the shot.

when it comes skeet begins to lose much of its value as game practice. In some cases advanced skeet shooting may actually cramp live-bird shooting, simply because skeet is rigidly programmed and live birds are unpredictable.

However, the expert skeet shooter is nearly always a topnotch gunner in the field, even though he doesn't get much help from skeet after many thousand targets.

Formal trapshooting has the advantage of unknown angles so that the shooter doesn't quite build himself a groove (except in doubles when the targets always go the same). The chief disadvantage of trap shooting as practice for field shooting is that the shot does not include mounting the gun, the gun being at the shoulder when the target is called for. Nevertheless, the rise of the trap target is very similar to the rise of many game birds. Like the skeet man, the trapshooter may take a little familiarization before scoring well in the field, but he has the fundamentals.

The hand trap with which one person throws targets for another is excellent practice, for the angles are unpredictable, but it takes a healthy forearm to make the pigeons really perform. It is dangerous to throw incomers with a hand trap unless there's some sort of shield.

Unless a permanent installation of some sort is available, I'd say the spring-powered practice trap is your answer. Mount it on some sort of frame so that you can haul it in a car and hold it down in the field with a couple of sandbags. Get an old fishing reel and fill it with good-sized cord that won't cut your hand. Fasten the cord to the tripper and you can walk all over the field, and release your own clay targets at will from any position, and you can do it alone. At one time I fired at something like 12,000 such targets. They were responsible for turning a terrible shotgunner into one who was only mildly sour in the field.

There are several special merits of this system. For one thing, it is necessary to walk back to the trap and load it after every shot. The exercise doesn't hurt, it slows the tempo of the whole thing, and it makes you think of the target you've just smoked or missed. Although most shooters are too gregarious to while away their shooting hours alone, I am convinced that's the way for them to make the most progress. When I have an audience for my one-man show I find myself reluctant to shoot at the angles I have been missing and tend to throw something I can hit. Human nature.

The best of this system is that you can repeat your tough ones endlessly. Most of us have angles we can't hit well, and often we don't take those shots often enough in the field to learn our mistakes, or even realize we're continually missing the same ones. Take Ben Williams. Ben Williams is a top field shot but had fired on very few targets until he went to work with my practice trap. Swinging a little open-bored 20-gauge over-under, he casually walked about the pasture inking everything the trap served up.

I watched in humiliation because I'd been telling him how tough it could be.

Then Ben missed. He threw the same target and missed again, and I perked up a little. Ben missed the third time—and the fourth, and he grew a look of wonderment. He missed again and turned to me.

"I realize now I have missed that shot all my life," he said. Whereupon he went to work until he had straightened it out.

Confronted by such targets, your expert is likely to miss in strings. The beginner, who seldom gets off two shots exactly the same way,

A highly satisfactory one-man practice setup. After loading the trap in foreground, shooter can trip it with a long cord, shooting from any point he chooses. Cord has been dropped here and shooter is mounting his gun as the target passes him.

will miss a few and hit a few. The expert tends to nail them until he finds a weak point and then misses them all. The answer is that he is firing the same way each time at a given angle—missing exactly the same.

My best example is Louis (Buddy) Nordmann, Florida quail and dove gunner, and no slouch at pintails either. I was throwing the targets for him, and he was simply walking around the field with the gun in one hand and facing away from the trap so each shot would require turning, mounting the gun, and firing from a new angle. He turned in a remarkable performance, breaking twenty-five straight on those surprise targets. Then I suggested he shoot a target from a position I'd had trouble with—one that looked like a straightaway but required a little lead. Buddy missed it eleven times straight, thinking each time he'd made a little mechanical error. Then he figured where it was going and my fun was over, for he didn't miss again. That's what I mean about experts. Once they analyze their mistakes they're going to hit. They're ahead of the rest of us because they can do it right if they understand exactly what it takes.

The purpose of the whole game is to prevent a grooved performance, for the live birds seldom go twice exactly the same. When you pull the cord yourself, that delay stands in for the delay in locating a bird that flushes unexpectedly. I hold the gun by the grip in my right hand, pull the cord with my left, drop it and catch the fore-end, mount the gun, and shoot.

Even that can become too much a part of timing, although it's a minor thing. After days of shooting like that, I had someone pull the trap for me and found myself on the target far too soon. I'd tend to see I was early, then fiddle with my swing and lead and end up with a miss.

"Crazy Quail" and its variations make up one of the simplest and most effective permanent practice installations. It's simply a pit with a trap mounted so that it can be pointed in any direction by an operator who sits on a seat that is rigidly attached to the trap, and the whole works can be turned in a complete circle. Thus the targets can go to any point of the compass, including over the shooter's head. Instead of keeping the pit at the same depth all the way around, we have it shallow on the side away from the shooter and banked up on his side for safety's sake. Thus, low targets can be thrown over much of the circle. Only those that go back toward the shooter must go high. This just may be the best practice setup of all, but the scores are very low and it's not too popular. For some reason competitive shooters prefer a game in which they can make long runs. There are few perfect scores of even ten targets at Crazy Quail.

Although they are expensive and require considerable area, the "walk-up" games are successful for training. The shooter walks along a path and clay targets, singly or in pairs and groups, are thrown up without warning from scattered locations. Few individuals will go to that expense, although it's a fine gun-club project.

Most shooters wish they could shoot their average every day, but nobody can do that. Most of us go in strings of hits and then strings of misses and seldom have "average" days. After more misses than usual it's time for quick analysis and a little pep talk, for you know you are as good a shot as you were last week when you couldn't seem to miss. With experienced shooters it's pretty well covered by shooting too fast or too slow, by raising your head or not getting it down at all, by stopping your swing. If you can get to some clay targets in a hurry, things will probably brighten up pretty fast. Keep your morale up and try hard, for there is such a thing as losing all confidence, doubting if there is shot in the shells, and becoming more careless as the misses go on.

My best shooting and my worst shooting come out about even. I once killed nineteen very wild sharptail grouse and Hungarian partridges without a miss, taking them as they came and went. I once missed exactly nineteen Wilson snipe in a row, and I was picking my shots as carefully as I could. I am neither that good nor that bad, but it is these lopsided scores that can lead to psychological problems.

HANDLOADING

Homemade shotgun ammunition can be quite economical, can shoot just as well as factory stuff, and can be built for special purposes in a few cases where the desired combination may not be available over the counter.

If you loaded hunting ammunition only and went after a variety of game during a season, it is unlikely you'd save money in the long run. For example, whether I really needed them or not, I used eleven different loads in 20-gauge and 12-gauge guns during the past season for birds ranging from snipe to turkeys. I didn't use enough of some of these loadings to make handloading worthwhile at all. By the time I had sorted out the right wad column, scrounged the proper cases, and adjusted everything for the particular powder needed, I'd probably have shown a loss, even if I counted my time as recreation. And hunting loads should be made with care and some pattern testing. If you like to build ammunition for fun, go to it, but unless you shoot a lot of practice shells, you won't save money on handloading. If you have definite ideas about special ammunition you can't buy, enjoy yourself, but you'll probably be disappointed if you do much bookkeeping. The savings seldom compare to those achieved in loading rifle cartridges.

The way to save money and produce handloads fast is to stick with a given combination of case, wads, shot, and powder, and that's very simple if you stay with practice or target ammunition. You can buy in quantity, and you work out all the rough spots of your loading operation. I have handloaded all my target and practice ammunition for years, but except where my target shells will work for game I use factory ammunition for hunting. I lack the temperament and patience for making a little of this and a little of that and changing or adjusting everything in between. Also, hunting ammunition should be thoroughly waterproofed, and that's an extra operation if you handload. And few handloads are consistent enough to be completely reliable in repeaters.

In thus maligning home-rolled ammo I realize I will likely offend some meticulous workmen who consider mere factory stuff crude. Not many of us are in that class.

Shotshell reloading is not quite as simple as I've been told, and having gone through five different loading tools and scuffled with the frustrating business of sticking together loads with a variety of case capacities and wads, I've concluded that the only answer is to load the simplest way. I'm now using plastic-sleeved wads and only a single kind of case for each gauge, so it's going pretty smoothly and the savings are well worthwhile.

I've run into slowing complications in loading for the 20-gauge, and if ever there was a need for standardization in loading, it's with the smaller gauges. The handloading difficulty with the 20-gauge begins with the fact that there's a smaller selection of components. Then too, since the 12-gauge is the big seller, the loading-tool people sometimes can't get too excited over the 20-gauge and may have makeshift accessories for it. Standardize, though, and all is well.

There's considerable false economy practiced on the empty cases. Some of the newer plastics can be loaded a dozen times or more, and it's economical to start with good ones, whether you buy them as new empties or in new factory ammunition. All of this hand-loading advice can be summarized by: Standardize on components and buy factory stuff for special uses where only small amounts are needed.

CLOTHING

Vests and gallused game bags are good, because they can be put on over anything from a down jacket to a T-shirt as weather dictates. Clothing should not be tight, for that hampers gun mounting. A few shell loops are good in emergencies. A complete vest of loops often dribbles ammunition when you take it off and sometimes when you are stumbling in brush.

Leather boots are best when it's dry. Rubber boots or rubber-bottomed packs should be worn more than they are, and I have some web-footed friends who insist on old leather because it's more comfortable to start out with. For some hunting there's not much need for safety colors, but when it's brushy a blaze orange cap or vest makes everybody more at ease. I like several layers of clothing that can be shed one at a time and stuffed somewhere in a vest or gameback. A couple of plastic bags can keep dirt and blood away.

There are more arguments about pants than anything else. Heavy canvas brush pants are good where there are briars. Pants faced with leather or plastic look sporty and protect well, although some of them hold moisture once they're wet. They can be pretty stiff when frozen. Long underwear worn under jeans are a good combination in all but the very worst briars, but they may not be socially acceptable everywhere.

Light rainsuits can be wadded up and carried in a pocket.

CHAPTER XV

Dogs for Upland Game

A GOOD BIRD DOG costs $500, the man told me. That's the average, no matter how you go about it, he said. You can buy inexpensive pups until you get one that turns out; you can buy more expensive pups until you get one that turns out; you can breed your own; you can buy inexpensive adult dogs; or you can go and get a finished one for $500.

That doesn't mean you might not hit the jackpot the first time around, but the chances are against it unless you spend nearly all the $500. Since the man who set the price for a good bird dog was operating a big game preserve and was running about sixty dogs, I listened pretty closely. He'd tried to get satisfactory dogs in every way he could, and the average cost kept coming out the same—$500. He had given away many of them; he had destroyed those he didn't think were worthy of the breed; but he had to have good dogs and he was getting them—for an average of $500 each.

Since then I have come to believe that his figure is a little low. If hunters weren't so easily satisfied by mutts they have learned to love, the average price for a good dog might be more than $500. Only a few gunners are capable of the coldblooded judgment that

Some of the essentials of a good upland hunt, not the least of which is the bird dog. Presence of the other equipment makes this one expectant.

causes a useless dog to be put away, and only a few are capable of facing up to the fact that the family pet is a lousy hunter.

In view of the expense of feeding a hunting dog, the veterinary bills and the hours of training, I don't consider the initial cost as a very important item unless you're bidding for a national champion, complete with cups and ribbons. In other words, if you think a $150 pup is better than a $20 pup you'd better go for the expensive one. The difference in cost is a minor part of the expenses you'll have during the next few years.

Only a small percentage of upland gunners keep a kennelful of bird dogs. A large share of those that hunt are family pets, only partly trained, and viewed with extreme tolerance in the field. You'll find dog experts who say family pets are no good for hunting, but it isn't the status of family pet that ruins a dog. It's simply a matter of a pet being kept whether it's a good hunter or not, whereas a kennel dog would be disposed of it didn't work out. The impersonal attitude that can be mustered toward kennel dogs is more logical from a hunter's standpoint than the kindly tolerance for the shedding rascal on the living-room divan.

German shorthair pointers are among the most biddable and efficient upland dogs. These are ready to be released during a field trial.

So if a dog is to be introduced to a family and is to adopt a hunter, its selection is even more important than if it is to be a kennel dog on a trial basis, subject to dismissal one way or another if it doesn't produce. Since a dog may live and hunt or refuse to hunt for ten years or more, any hunter should think a long while before choosing that part of his family.

Breed and pedigree are important guidelines, but bird dogs are individuals. Every breed has characteristics of its own, freely ignored by individual dogs who haven't read their pedigree papers. There are collies that point quail beautifully and mongrels that retrieve woodcock, but such quirks of heredity can't be counted on no matter how careful the training. Despite the throwbacks and offshoots, your best bet is a purebred dog from an ancestry that has been doing for generations what you want your dog to do.

Name of the breed isn't all of it, of course. There are English pointers that fan the horizon in field-trial speed and there are English pointers that root about the cover in plodding gravity, almost underfoot. German shorthairs are supposed to be close workers, but I have seen stub-tailed whirlwinds that must be followed by panting saddle horses. Brittany spaniels are supposed to be fairly timid, but there was one named Pepe in Arizona who was willing to chase anything that crossed the state border.

Now within the breed are strains for special purposes. Since the English pointer is the most consistent field-trial winner, the pointer is accepted as a big-goer, but there are strains developed for close-in brushpatch operations and for ruffed grouse in the thickets. I once tried to make a close-in gun dog of a field-trial pointer, a project that ended in complete failure and near nervous collapse for both of us. It may be I ruined him for his original mission, a case of stupid meddling. The English pointer was bred to run, so let it run.

Geting the most out of a pointing dog, or a flushing dog for that matter, is hard enough if you select one bred for exactly the job at hand. Jacks-of-all-trades seldom compete well with specialists, and for that reason it's nice to find a dog that is actually a native of the part of the country where it is to hunt—at least one that came from a line that hunts the same kind of game. There's a lot of difference between a ruffed-grouse dog and a bobwhite genius.

I've had my share of experience with the general-purpose pointing dog. Kelly was a big Brittany with fire who pointed eighteen species of North American upland game for me. I don't say he was a champion at any one bird, but he held his own, adapted to any terrain or bird within an hour or so, and got the job done. The Brittany has been coming on strong in recent years. I am inclined to tout it as the best all-around dog for all feathered game, because it is highly adaptable, can live happily in an apartment or a one-man tent (with the man), and usually accepts any new bird as just part of the work. When it comes to specific game it's another story. Few dogs have been asked to hunt every upland bird in North America. In fact, although there must be others, old Kelly is the only one I know of at this writing.

So many of the birds run that I could not call him a particularly staunch dog, and I consider the bobwhite quail his weakest area. Having followed running pheasants and drifting Hungarian partridge for much of his career, he had a tendency to crowd quail, evidently unable to believe they were not moving. Many times he

A well-trained springer spaniel can be a jack-of-all-trades, and his retrieving instincts are often stronger than those of pointing breeds. (Photo: Florida State News Bureau)

has walked cautiously into a covey and put them up.

Whether it is generally true of all-round dogs or not I do not know, but he had a distinctive preference for large birds. It was hard to keep his attention on mountain quail if he could hear chukars calling, so I assume the heavy scent was simply more attractive for him. I suspect that chukars, pheasants, and sage grouse were his favorites.

He was not difficult to control except for those times when he could not resist a jackrabbit. He ran so hard that he continually gouged his eyes and injured his feet. He ran once until he simply passed out. This is not good, but it was a part of his enthusiasm and he never learned to pace himself. He was a very poor retriever but excellent at hunting dead or crippled birds. When he found a dead bird he would bring it out where you could see it and then lay it down. He simply did not believe in bringing it to you. With all of these faults he was one of the best dogs I have ever seen work. If a man gets only one good dog in a lifetime, as the saying goes, I have had mine. I am not partial to the Brittany except as an all-round and readily adaptable dog. May Kelly rest in peace.

The English setters are to the North what the pointers are to the South, carrying a heavier coat for cold weather and adapting to closer cover and hunters who nearly always walk. The Irish setter, nearly ruined as a hunter when bench lovers took it over, is coming back in some strains. The Gordon setter, a slow worker, is not as popular as it once was. The European imports such as the wire-haired pointing griffon, the wire-haired German pointer, the Viszula, the weimaraner, the German shorthair, and the Brittany are highly intelligent dogs, sometimes expected to perform the impossible in adaptability. The flushing breeds, led by the springer spaniel, are at their best on pheasants, sometimes on woodcock and grouse. Retrieving specialists like Labs and Chesapeakes are taught as close-in hunters, and I have seen a Lab that goes well on bobwhites in the brush, moving slowly in half-points and boosting tight-holders with her nose.

Dog training can't be a full-time occupation for most hunters, and although it might be possible to teach a poodle to point, you're better off to start with the essential instincts built in.

Dog men and hunters are not always the same people, there being more of the latter, and few gunners ever follow a truly finished dog of any breed. Most of us get by with helpers who would never score in either field trials or bench show. The meat dogs do their work with brains and persistence, often with a lack of style, and nearly always with tolerance from the man with the gun.

TRAINING

Since most of us work with half-trained dogs by professional standards, we can expect some outstanding failures and will have miserable days unless we can convince ourselves that the culprit is not really our flesh and blood but just a dog with a mind of its own, however simple. Happiest is the hunter who can laugh at his dog's mistakes, enjoy its successes, and never feel the need to defend his beloved friend against the entire world. If a critic is unhappy with your dog, let him grumble and criticize and you can agree with him. But if he really doesn't like it, let him use his own dog or stay home. Too many friendships are frayed by dog arguments, and it isn't worth it. Be careful what you say about a man's dog. He may not have the broad mind you should have.

Neglecting to train your dog properly is generally excusable, because you may not have the time, however many books on dog training you own. At least you can be objective about reward and punishment. Punishment should fit the crime in the certainty that the dog knows the reason, and personal anger shouldn't enter into it. It shouldn't be an outlet for frustration.

The refinement of dog training is almost endless, but if the animal has pointing, hunting, and dead-hunting instincts it is likely to be serviceable if you'll teach it to come to whistle or call, to sit or stay on command, to whoa on command, to heel, and to follow simple instructions as to the direction to hunt. It'll generally pick up some other admonitions, such as orders to hunt close or go easy.

If you can make your dog a scholar through long training, so much the better, but you'll kill plenty of game over one that knows only simple commands. There's disagreement as to when training on game should start, but all experts agree that discipine should come at an early age. I know one hunter who doesn't bother with game until a dog is a year old and he does very well, although some trainers insist he has wasted six months or more.

A gun-shy dog isn't worth bothering with unless you are prepared for long hours of work, and even that may not do the business. A two-year-old of a pointing breed that isn't pointing and hunting probably isn't worth feeding. The less training you do, the more essential it is to have a dog with strong hunting instincts. It takes a good prospect to pay off for a hunter who doesn't work much with it. Choose carefully.

A good Jeep setup for bird dogs. Manon Halcomb of Florida uses four dogs in a day's hunting.

READING A DOG

But every dog owner should learn what his dog is about. There are hunters who make no effort to read a bird dog's actions until that moment when it's on point. They whistle it away from birds; they bawl it out for running over birds downwind; they make it hunt dead in the wrong place when it wants to trail a cripple; they hurry it when it works on a puzzle; and they accuse it of false pointing when the bird has just left unseen, leaving a strong scent.

All of this injustice comes from a creature with a nose so inferior to the dog's that he cannot even understand the principles of scent and its travel. It might be good for every bird hunter to set a small smoke bomb in a field on a fairly quiet day and see how the smoke goes—up, parallel to the ground, fast, slow, or in a gently widening haze. That's something like scent, an elusive thing that performs differently with humidity, heat, and cold. No one can see it and you can't smell it, so you'll have to interpret it through your dog's actions, and once you learn to do that you will have to confront the fact that there are times when birds put forth little or no scent.

In crude interpretation of what a dog is faced with, we can classify bird odors as direct and indirect. Direct odor comes straight from the birds themselves, and that's what the high-headed covey dog is searching for, capable of catching it at high speed. That's the "body scent" the big-going quail dog strikes when it makes its sudden stop, a dramatic demonstration of strong pointing instinct. It is mainly free scent, and although it may be somewhat slowed in its drift by grass, weeds, or brush, it is riding in air. Generally it is strong, and it usually indicates the birds are close. If there's considerable air movement I doubt if any dog catches body scent from upwind.

The bold dog that runs hard is most likely to catch scent and point quickly. It is often stated flatly that such a dog is necessary for holding some kinds of birds. I won't say it's any sort of hypnotism, but a bird that might fly from a slow-going dog is likely to freeze solidly when the dog comes fast. The theory is that the dog, which appears as a predator to most game, is so close and coming so swiftly that the bird instinctively attempts to hide instead of flushing. It works on most species part of the time, on some species nearly every time. Quail are especially susceptible to the fast-moving dog. Sharptail grouse, prairie chickens, and Hungarian partridge are often held by such points, but it is not a hard and fast rule, and many times I have seen a dog going full-bore in open country, throw on the brakes suddenly, skid to a stop, and hold the birds only momentarily. A second or two after the dog points, the birds fly, having squatted in indecision for an instant and then going up.

The plodding, ground-trailing dog is less likely to hold the birds solidly, but they frequently run from it instead of flying. It may be bad to have birds running, but that's better than having them flush far out of range. The perfect approach is the dog that will work both ways, and one of the best pointers I have seen on open-country birds hunts with a high head until he catches a faint scent and then reverts to unstylish operations with his head fairly close to the ground. Of course if he hunted the ground all of the time he simply couldn't cover enough area to be efficient.

Running or walking birds can be a puzzle for both dog and hunter, but the ground-trailer comes on strong in many situations. Some of the best pheasant dogs will work a moving bird until it comes to a spot where further ground travel would expose it. Then the bird stops and the dog stops too, and if you're lucky the gun is close enough for a shot. It can be deadly business. It works repeatedly with chukar in rough country, birds that are seldom willing to walk downhill. They move ahead of the dog, which may be creeping in disgraceful fashion from a style standpoint, and suddenly find themselves at the top of a rise, whereupon they flush. Chukar hunters often trot along with their dogs for long distances, and there may never be a solid point. Needless to say, such a performance would be embarrassing to many field-trial people, and if you want to be blunt you can call this using a pointing dog as a flusher. Certainly it may be bad training for birds that hold tightly. The advantage of the pointer, of course, is that you can let it run wide in the hope it'll find distant birds without putting them up.

It will cause acid argument in some circles, but dogs can be too staunch under some circumstances. I have seen a pointer hold rigidly while you walked past it and beat the grass for 40 yards ahead with no result. Its instinct told it the scent was strong enough for a point and it was time to stay put, while the birds left at top speed on the ground and might be found 200 yards away.

The indirect scent is that gleaned from vegetation in most cases,

*The grand manner of following dogs. A shooting dog field trial
gallery moves out on a Southern plantation where rubber-tired shooting
wagons and Tennessee walking horses are standard equipment.*

and it can be followed for long distances when the dog is willing
to work it out. Some dogs simply won't bother with the delicate
traces of old scent on grass stems. You can see this with two working together. One slows to a walk and laboriously works out the
trail. The other catches the scent all right, goes birdy for a few
seconds, and then continues its high-headed gallop. It doesn't want
to bother, for it's looking for a snootful, and it may find more birds
in the long run. It may find none at all. I have seen a good singles
dog pin a Hun and have a typical covey dog back momentarily,
then cautiously retreat a few steps and start feeling for a covey.
It simply isn't intrigued with the odor of a single bird. Which is
the best dog? I suppose it's a matter of which one you own.

There sometimes comes a moment when you must take over
from the dog, even though it should be allowed to manage its
department most of the time. Old scent isn't carried well on very
short grass or cultivated ground.

"Pick 'em up," the fox hunters said, "the doggone fox has crossed that plowed field just the way he beat us last Saturday night!"

Granted a foxhound can follow fresh scent across plowed ground, he's apt to lose an old trail there. Bird-dog men can learn from hound experts. There's the case in which a pointing dog works what appears to be a hot scent and then loses it at the edge of short grass or cultivated land, sometimes even at the edge of a Jeep road in open country. Now is the time for you to pick a likely spot on the other side of the dead area and put it to work there. Usually the first assessment is that the birds have flown, but it isn't necessarily so. You walk across the open spot that holds scent so poorly and find your dog is back in business—often you find you're in business before it can point, for they may have held after crossing the open space. So you put your birds in your coat (or curse your marksmanship) and instead of clumping on across the ridges you turn around and try to figure what really happened. You'll be surprised at how often the whole thing pops out like a detailed chart. That's how you get bird knowhow and find you and your dog suddenly begin to understand each other.

WHO FLUSHES WHAT?

Two of us, accompanied by a tattered little pointing dog, arrived at the beginning of sharptail-shooting season in Canada. The bird-dog-training season had just closed, and I looked up a Southern trainer who was just leaving for the land of Spanish moss and magnolias with his pointers loaded in the truck and his horse trailer hooked behind. I thought he could give me some hints as to where the birds were living.

He was cooperative, but he shook his head.

"The sharptails are too old for pointing dogs now," he said. "They won't hold. You'll ruin your dog. We train on young birds that don't fly much."

All right, but for the time being at least we weren't quail hunters. We were sharptail hunters, and there was no thought of our dog being ruined for quail, so we put him into the sand hills, where he ran up sharptails that wouldn't hold, pointed into hopeless bramble patches, and now and then pinned an adult sharptail. It was good hunting by crude characters who had forgotten bobwhites for the time being. Perhaps it placed a permanent blight on our dog, but he has pointed many a bobwhite since, another example of the jack-of-all trades that is a big winner at nothing but a loser at nothing either.

The pointing dog called upon to flush birds on occasion is usually a spotty performer, and he who demands such varied tactics must accept some erratic maneuvers, but there are occasions when the dog must do the flushing if anything flies. One of the best pheasant dogs I have ever watched had a spooky performance for pheasants in dense thickets. He would point into the thick stuff, and when the gunner arrived he would rush at the thicket, stopping just short of the tangle. This maneuver would cause many birds to flush when they might otherwise simply run from the shooter. Anyone who plans to *train* a dog to do such things is probably due for searing disappointment and a nervous breakdown. Such things are the dog's idea, and only mental telepathy could bring it about unless the dog plans it.

I once followed a good pheasant dog through some high grass when he was obviously after a running bird. It was a series of flash points and then brisk stalking, and when I finally had a solid point and came alongside, the dog was turning his head rapidly from left to right, expecting the bird to go up. When it didn't, I was badly shaken to find the dog jumping up and down without leaving the spot where he had pointed. The bird went up from only 15 feet away. Without the jumping act it might have continued to run, a possibility apparently weighed by the dog. Such goofy but effective tactics come only from long experience.

The dog that has followed many moving birds is on the ragged edge of the breaking habit, and this is where many good ones go wrong. I once took a Brittany directly from ptarmigan hunting and put him on ruffed grouse. He'd learned all sorts of bad habits from the ptarmigan, mainly because they tended to walk around under his nose, a strain few canine brains can withstand. He'd bounced a lot of ptarmigan, and the halfhearted punishment he'd collected hadn't made much impression.

Anyway, he pointed, jumped, and caught two young ruffed grouse on his first day with them. For a while I despaired of ever having a pointer again, but he came out of it fairly well. Similar problems can come from careless use of planted birds that fly weakly and are caught by breaking dogs.

Where dog training is concerned, some of the worst birds can be mountain and valley quail in thick river bottoms, birds that refuse to hold or fly but scamper around in thick cover a dog can't manage easily, and then continue the debacle by hopping into the low branches of a tree or bush where the dog can neither see nor smell them. In some areas, ruffed and blue grouse do the same thing, especially if they've had little hunting pressure. The dog's bell stops its tinkling, and in a few seconds you hear a brief whir as the bird goes into a tree. After watching this a few times the dog is apt to make a wild lunge in anticipation of the brief flight. Quail and grouse in trees are hard to find, let alone flush, and dogs get strange ideas while their masters throw sticks and stones at firmly perched grouse or quail.

There are some canine geniuses that will point staunchly where the gunners can kick up the birds and then turn into cautious flush dogs in spots where humans can't travel. This happens sometimes in the South, where badly frightened quail will hole up in small but thick palmetto patches, so dense that human travel is almost impossible. There's more room near the ground, and the dog may find going much better. The birds will hold very closely in most cases, and some dogs learn to boost them out with their noses. That's the kind of singles shooting that builds a quick bag if the shooters are at the edge of a small palmetto clump. The bird makes considerable fuss as it rises, and it's generally one bird at a time, even though several may be hiding close together.

Generalizations about bird species are often disproved. There's one thing that shows up time after time: Birds in the same cover tend to act somewhat alike, regardless of species. "Gentleman Bob," the tightly holding quail, will sometimes scamper about freely in very thick stuff, even though under a dog's nose. Get a valley quail in the open sage and it may act like a chukar or a sage grouse. Get it in impenetrable thickets and it plays ruffed grouse. For that matter, if you catch a ruff eating grasshoppers on a grassy meadow it may act considerably like a prairie chicken. All of this comes out that a pheasant hunter from Idaho draws should think twice before saying a Nebraska cornfielder is out of his mind. I don't know anybody who has hunted everything everywhere. Dogs, birds, and

Jim LaValley and his weimaraner with a brace of Montana pheasants.

hunters vary with locale, so we'd best temper flat statements about any bird or dog.

Dry days are poor days for scent, which generally travels best in damp, slowly moving air. High winds can whip odor into baffling shreds, sometimes for long distances, sometimes so close to the ground that it is missed by a high-headed covey dog. A covey of feeding birds may put out a wall of scent; a covey crouching in the rain may be almost scentless. These things are true of all game birds.

I recall a day when I hunted with Manon Halcomb, a veteran of southern quail coverts and always an owner of good pointers, generally about three of them. There seemed always one dog that was in solid, one that was still on trial, and a third ready to be replaced if it didn't come around in a hurry.

It was dry and warm that day, but the dogs pointed a covey and then found a single after the covey rise. That bird turned and came over my head, and for once I let it go until the distance was right and then centered it. A puff of feathers settled slowly, but the bird hurtled on through a hole in some scrubby oaks. We went over there with the dogs and watched them comb the short grass with no result, and we decided we'd lost a cripple and sat down to eat our lunch in disgust.

"There's your bird," Manon said, pointing to a very dead breast-up bobwhite he'd just noticed. "Fool dogs have walked all over it. Let me get that pup."

So Manon called the pup, and after a few moments of sniffing about within 10 inches of the dead bird, the dog looked inquiringly up at its boss, one foot on the bird's wing, evidently having smelled nothing at all. Manon called one of his more experienced dogs, and that one couldn't find the bird either, even though directed to within a foot of it, so we picked it up and decided it was one of those cases when there simply wasn't any traceable scent.

It was an hour later that the dogs pointed another single several miles away while we were riding the truck, and Manon walked it up and knocked it down. It sprayed feathers and went down end over end, evidently stone dead in the air. Although it landed in a thin stand of weeds, the dogs never found it.

All of this prepared me for another point in brushy cover—a big covey that went up raggedly, and I picked a single bird that bored up a hill. I hit it and watched it tumble into the grass, and there I stood, other birds buzzing about my ears and Manon's 20-gauge coughing off to my right somewhere, but I wouldn't take my eyes from where my downed bird fell and I never fired a second shot.

Manon said, "Dead birds—fetch!" and the dogs brought him a double.

"Mine's up there," I said. "I know exactly where if the dogs can't smell it."

But I needn't have worried, for one of the pointers, the same one that had been unable to smell a dead bird at 10 inches and had failed on a second chance, put its head in the air a full 30 feet from my kill and trotted straight to it. For some reason that bird put out strong scent. For some reason the others hadn't. Until we can smell through a pointer's nose we'll never really understand.

An expert dead-hunter is a ground snuffler, whatever he might do the rest of the day, and the best cripple finder I ever knew became a ground trailer the moment you said, "Hunt dead." The racing dogs that "slam into points" in midstride are the ones that poetry is made of, but there are dogs, perhaps the same ones, that cautiously unravel bird trails in complex patterns of feeding or hiding, trails that some big-goers will abandon after a brief examination. Think of the woodcock trundling about a thicket in Alabama or the slinking pheasant threading its way through a strand of tules in a Western draw. Such game must be followed, generally ground-trailed, and the classic pointing stance may not do the job.

The routine is supposed to be a simple case of a dog pointing and the hunter walking past him and kicking up the birds, but there are birds that won't perform that way and there are hundreds of cases in which the dog has to put them up or they won't be put up. It's happened to me with mountain quail, scaled quail, Gambel's quail, pheasants, chukars, Huns—and so on. So you stomp around awhile and finally tell the dog to find the birds and put them up and it does. Have you taught him to break point? Well, maybe so, but what do you recommend? Many times the recommendation is to hunt only birds that hold solidly. I'm sorry, but the lease has run out on my plantation.

I have read that the only pointer to be used on pheasants is a dog that's "no good anyway and breaks point when the bird moves." I had a very good dog, I guess. Anyway, he'd point a pheasant and stand there until hell froze over and the pheasant had strolled into the next county. I never killed many pheasants, but I sure had a classic pointer. He did the same thing on Huns and sage grouse (I guess that's what they were, but I never caught up with them). So the treasured meat dog has point leavened with bird and man sense. It is unorthodox or it wouldn't be what it is, and unless it is a strict specialist you must overlook the times when it tries to work a bobwhite like a ptarmigan.

Most birds move under the point, at least to some extent, and some birds don't even hesitate in their travel when the dog comes upon them. Some dogs can tell instantly that birds are moving, even without ground-trailing, and such perception is in the same category as the knowledge of which direction a trail is going.

I have seen a very few dogs that would circle and cut off running birds, obviously doing it deliberately. Other dogs, evidently of just as much ability otherwise, would hunt a busy lifetime without ever figuring it out. I suspect that such a trick is learned accidentally and sticks somewhere in canine memory. It's an especially good move since birds that are headed will hold tighter than those that are simply followed up. Evidently the confrontation confuses them and they are baffled to find their escape route cut off. Running birds are the main dog problem of Western hunting, and the speed of

A point in the open country of Alberta's sand hills.

such racers as the scaled quail is much greater than the uninitiated can imagine. Frankly, any dog that can handle scalies well and do a good job on woodcock the following week is some kind of canine Plato.

Dogs that live by their noses make use of their other senses to a varying degree. It's a good thing they don't have very good eyes, for not many dogs can hold a point while watching birds walking around ahead of them. I have seen pointing dogs that actually caught the sound of moving birds in the grass, pricked their ears, and changed their stance to face the sound. Maybe that's not classic, but it's pretty helpful.

Some dogs learn the sounds of birds. The aforementioned Kelly never learned to follow the call of bobwhites, paying no attention to birds tootling all around him, but he snapped to attention and became hard to hold the moment he heard a chukar a quarter-mile away on a mountainside. Other dogs will work unerringly toward a calling bobwhite. Most of them are alerted by pheasant cackling after a few trips.

With experience, most dogs learn the logical cover for the game they are after, and most of them learn to play the wind to best advantage. Pups that have had a snootful of bird scent sometimes want to hunt upwind, regardless of the direction the hunting party must take. Covering the area thoroughly is something some otherwise good dogs never learn, and some speedsters retrace their ground repeatedly, thus covering less area than slower but more logical operators.

ENDURANCE

There are good dogs that never learn to pace themselves, running wide open from the moment they're put down until they either play out entirely or are picked up. Shooters with plenty of dogs can use speedsters to good advantage, leaving the individual down for only an hour or two and replacing it when it begins to fade. The man with only one dog and two or three days of hunting ahead has a problem; nevertheless, it's usually easier to tone down a too-wide type than to put go into a dog that prefers heeling to hunting.

It is in open country that overenthusiastic dogs usually shoot their wads too soon. They'll generally last longer where terrain or vegetation makes racing difficult. Usually, a too-eager hunter will be toned down on the second day and begin to save himself; some never learn, and there is a danger of trying to make gun dogs of true field-trial racers, since some simply will not adapt. Leave them doing what they do best.

A dog that plays out too quickly usually doesn't get much hunting time and tries to do it all at once. Fresh from the kennels, where it spends too much of its life, it loses its cool when it smells the cover and possibly the birds. For a wild one, the experts recommend more time running loose if there's a place for it. Less enthusiastic dogs may hunt better if they spend more time in closer confinement.

It's not just a matter of getting worn out fast. In warm climates some goers are permanently injured by overheating. Some of those that rip and tear at the brush and everything else in their way are prone to injury, generally to the feet.

In a four-day chukar hunt in rugged terrain I watched one dog thrive on it while another became almost a stretcher case. They covered about equal amounts of ground and appeared about equally enthusiastic. With his rations boosted because of the hard work, one actually gained a little weight while working the cliffs and canyons. The other one became almost exhausted early the first day and had to be rested. By evening of the second day he had very badly worn feet, and when they began to bleed we put him up. Our other dog had no foot damage and was going as strongly at the end of four days as he had at the beginning.

Nobody can prophesy a canine performance by simply looking at the dog, but a few minutes of watching these two could give you a pretty good idea. The durable dog was lightly constructed, short-backed, and ran almost silently. His chest was deep but not broad. The other dog was heavier, had front legs placed wide apart on a thick chest, and ran hard. You could hear him pounding his feet on the rocky slopes. After watching and listening for a few minutes you could guess who was going to be around at end of the hunt.

The build for a durable hunter can vary greatly with breed, but the dog that is overly stocky for its breed, seems to run with effort, and beats the ground with its feet can't be expected to last long at high speed. If it moves slowly, don't blame it, for that's what it may be built for. Heart and desire can make up for a host of physical deficiencies, but the dog gets a head start if it has the equipment to start with. Professional dog trainers can be pretty decisive about a dog's appearance.

There are cases where physical deficiencies can actually be of help. You've heard of the three-legged grouse dog that moved slowly enough to be deadly in the brush. I know of one English pointer named Patty who has some sort of hindquarter ailment. She doesn't suffer with it but isn't very agile, and her progress through the piney woods is a sedate trot. She is deadly in thick brush where other leggy pointers are apt to disappear.

All of this comes on like coldblooded judgment of man's best friend, and perhaps it is. If you have sentiments like mine you're wise to resist sudden attachments to pooches that haven't proved themselves—unless you want a fat house pet instead of a hunting dog.

The attachment of hunters to their dogs is difficult to explain, but perhaps it is tied to the fact that however strong their mutual regard they can never really converse as two humans. So the loss of a longtime field companion is a special kind of sorrow, and no one knows what to say to a dying dog. I failed to find any words when I was a kid and I have failed since as an old man.

CHAPTER XVI

Places to Hunt

There are still broad expanses of upland-game country, virtually untouched because they are not advertised and generally in areas where some other form of hunting attracts the attention of both native and tourist. It is a concept difficult to understand for a man who finds a wall of posters where he used to hunt and who has seen his cover dwindle through development or clean farming.

The outstanding exceptions are pheasant and turkey hunting. I would guess that there is more long travel for pheasants than any other upland bird. The pheasant is "big enough to be worthwhile," and without detracting from the ringneck's appeal it must be admitted that under certain circumstances and in great plenty it can be bagged easily by once-a-year gunners, often without dogs and operating in a picnic atmosphere.

Turkeys, of course, are almost in the category of big game and extremely difficult for hunters who do not know the country well. Many shooters who have no real interest in most upland game are eager to hire guides for turkey hunting.

If there's a secret to finding good hunting for a given game bird, look for an area where it is overshadowed in popularity by other game. The popularity doesn't necessarily have much to do with the plenty or scarcity of either species. Here are a few examples:

Ruffed grouse (willow grouse) are extremely plentiful in much of Alberta and British Columbia, and in some of that country they are easy to hunt, but that's big-game country. You can say that those aren't shotgun people for the most part.

Winter woodcock hunting is excellent in Louisiana, Mississippi, and Alabama, but the woodcock are overshadowed by the quail and largely ignored.

The scaled quail and Gambel's quail, as found in the Southwest, do not seem to have the gunning pressure of the Eastern bobwhite. Of course there are local exceptions, but the desert species should be able to hold their own for a long while.

If you are willing to go to the trouble, all of this upland game can be had, even without local guides, and usually without much expense other than lodging and licenses.

In a strange place and often after birds I know very little about, my first choice of an information source is the state or province conservation agency. I am quite aware that many a game warden, game protector, wildlife officer, or whatever his local designation is is not a hunter and may have little knowledge of the game I'm after, but he nearly always gets me to the right source pretty promptly. It has worked from Alaska to the Mexican border, and I am amazed at the hunters who never tap this source.

Sporting-goods stores are information sources. Get maps whenever they're available. You can take advantage of one bit of psychology that hangs over every community, and that's local pride in the area, and probably in its game. If your public relations is good you may get into some good hunting simply because a local resident wants the outsider to see that it's there.

Now and then you come upon someone with the crotchety idea that it's the foreigners who are killing all the game, cutting the fences, shooting the livestock, and desecrating the community in general, and although most records show the vandals are nearly always residents from near the scene of their crime, you may as well back off from such folks. On the other hand, most locals have an added interest in helping someone who has come a long way.

In most rural communities the sportsman from the nearest large city is in disfavor. In Colorado, it might be Denver; in Georgia, it might be Atlanta. This is a unique outlook, but it can have some basis, since large parties of hunters very frequently come from nearby cities and the kind of people who cause trouble in the field are usually occasional hunters who don't travel very far. It is surprising how many landowners will ask you where you're from when you seek permission to hunt.

Private leasing of small-game areas is against the principles of some outdoorsmen, who feel the move should be toward public access and that private leasing sabotages both the conservation agencies and the occasional sportsman. No two cases are exactly alike, but leasing is snowballing and there are communities where it's a matter of rent it or forget it.

Sometimes the annual fee isn't large because the landowner is confronted with too much hunting, has been reluctant to post his property, and is looking for an easy way out. He simply doesn't like to refuse hunters, and when a leasing individual or group is willing to handle the posting and take the blame (if that's the right word) for closing the area he can wash his hands of the knotty permission problems. I know one big rancher who wants to know who's on his property but refuses permission very rarely, and then only when the requester proposes something that might damage land (usually an oddball vehicle he wants to hunt from).

Commercial game preserves come in all dimensions and qualities. Generally, the better the hunting the more the cost, and the management of a pay-to-hunt establishment is wondrously complex. The high rate of mortality among shooting preserves is mute evidence of the problems involved. The artificiality of the situation varies tremendously.

Remember the manager is trying to present birds in as nearly a wild situation as possible, but remember that he must present them to some customers who can't walk 50 yards and to others who can hardly hit a balloon on a string with a skeet gun. He may blanch in horror when a client arrives with a well-worn gun, tattered brush pants, and long shooting experience. He may even say his form of shooting just isn't designed for experts, but he may have a special field for such shooters; he may even have some wild-bird shooting available not far away. And not all pen-raised birds are a cinch.

Pen-raised game birds can be bought at a wide range of prices. Those that act like wild birds must come from appropriate strains and must be reared in surroundings where they will see as little as possible of those who tend them. This makes the rearing more expensive, of course. Some preserve birds have all the wild tendencies of barnyard chickens, and the same preserve operator may have wild ones one month and overly tame ones the next.

The ring-necked pheasant is the bread-and-butter bird of the preserves. It's large enough to make a big impression at the table, it is neither too easy nor too difficult to hit in the air, and it loses little of its wild characteristics when raised in captivity. It behaves like a wild bird almost immediately after its release. The bobwhite quail is without a peer as a preserve bird if it comes from good stock, but the quail tends to become tame unless carefully handled and bred. The chukar partridge on the preserve is quite different from the truly wild bird but is a popular target.

Even agriculturists who should know better tend to think only of multiplication tables and subtraction when confronted with a game resource. When the bird population goes down they blame predators and hunters, because these things can be seen. They think in terms of two birds plus a satisfactory hatch equaling seventeen birds to be present the following fall. A bird taken by a hunter is listed as a bird gone forever, and to them all living game birds are brood stock. Tell such people that two pheasants this year will probably mean only two pheasants next year, even if the hatch is satisfactory, and you will receive a pitying stare or violent disagreement.

The hardest facts to sell are those concerning natural mortality. Of course it varies, but it's conservative to say that about 70 percent of the quail or grouse that are around early this fall won't be around next summer, whether anybody fires a shot or not. It is possible under special circumstances to overshoot a given population, but it happens very seldom.

There is a natural regulation that takes over when a game population is down. First, the remaining birds are usually the strongest and therefore the hardest to find and shoot. Second, the tough hunting reduces the number of hunters automatically and reduces the kill. Third, natural predators become scarcer or turn to other prey.

None of this is guesswork, for it has been proved repeatedly under controlled conditions. Time after time, long closed seasons have had no effect upon game revival following a poor season or two. The comebacks usually match those of nearby areas where hunting is continued throughout the "down" period. In some cases the hunted area actually has a stronger comeback, but I have been unable to get biologists to say scattering the birds through hunting is beneficial.

This is not to say no birds can be overharvested. I have heard management people say that sage grouse can be quite vulnerable on limited range, and where cover is scanty pheasants may be too easily killed. Some managers believe split and broken seasons are necessary to keep quail populations intact; others say it is a useless device. It probably depends on the specific area involved.

Game biologists can make mistakes as well as anyone else, but I'll go with the trained man most of the time, and few professionals have so much competition from amateurs. New ideas are sometimes kept quiet because the public isn't ready for them, and practices often lag years behind knowledge.

Although other self-styled game experts can be a nuisance, the landowners can promote really tragic projects. In recent years there have been thousands of square miles of prime pheasant cover closed because farmers did not agree with game biologists. Using mass closures as a weapon, the farmers have tried to force their conservation agencies to follow their ideas, and have succeeded in some instances. I do not say the farmers are always wrong, but I'll go with the professional most of the time, and he has enough trouble with political pressure, let alone having his game areas closed. Closed areas multiply pressures on open land and snowball as landowners on the fringes of closed sectors find their property crowded.

There are strong, often misguided, drives against hunting on the grounds that it is cruel, that it destroys a natural thing that cannot be replaced, and that it appeals to man's baser instincts. Arguments in favor of hunting are often made helplessly when it is found that anti-hunters lack enough background to discuss the matter intelligently. Hunters and fishermen who have paid the conservation bill for many years find themselves speechless in the face of sentimental arguments so naive that logical responses will miss completely.

These few facts must be the basis of pro-hunting argument:

The hunter's money pays for the lion's share of game conservation. Game is a renewable resource and cannot be stockpiled from one season to the next (especially true of upland birds). Nature's methods of pruning a game population is infinitely more cruel than those of the hunter.

Conservationists have found that the upland game hunter is less vocal than big-game hunters, and professionals often confess that squeaking wheels get most of the grease. It is, they say, the nature of the bird gunner to be quieter and less aggressive. Perhaps he is.

Index